SAP Sales and Distribution Quick Configuration Guide

Advanced SAP Tips and Tricks with Variant Configuration

SYED AWAIS RIZVI

ITSAS LLC PUBLICATIONS

Author: **Syed Awais Rizvi**

Executive Project Manager: Syed Imon Rizvi and Syed Ali Qasim

Technical Editor: Raza Naqvi, Alizer Rizvi

Graphical Development and Editor: Imtayaz Abbas

Production Manager: Syed Riyaz Hussain

Project Coordinator: Syed Raza Naqvi

For feedback and comments rizvir at gmail and http://phtime.com/

ISBN: 1942554060 | ISBN: 978-1-942554-06-6
Color Edition
ISBN-13: 978-1539985228 | ISBN-10: 1539985229
Kindle Edition
ISBN-10: 1-942554-00-1 | ISBN-13: 978-1-942554-00-4

Library of Congress Control Number: 015905475

DEDICATION

Start with name of God, most gracious and most merciful.

God! Send your blessings to our Prophet Muhammad (peace be upon him) and his Ahl al-Bayt.

Thanks to my dear Mother and Father.

Special thanks to my dear wife Sairah for all the support and understanding.

Thanks to my family and friends for all the support and inspiration.

There is no greater wealth than wisdom, no greater poverty than ignorance, no greater heritage than culture, and no greater support than consultation.

-Imam Ali (A.S) Nahgulbalagah

Disclaimer:

50 Plus Topics in Chapter 1 "Introduction to SAP"

Including

- **SAP Introduction**
- **GTS**
- **GRC**
- **EHP**
- **Fiori**
- **Screen Personas**
- **Project Management**
- **System landscape**
- **Finance related Topics**
- **S/4 Hana**

30 Plus Topics in Chapter 10 "Advance Tips and Tricks"

Including

- **Variant Configuration**
- **16 determinations shortcut**
- **SQVI (Table Join and reports)**
- **Debugging**
- **Pricing**
- **Table Edit**
- **LSMW**
- **Short Cuts (Parameters)**
- **EDI**
- **BAPI**

Introduction to the Book

My Motivation of writing this book comes from a need of simplification of an SAP SD. To learn basics first chapter starting from foundation learning. Would like to learn SAP essentials with simplification then this book is for you. In this book complex subjects defined with mind maps. To make learning fast this book utilize mind maps to make complex subject easy to understand. First chapter is all about SAP and information technology foundation learning. All the topics prepared with simple and short definitions to make reader understand the topic. If you are on time crunch and want to start learning fast skip to the configuration, then start with chapter two. Chapter two start with sap SD enterprise structure setup. Many topics become easier to understand with pictures, so you can find many mind maps and SAP screenshots. Every chapter has Brief summary that will help reader understand and pick the chapter to study. This book written for SAP ECC R/3 Sales and distributions.

Feedback:

Feedback or comments are welcome emailing rrizvir at gmail.com Please do leave a comment and review.

Why This Book?

This book starts with foundation learning with basics and easy to understand simple definitions. For complex topics book offers mind maps where learning become very fast. This book focuses on simple and easy to understand approach. This book will help anyone who wants to learn from very beginning or anyone who would like to improve their skills in SAP SD configuration.

Learning with Mind Maps:

Mind Maps helps representing complex topics with a simple understandable pictorial representation. Mind Map simplifies complex subjects to make the learning process easier. SAP Sales and Distribution Quick Configuration Guide utilize mind map to explain configuration for complex topics.

Who can benefit from this Book?

- Consultants
- Business Analysts
- Managers
- Beginners

CONTENTS

CONTENTS

BILLING & CREDIT MANAGEMENT........ 191

AVAILABLE TO PROMISE 213

Disclaimer:

This publication contains references to the products of SAP AG. SAP, R/3, SAP NetWeaver, Duet, PartnerEdge, ByDesign, SAP BusinessObjects Explorer, StreamWork, and other SAP products and services mentioned herein as well as their respective logos are trademarks or registered trademarks of SAP AG in Germany and other countries. Business Objects and the Business Objects logo, Business Objects, Crystal Reports, Crystal Decisions, Web Intelligence, Xcelsius, and other BusinessObjects products and services mentioned herein as well as their respective logos are trademarks or registered trademarks of Business Objects Software Ltd. Business Objects is an SAP company. Sybase and Adaptive Server, iAnywhere, Sybase 365, SQL Anywhere, and other Sybase products and services mentioned herein as well as their respective logos are trademarks or registered trademarks of Sybase, Inc. Sybase is an SAP company. SAP AG is neither the author nor the publisher of this publication and is not responsible for its content. SAP Group shall not be liable for errors or omissions with respect to the materials. The only warranties for SAP Group products and services are those that are set forth in the express warranty statements accompanying such products and services, if any. Nothing herein should be construed as constituting an additional warranty.

This book is written by Syed Rizvi with his own personal views and understanding; this book is not representing any company, products, and registered trademarks. The author does not assume any responsibility, error, and omissions and the book is based on "AS-IS". All the screenshots are copyright by SAP AG. This publication expresses no warranty, damages, guaranty, and liability whatsoever professional or any kind, direct or indirect. This book does not express warranty or guaranty, articulated or indirect to the accurateness or comprehensiveness of any information published herein of any kind.

Notes

CHAPTER 1

Foundation Learning

What is in this chapter for me?

Information technology complexity increasing day by day. It is not easy task to start learning complete new technology, so it become more important to start from basic foundation learning. With foundation learning reader start from SAP introduction to brief overview about SAP ECC with related essentials information topics t. Foundation learning is very useful for beginners as wells as intermediate learner. First chapter also covers topics from project management, which is essential for any project. In first chapter reader also learn SAP related terminology.

Being cheerful and friendly with people is by itself half of wisdom.

Imam Jafar Al-Sadiq (A. S.) (Behar, vol. 76, p. 60)

Learning Objectives:

- Introduction to SAP
- Learn about SAP modules
- Learn about SAP related terms
- Learn about project related methodologies introduction
- Learn business related terms

Introduction to SAP:

SAP AG is a name of German Software Company, which is famous for their SAP ERP system globally. SAP commonly known for ERP application. SAP stands for Systems Applications and Products in data processing. In any business, three departments are very important, finance, logistics, and human resource. SAP provided modules under accounting, logistics, and human resources. Many models are available for accounting, logistics, or human resources. SAP modules designed to represent independent business departments. One of the key benefits of SAP ERP modules is that they are, integrate, and centralize with business functions.

SAP modules offer best practices and "industry standards."

IS-Retail
IS-Oil and Gas
IS-Auto

SAP Three Tire System:

ERP industry constantly changing with new technology for performance. SAP ERP's called "SAP ECC," that stands for ERP Central Component. SAP ERP represented by three-tier based system with each tier representing each section of the software application.

- **Application (Application Server)**
- **Presentation (Computer, mobile, web, etc.)**
- **Database (Database server)**

Subsequent Figure Present the three-tier system.

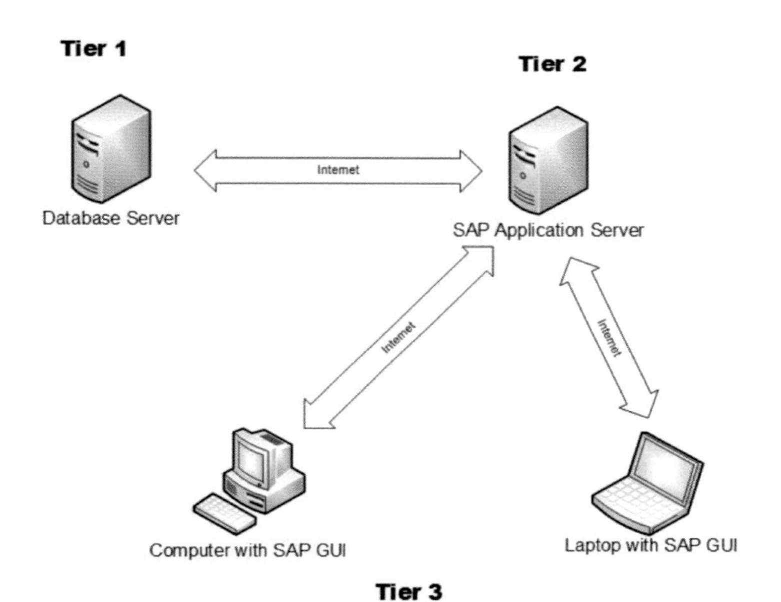

Legend		
Legend Subtitle		
Symbol	Count	Description
	2	Server
	1	Laptop computer
	1	PC

Figure 1

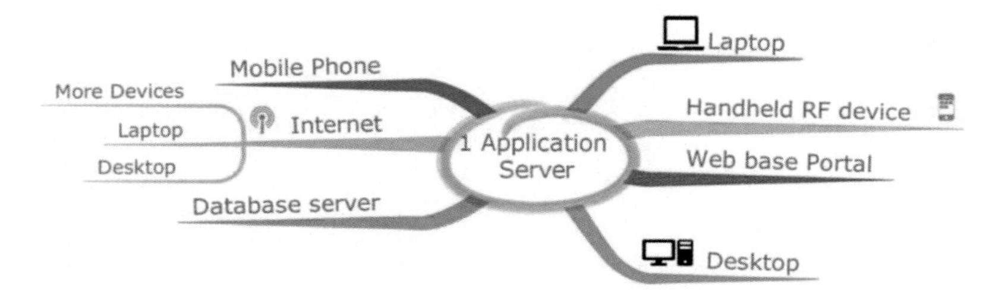

Figure 2

Application Server:

SAP GUI interact with SAP application server to access SAP database. SAP application server is a center point to access database server and to serve SAP GUI. SAP application server can be connected with different types of databases. SAP application server name used in SAP GUI connection.

Presentation:

In order to access SAP, we need a software installed on a computer called SAP GUI. With SAP GUI, we can access SAP R/3 application. GUI is a SAP presentation layer to present SAP application on a computer. SAP GUI also come with upgrade for example version 7.4 or 7.2.

Database Server:

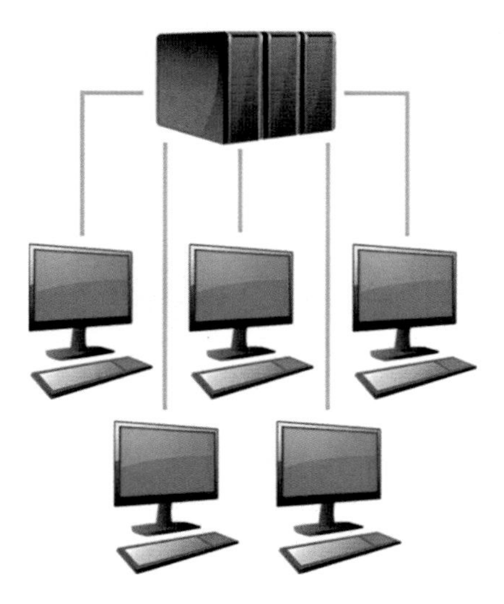

Database represents a collection of tables. SAP database reside on a separate server called SAP database server. SAP database server is a one component of a three-layer SAP ECC system.

SAP S/4 HANA

SAP S/4 HANA is a upgrade from SAP R/3. S/4 HANA stands for SAP business suite build with in memory computing, where database stays in memory. One of key reason SAP HANA was developed is to improve performance and reduce database footprint. SAP HANA offers in memory computing where application reside on a memory with some part of the database resides on a memory too. With SAP innovation SAP application server and SAP Database server reside on memory. SAP HANA also used a column base store for improved performance.

For more information on SAP HANA check free courses offered by SAP, https://open.sap.com/.

SAP Modules:

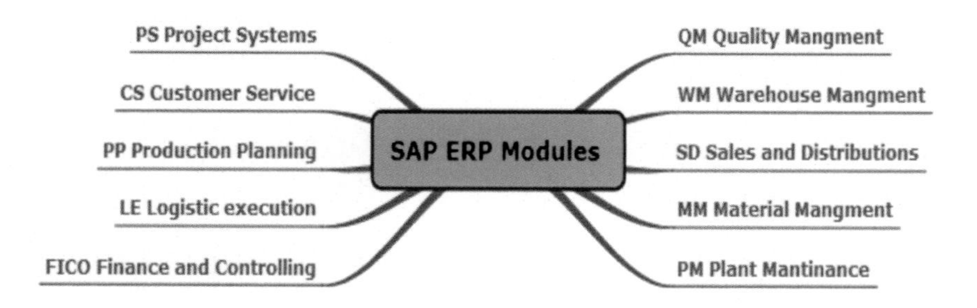

Figure 3

Any business consists of many department, SAP ERP solution divided into many modules for the different department to accommodate business functions. Most businesses has three main departments:

- Accounting
- Human resource
- Logistics

Business departments can be divided into many more sub divisions. The sub division of these main unites of business are represented as modules in SAP.

SAP FICO:

FICO stands for finance and controlling. SAP FI and CO represent two different finance modules which goes together hand to hand. Figure 4 show some of the accounting modules in SAP.

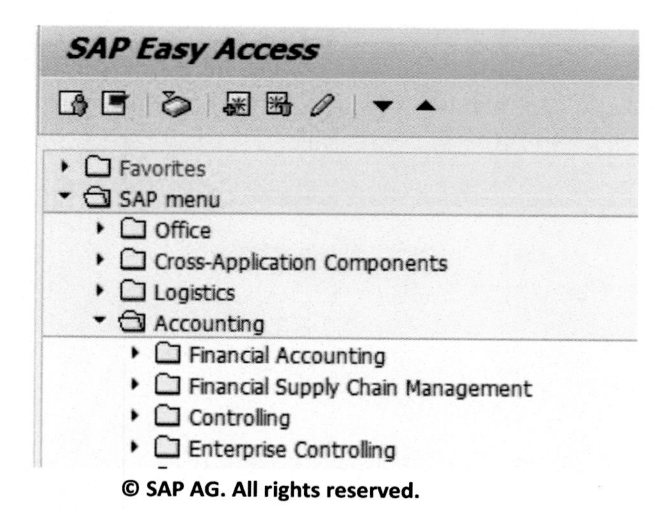

Figure 4

MM Material Management / WM Warehouse Management

MM stands for material management, and WM stands for warehouse management. SAP MM/WM is part of a logistics, where MM handle procurement processes and WM handle warehouse processes. SAP MM processes involve procure to pay, also abbreviated as P2P.

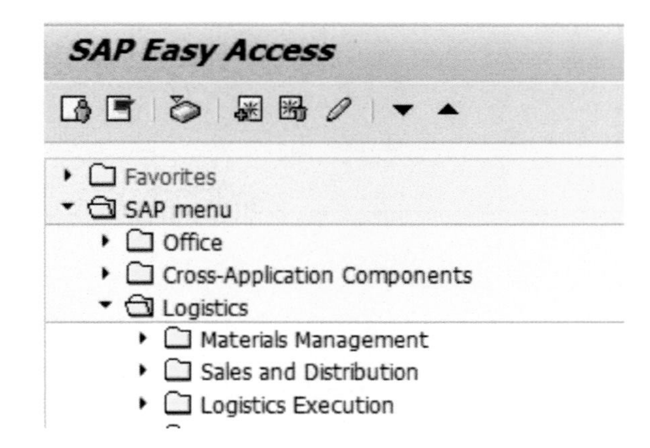

Logistic Execution:

Logistics execution module is also part of a logistics domain. Following represents few of logistic execution related functionalities:

- Inbound Delivery
- Outbound Delivery
- Warehouse Management
- Shipping
- Yard Management

SAP Sales and Distribution:

SAP Sales and distribution feature functionalities for order to cash cycle. SAP SD offer functions for sales, pricing, and billing. SAP SD integrates with FICO, MM, PP and many more modules to accommodate the process.

GTS and GTM

SAP GTS stands for Global Trade Compliance. SAP GTS and GTM modules feature full range of functionality with industry standards best practices of imports and exports. SAP GTM stands for Global Trade Management. SAP GTM manages compliance from the standpoint of globe. SAP GTS integrates the logistics and financial areas to custom compliances. SAP GTS provides following functions:

- Denied Party screening (Customer Master)
- Sanction Country Screening (in transactions, order, delivery, invoice)
- Screening on Products License (Material Master)
- Denied Freight forwarder screening (Vendor Master)
- Dangerous goods
- Harmonized tariff code management
- Drawback functionality

SAP GTS provides functionality with imports, Exports, custom related processes with government compliance controls, so that corporations stay up to date with regulations, avoid fines, and penalties. SAP GTM is part of ERP while SAP GTS is part of GRC.

SAP GRC:

SAP GRC stands for Global Risk and Compliance. SAP GRC software comprise of SAP product which utilizes the following areas:

- Financial Compliance

- Trade Management
- Environmental Regulations
- User provisioning, roles and authorization

Financial Compliance includes SOX, Roles, fraud, and risk related processes. Trade management includes ITAR and EAR compliance.

ABAP:

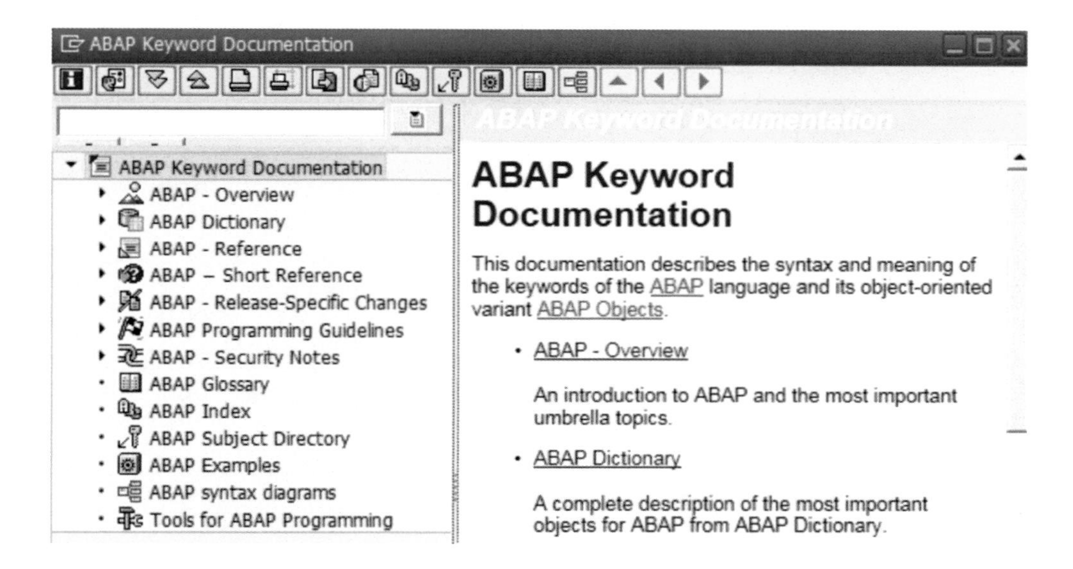

ABAP stands for Advance Business Application Programing. ABAP employ in SAP to interchange or enhance the SAP standard. ABAP programming language comprise basis of SAP programs. To read ABAP programing, practice the following t-codes. These t-codes also provide examples how to utilize the syntax in programing.

T-codes:

1. ABAPHELP
2. ABAPDOCU

ALV:

ALV stands for ABAP list viewer. SAP reports feature an ALV option to select different variations and selection options for the data to display. With this, users able to hide, display, or suppress fields or header and item level information into the report. It's a very flexible tool for reports.

Project Methodology:

Methodology represents systematic, organized, proven model or method that allows for implementing objectives. Methodology represents a model of work that has been tested and performed many times for expected results. Use of methodology ensures the expected result from desire projects. Use of methodology is proven in many areas to accomplish success in calculating manner.

By utilizing Methodology, one able to predictable result. Methodology able to represent effective if followed entirely, otherwise partial approach can cause harm. Methodology feature a set of rules and parameters with phase-wise approach.

Example of methodologies:

- Implementation methodology
- Business modeling methodology
- Research Methodology

SAP Activate:

SAP Activate represent SAP latest methodology gear toward rapid implementation for SAP S/4 HANA. It is primarily driven from agile methodology and aligned with PMI standards. SAP Activate methodology represented by suite of methodologies each for different SAP application. Following are phases of the SAP activate methodology phases:

- **Prepare**

- **Explore**
- **Realize**
- **Deploy**

Agile Methodology:

Agile is the new emerging project implementation methodology to offer better success rate. Agile methodology is consisting on iteration cycles where each cycle features section of product to be developed. In each cycle portion of functionality is tested for approval.

Scrum gain the popularity due to success rate of the software implementation. Scrum features deliverables similarities to other methodologies however they are delivered in cycles.

Agile Cycles:

What represent a project cycle? "Agile" mythology features small incremental cycles. Each Cycle feature deliverables and a set of activities to consider and complete. Project cycle represent a developing and completing portion of functionality.

ASAP Implementation Methodology:

ASAP stands for Accelerated SAP. It's a project implementation methodology developed by SAP. It is also called an SAP road-map implementation.
ASAP Methodology Roadmap is divided into five major phases.

- **Project preparation**
- **Blueprinting**
- **Functional Developer or Realization**
- **Final Preparation or goes live preparation**
- **Go-live**
- **Support**

Project Preparation:

It is utmost important phase of the project where business plan for the rest of the phases. Project preparation involves getting ready for the project, commercial discussion, and finalization of SOW. In preparation companies represent a proof of concept and benefits of new functions.

Project Preparation involves:

- Team and stakeholder identification
- Role and responsibility assignment
- Team building activities
- Process of approval
- Scope and Objective

Scope of the project means what modules, functionalities, systems and components planned for implementation. Scope supposed to be very clear, so everyone is working on the same target. Team building activities are required in the discovery phase for team identifications.

Blueprinting:

To better understand project teams from different streams, gather process requirements. Requirement gathering start with requirement gathering workshops. In workshops analyst documents the current processes. The captured business processes analyzed for fit and gap analysis. Gaps are aligned with RICIFW. RICIF consist of: Reports, Interfaces, Conversions, Forms, Work flow.

Realization:

System built activities start in realization phase including configurations, testing, functional specification developments, RECIF developments, etc. Test scripts are executed with test plans and scenarios. The deliverables are for testing the cycle. It is as follows: test plan, test scripts, document user acceptance documents etc. In the realization phase, activities are involved around following deliverables:

- System Configuration and customization
- Testing Scenarios
- Functional Unit testing (FUT)
- Technical Unit Testing
- System Architecture
- Data Migration Documents

Go-live Preparation and Go-live

For great part of the project, this is the last phase for final push to go-live. The deliverables and activities involved for Go-Live Preparation phase are the following:

- Fall back Plan
- Data Cleansing and finalization
- Data Migration Mock tests
- Go-live of system

Best Practices:

Best practices represented the industry's standard. Best practice given the industry the highest value after international standards of ISO 9000. SAP process and function are based on SAP best practices.

SAP Best practice represented by out of box functionalities, process design etc. Adoptable best practice can help companies to stream line their processes.

Tips:

- Best practice improve business process
- Best practice also provide industry standards
- Best practices do not require ABAP programing

SAP Configuration:

SAP out of the box requires preparation configuration setup for master and transactional setups. Customization in SAP called IMG. IMG stands for Implementation Guide.

To customize one can use T-code: SPRO

- Configuration perform by analyst, consultants, and configurators.

OSS Notes:

OSS note stands for Online Service System. OSS represent support system by SAP. SAP provide service pack and version supports. SAP also provide support for bugs or issues through OSS. To view OSS notes, user require an S- ID issued from organization or SAP.

Tips:

- OSS notes can be searched on https://support.sap.com/
- Obtain a S-ID from SAP Basis or security team or SAP
- OSS notes incident support require detail document for SAP to investigate.

EHP:

EHP stands for Enhancement Pack. Every new version of SAP follow with many enhancement packs. Enhancement pack provides new features and upgrades to the latest version of SAP ERP ECC.

The latest version of SAP ERP ECC 6.0 enhancement pack "**SAP ECC 6.0 EHP 8**"

SAP Fiori:

SAP Fiori provides a web base use of ERP functions mainly for SAP S/4 HANA. SAP Fiori comes with bundle of applications with integration. SAP Fiori web base application allows access for mobile device and tablets. SAP Fiori feature released a set of application based on ERP module's functionality.

For more information http://help.sap.com/fiori_products#section1

Project:

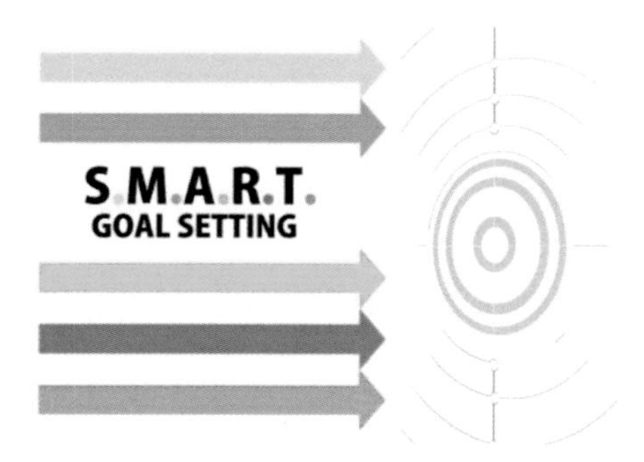

Any strategy for a task with beginning and end can be called project. Project cannot be completed without consideration of project plan, project scope, and resources. Many methodologies are available for project implementations.

Project Phases

Phase can be defined as period of time with set of goals. Project divided into many phases. In project phases, particular activities are defined for each phase. The activities and targets require to accomplish before the next phase.

Blueprint Documents:

What topics included in Blueprint document is decided by project manager, team lead or team members. It is essential for business to understand and also provide a feedback on all of the templates that will be used in project. Depend on the project goals many topics can be included or excluded in blueprint document. Following are some of the brief topics that can be utilized in blueprint document.

- AS-IS Business Process
- AS-IS process flow Diagram
- Pain points and requirements
- To-be process flow diagram
- To be process details
- Gap-analysis standard or GAP
- RECIF Process
- Business process owner and BA details
- Project name and doc version
- Status of the document with version history
- Roles and Security
- OCM Change Impact
- Feedback from Business

Blueprint document Mind Map

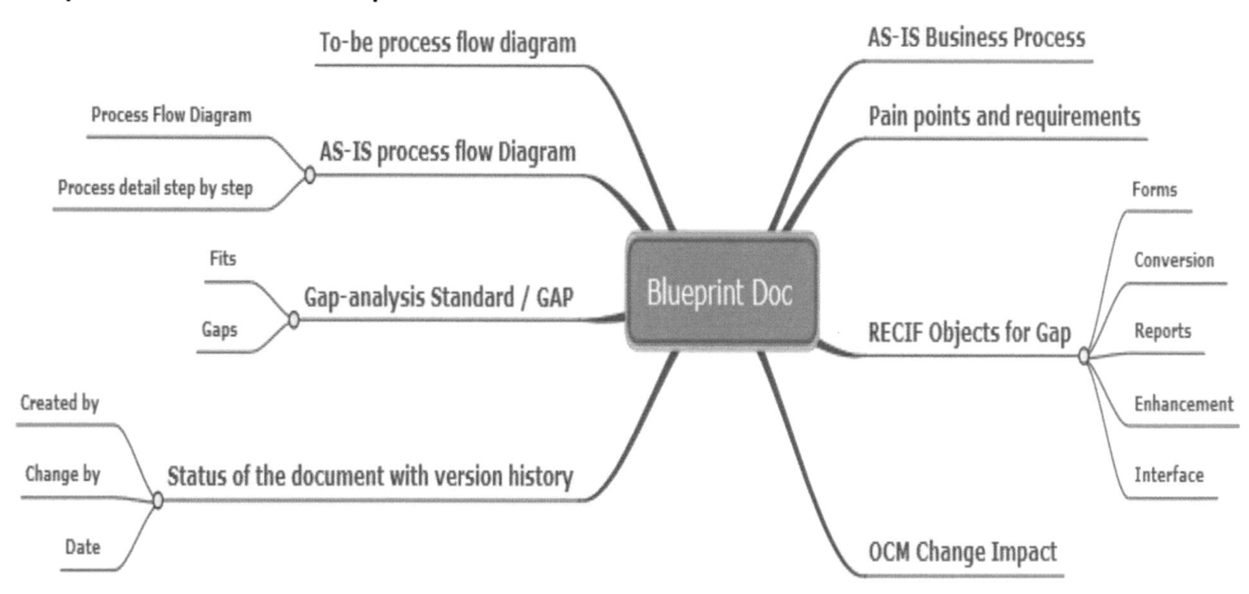

Project Issue / Opportunity Management:

Every issue is an opportunity for correction. Issues are part of a project. Issue never stop coming even after project implementation or in project implementation. Manny companies maintain issue and risk log to improve.

Issue Log:

Keeping an issue log is ongoing process to track bugs in a software before and after implementation. Issues are logged based on system performance, user complaints, testing etc. Many tools are able to utilize and manage issue logs.

Project Risk Management:

Risk is part of our life, starting from driving on a road to taking stairs etc. Risks can be defined as predictions of issues in future. Risk expected to be identify in any stage of the project. The biggest risk exist when project managers, stakeholders, and team members ignore potential risks. Risk also supposed to be kept in a risk log and tracked to avoid future issues.

PMO:

PMO stands for Project Management Office or officer. Project managers are experienced individuals who look after the project.

Project complete life cycle:

Any project that is completed from start to finish is considered a full lifecycle.

SOW:

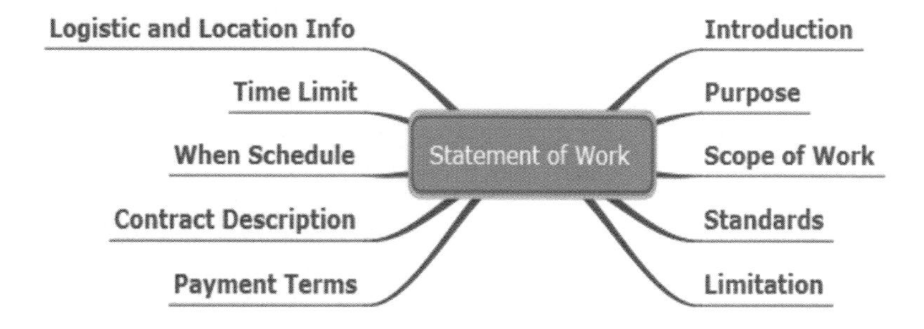

SOW in Mind map

Introduction:

SOW stands for a statement of work. It comprise of legally binding document, engagement or service contract.

ERP

Representation of ERP in mind map.

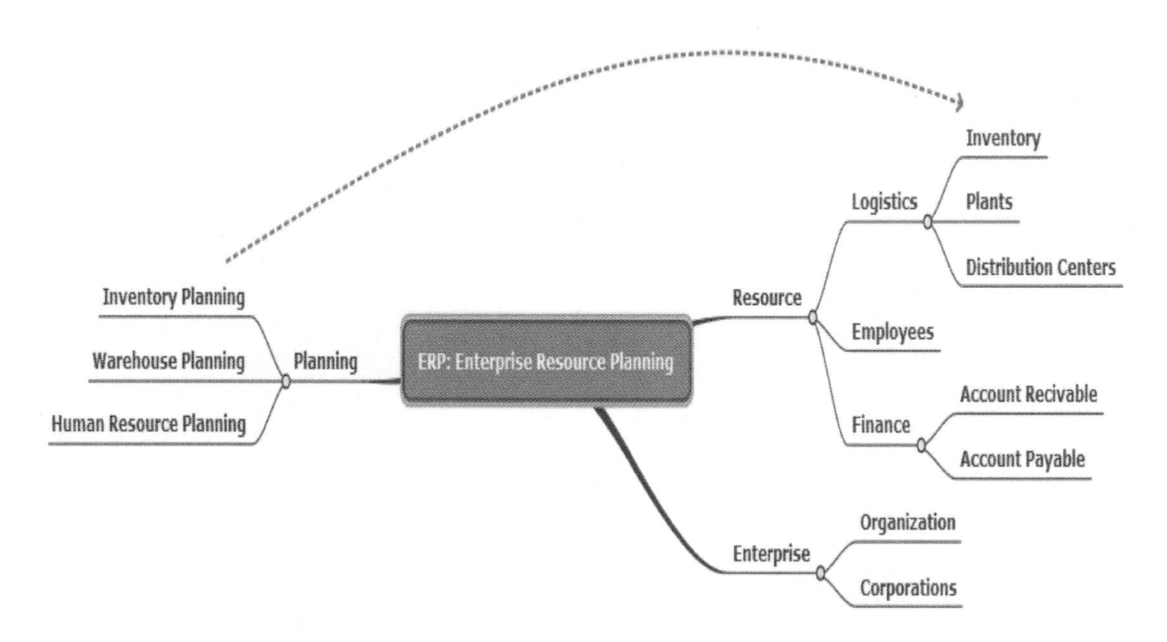

ERP Stands for Enterprise Resource Planning. Few of the ERP functions are defined in figure and show how enterprise resource planning works. Many business departments are managed by the organization, thus the ERP software becomes a necessity that able to handle multiple departments and resources centrally.

Enterprise:

Enterprise represents a business or organization. Any big organization with many departments can be callified as enterprise.

ECC:

ECC stands for ERP central Component. ECC abbreviation employ by SAP to identify its new release of SAP. Usually ECC term practice for SAP version ERP 5.0 ECC OR SAPERP 6.0.

Service Pack:

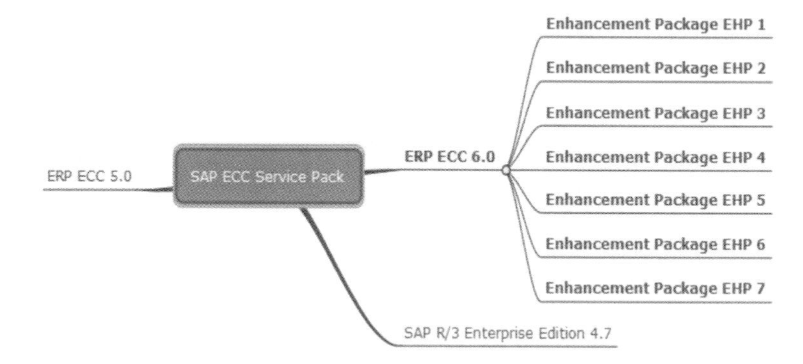

Service pack refers to upgrade to specific version of SAP. New service pack offers new features and bugs fixes with it.

System Landscape:

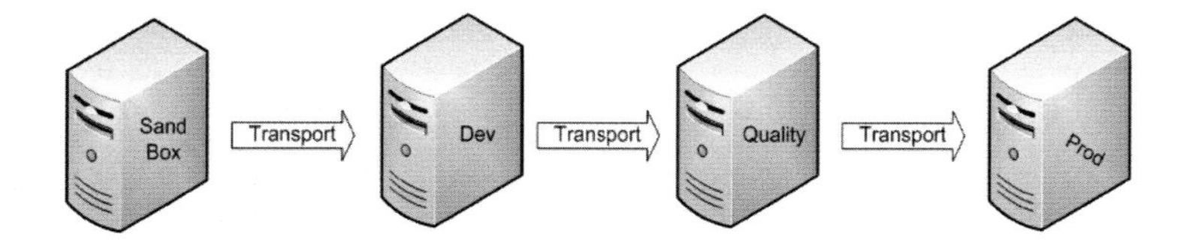

System Landscape

We use system landscape to develop identical objects to prepare it in deployment system, test it, in test system and finally copy the finish product to production system. System landscapes mostly consist of three or more identical environments for project life cycle. In a project, we develop functions in a "development system" and then it get copy to "quality server" for testing. After the successful testing, it will be transported to the "production system".

In general, system landscapes consist of three system environments:

- Development
- Quality
- Production

Development System:

Development system utilizes for system configuration and custom developments. Many projects also maintain sand box with addition to development system.

Quality System:

Quality system used when project team needs to test the changes. Quality system also utilized for user acceptance testing, regression testing etc.

Production System:

Any system that is used for real time transections is call production system. Many companies start using SAP live system after the project cycle is completed.

ABAP:

ABAP stands for Advance Business Application Programing. ABAP is SAP language for SAP system enhancements. ABAP programing is used for new enhancements, transections, report etc. ABAP is SAP langue for development.

T-codes:

- ABAPHELP
- ABAPDOCU

ALV:

Most of SAP report features in ALV, ALV stands for ABAP list viewer. With ALV user has option to select different variations and selection to slice and dice the data. With this, users able to hide, display, or suppress fields or control header and item level information into the report. ALV is a very flexible tool for reports.

BAPI:

BAPI stands for Business Application Programing Interface. BAPI is also called the functional module. BAPI is technical component of SAP for development and enhancements.

Document:

Electronic document concept is same as paper documents. Paper documents used for record keeping and electronic document is also used for similar purpose. Computer files saved in electronic document. In computers and servers all electronic files saved in database as electronic documents.

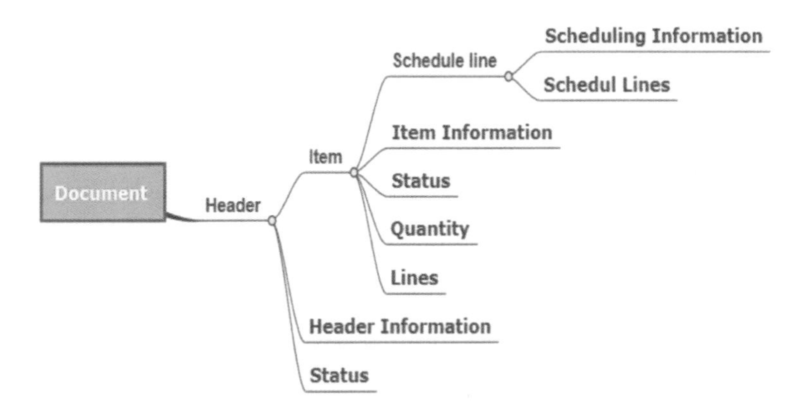

Document represents information or proof record or record.
In a SAP SD document divided into three parts. Throughout SAP most document concept stay the same for document header and document item.

1. **Header**
2. **Item**
3. **Schedule Line**

Header represents a controlling, item represents the content of document, and schedule line indicates additional controls from line item.

Header Data:

Header data defines the type of document and it controls the behavior of the document.

Item Data:

Item data copy header data information into all of the lines items.

Schedule Line Data:

Schedule Line Data contains scheduling information of a document.

Database:

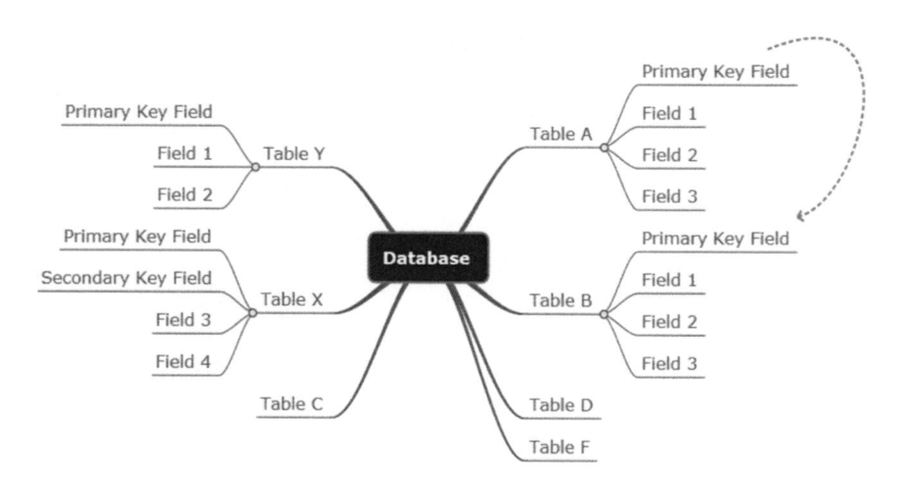

Logical collection of tables can be called tables. The table consist of rows and columns, with reference to database. Database servers maintain databases.

Number Range:

Number range is an identifier which controls document number, sequencing, limit of numbers and manual numbers. Mostly number range controls the number of transactional data. Number range represent a SAP configuration for transactional or master data. Series of number ranges utilized differently for different transactions. In SAP two types of number ranges exist:

1. **Internal Number Range (Automatics)**
2. **External Number Range (non-automatic)**

Internal number range automatically selected by a system, and external number range will not assign a number to new transection.

Internal Number Range:

Internal number range used where we want system to automatically assign next number to master data or transactional data.

For example, if customer is created with internal number range then system automatically select a next available number from internal number range.

External number range:

External number range used where we want to assign number for master data or transactional data manually.

Example of Internal Number range:

If customer created with external number range, then system will not assign new number instead system will give error massage to enter the number for new customer.

Table:

Tables contain information in rows and columns. Data utilized for programs and software data store.

Field:

In a table field located in rows and columns intersection. Each field features properties form header field. Each field features many controls. Field characteristic defines at header level. Following represent several properties of a field.

- Field Name
- Technical Name
- Key Field
- Data Element
- Data Type
- Length
- Decimal Place
- Short Description

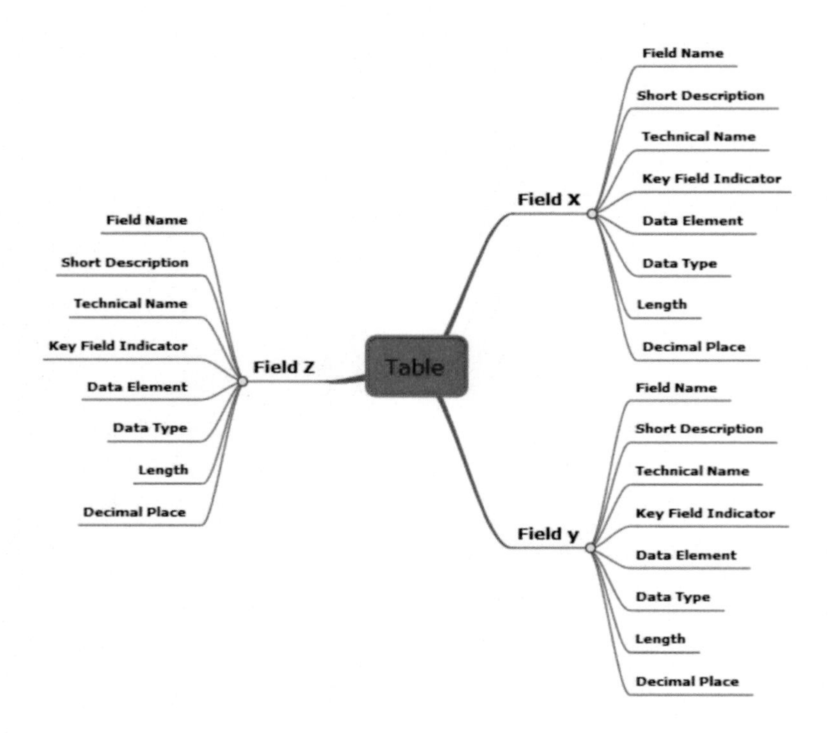

Field Status Group:

SAP feature four field statuses and it called field status group:

1. Required
2. Suppressed
3. Optional
4. Display

In SAP field status group control each field able to display, hidden, suppressed, or optional in the master data or transactional data.

Display:
Display status of the field only displays the content and cannot be change. When field status represents on display status, it only displays the content of the field.

Suppress:
Suppress means hiding the field from the screen.

Optional:
Optional field status is utilized as an option. When field status represented as an optional, the user able to fill the data or leave it empty.

Required:
required field status require entry for data processing.

Data in SAP:

SAP feature two types of data.

1. Master Data
2. Transactional Data

Master Data:

The data that hardly changes and utilized in transactions. Example of master data in SAP are:

- Customer master
- Vendor Master
- Pricing Master

Transactional Data

Data that changes often called a transactional data. Transactional data always based on a master data with variations of transactions. The sales document, delivery and billing document represents good example of transactional data.

EDI:

EDI stands for Electronic Data Interface. EDI framework used between EDI capable system to transmit or receive data. EDI defined with industry standards to send and receive various transection include: orders, invoices, delivery etc.

IDOC:

IDOC stands for Intermediate Document. IDOC's made for EDI interface and interfaces. IDOCS able to view with t-code IDOC. IDOC also able to utilize for data migration along with LSMW.

SQL:

SQL stands for Structured Query Language, SQL represent query of database. SQL utilizes to call tables and data employ SQL commands. It is based on ANSI.

ANSI:

ANSI stands for the American National Standards Institute. ANSI helps in the development of standard, and for more information, please go to the link http://www.ansi.org.

BASIS:

Basis refers to the SAP system admin and security module. A basis consultant installs, upgrades, maintains, secures and administer the system. The basis consultant role is to authorize the setup related activities in projects and in system support. Basis analyst also upgrades systems and enhancement packs.

Synchronous Interface:

Synchronous means real time data processing transaction. A good example of synchronous process is when data is synchronous between two or more phone calls. It is utilized in interface related documents if the interface is synchronous.

Asynchronous Interface:

Asynchronous is opposite of synchronous, it is not real time. For example, when the process involves periodic update then it considers asynchronous. It is utilized in interface related document if the interface is asynchronous. For example, mail via postal service takes time to arrive to its destination. .

AR (Account Receivable) and AP (Account Payment):

AR refers to accounts receivable, which is utilized in the revenue for the sales income.

Accrual and cash Basis Accounting:

In accounting, revenue is calculated on the basis of either cash or accrual. Accrual mean added up and keeping track of it. On the accrual basis of accounting the amount is tracked and eventually it is posted for accounting purposes. Cash basis accounting is posted as soon as the transaction is processed in the system or accounting.

Profit Center:

Profit center related to accounting, it keeps track for profit and cost. Profit center is utilized in SAP finance and controlling module.

Cost Center:

Cost Center is an internal company accounting component. Cost centers are utilized to put expenses toward the accounting in order to track the cost.

Process:

Process is an activity which takes inputs, adds value to it, or changes it and produce outputs from it.

Process Flow Diagram:

Pictorial representation of process is called process flow diagram. There are many different methods to draw process flow diagrams. UML method is one of the example of process flow diagram methodology.

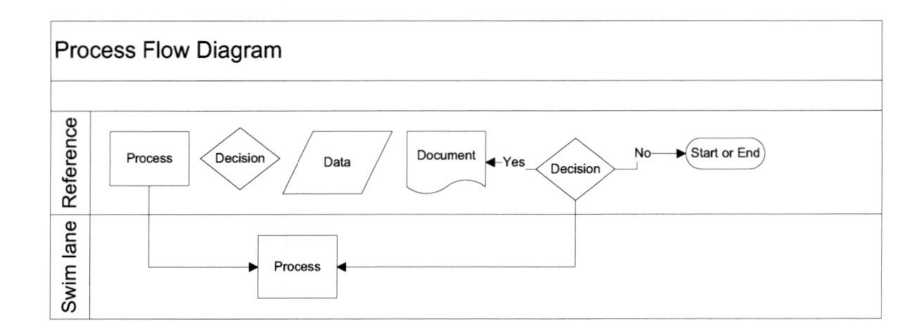

Workflow:

Workflow is a system of work that goes through business approvals and administration approvals. SAP Workflow feature a process of approvals in system. Also, in SAP, workflow is part of RECIFW that is counted toward system change, other than the standard functionality of SAP ERP.

Use case:

Use case is a pictorial representation of process. Use case helps visual process flow for better understanding. The use case features Actors in stick figures interacting with system define in the middle. Use case is created in requirement gathering and documentation for the project.

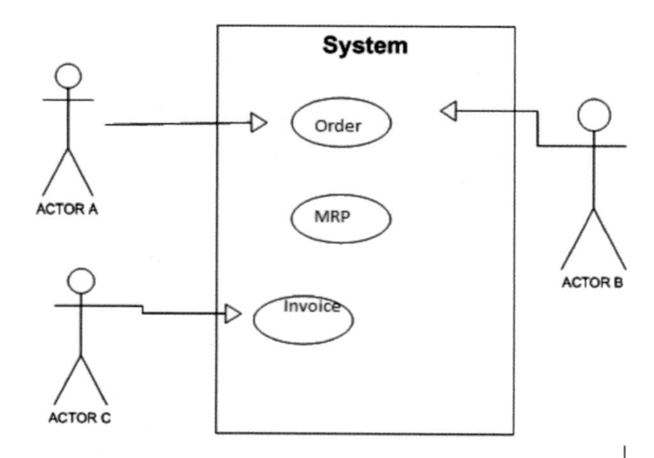

General Ledger Accounting:

General ledger accounting is an account for all business transactions. GL is utilized for profit, loss report and financial calculation etc. It is very important for businesses to keep track of transaction for legal and accountability. The SAP feature general ledger accounting is integrated with all of the modules to keep track of all financial transactions.

T-Account:

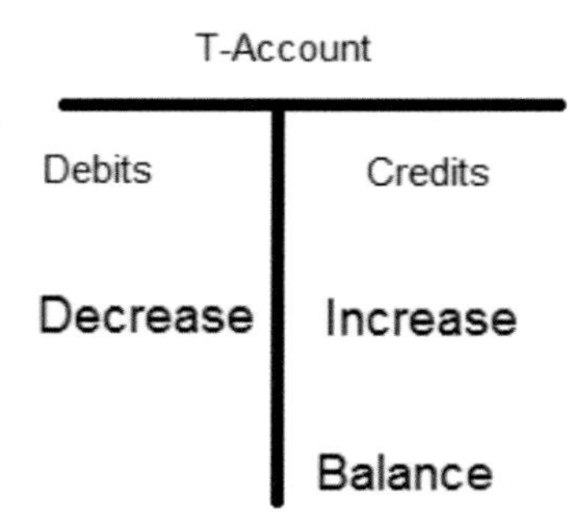

T-account is utilized in accounting with journal entries. On the left side of the T-account is debit and on the right side is credit. In the figure above, we able to see that the left side is the debit and that the right side is credit. At the end of the T-account, we able to see balance from both sides of transactions and keep track of journal leader balance with sub T-accounts.

Journal entry:

In T-accounting each transaction is entered either on debit or credit, this is what is called a journal entry.

Credit

Credit means an increase in amount or gain. Credit refers to entry in accounting when balance increases. When we over pay our bill then we will receive a credit balance transfer back.

Debit

In accounting, debit refers to the decrease in the account. For example, debit means to pay out something so it decreased amount is transfer out of the balance.

Credit and Debit memo

Credit and Debit memo is an invoice document in SAP.

SME:

SME stands for Subject Mater Expert. Subject matter expert is a title given to technology or business-related knowledge.

SAP Consultant:

SAP Consultant is a title for the role in which his/her responsibilities fall into the project implementation or support role.

OCM:

OCM stands for Organizational Change Management. OCM streams help businesses prepare for the new system. OCM teams works with management for organizational changes.

Stake Holder:

A stakeholder is an individual or group of individuals who are responsible for the project from business side. The project manager reports to the, stakeholders about project progress. Stakeholders able to approve the additional scope of the project or remove it, based on projects vision.

"Z" and "Y" customization:

SAP recommends customization to start with "Z" and "Y". When customization start with "Z" or "Y" it will not be over written on upgrades.

Role and Responsibility:

Business:

Role and responsibility always defined clearly in successful projects. Role and responsibility personify importance to define clearly in business role as per compliance and regulations.

SAP User:

SAP user are defined with roles and access for transactions. Different transactions allows create, change and display access.

T-code:

T-code stands for transaction code. The easy access menu feature a transaction bar, as seen in the screenshot. In this transection bar a user entered a T-code.

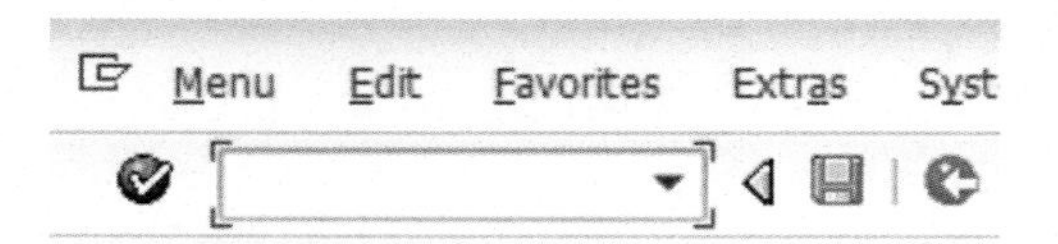

Tips to remember T-code:

Here are some tips to remember T-code alphabets.

Character	Description
N	Number
V	Sales
F	Billing
M	Material Master
01	Create
02	Changes
03	Display
05	Report

To get reports for any module from EASY Access Menu use T-code: **SAP1**
this will only show a report from every module.

For sales related MENU use t-code: **VA00**

For Customization (Implementation Guide also abbreviated into IMG) T-code is: **SPRO**

/o	Open New Session
/n	To end the current transaction
/i	To delete the current session
/nend	To log off with saving
/nex	Exit without saving

SAP Easy Access Menu:

The SAP Easy Access Menu is the initial screen after logging into the SAP GUI. The easy access menu able to customize with GUI options. In general the SAP easy access menu able to have six separate sessions running at the same time. The easy access menu feature a transaction bar code bar T-codes. The easy access menu able to customize and assigned to the user or to a group of users.

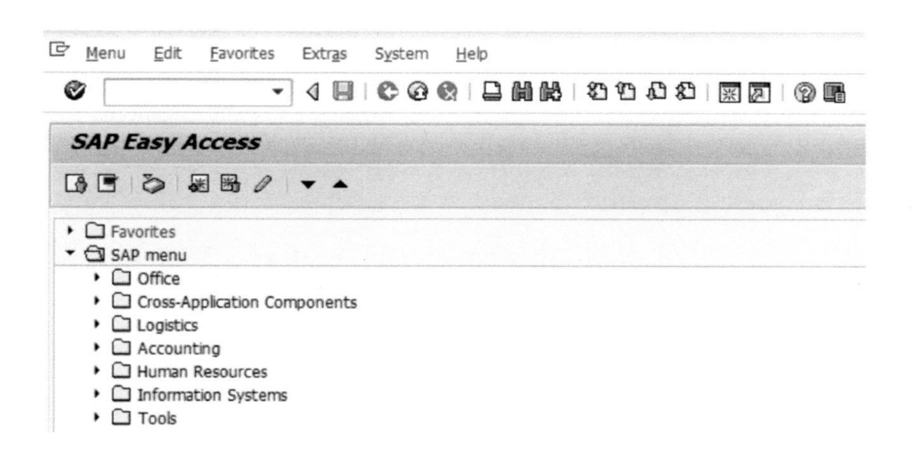

Easy Access Menu buttons and shortcuts:

Button	Description	Shortcut
	Enter	
	Command Field for T-codes the triangle close the command field	
	Save	ctrl + S
	Back	F3
	Log Off (from current session)	Shift + F3
	Cancel	F12
	Print	Ctrl + P
	Find	Ctrl + F
	Find Next	Ctrl + G
	First Page	Ctrl + page up
	Page up	
	Page Down	
	Last Page	Ctrl + pg den

	New Session	
	Create shortcut	
	Help	F1
	Customize Local Layout (change Color, themes, font size, etc.)	
	Add to Favorites	Ctrl + shift + F6
	Delete Favorite	Shift + F12
	Change Favorite	Ctrl + shift + F3

•

SAP Messages Types:

SAP error messages are defined in different categories. Some errors are not able to bypass. If a warning which is normally red comes on, it means it's a hard error and cannot sustain to ignore. Not all errors are not hard errors, these errors are called soft errors. The warning error color is yellow and it able to ignore, however the user will see warnings. In the event that the transaction system issues a message, it means that the status of transection changed by the user. An SAP, messages is defined in different categories, with their own message types. Each process feature a message type in SAP. It gives a status to the user that results in success and failure:

1. Warring
2. Error
3. Exit
4. Success

Each process feature a message type in SAP. It gives a status to the user that results in success and failure.

Message Type	Screens hot	Description
Information		The message type is for information purposes, by clicking the icon it will open a new window with information.
Warning:		It feature warned you on the next step. It able to correct before the warning is ignored. (The user able to ignore it by pressing enter) The warning may appear more than once based on transactions. It appears on left bottom of the screen.
Hard Error		Message gives a hard stop. Unless the correction is made, it will stay at error and will not process.
Exit		Message exits the trisections and gives a short dump or stop the transaction.
Success		Success message with document number or if this transaction is successful this will appear. It appears on left bottom of the screen.

Notes

CHAPTER 2

ENTERPRISE STRUCTURE

Companies created as per country and government regulations. In SAP SD business organizational unite represented in enterprise structure elements. In this chapter, find a brief overview of SAP Sales and Distribution enterprise structure configuration guide. This chapter also cover part of finance and logics enterprise structure setup.

- Enterprise Structure Introduction
- Company
- Company Code
- Credit Control Area
- Sales Organization
- Distribution Channel
- Division
- Sales Area
- Sales Office
- Sales Group
- Plant
- Shipping Point
- Shipping Point Determination
- Business Area
- Visual Validation of Business Area

Learning Objectives:

- Learn how to configure SAP SD Enterprise structure
- Learn enterprise level finance and logistic integration
- Learn how to configure with transection code and configuration path
- Learn how to configure enterprise structure to optimize and minimize master and transactional data

Introduction to Enterprise structure:

Enterprise structure is a representation of organizational unites in the system. After finding AS-IS structure, project team discusses with business how to setup business organizational unites in SAP. The enterprise structure setup requires project team to design and take business feedback. Enterprise structure design is essential for master data and transactional data complexity. It is best to not create unnecessary sales organizations, distribution, and division, which will end up creating many sales areas.

In SAP Company, code is a representation of legal entity. Each company can have multiple company codes assigned to it. Each company code can have a sales organization, division, plants, warehouse etc. The client represents the logical database instance. Sales organization assigned to a company code. Each plant assigned to company code. Storage location assigned to a plant.

Enterprise structure diagram:

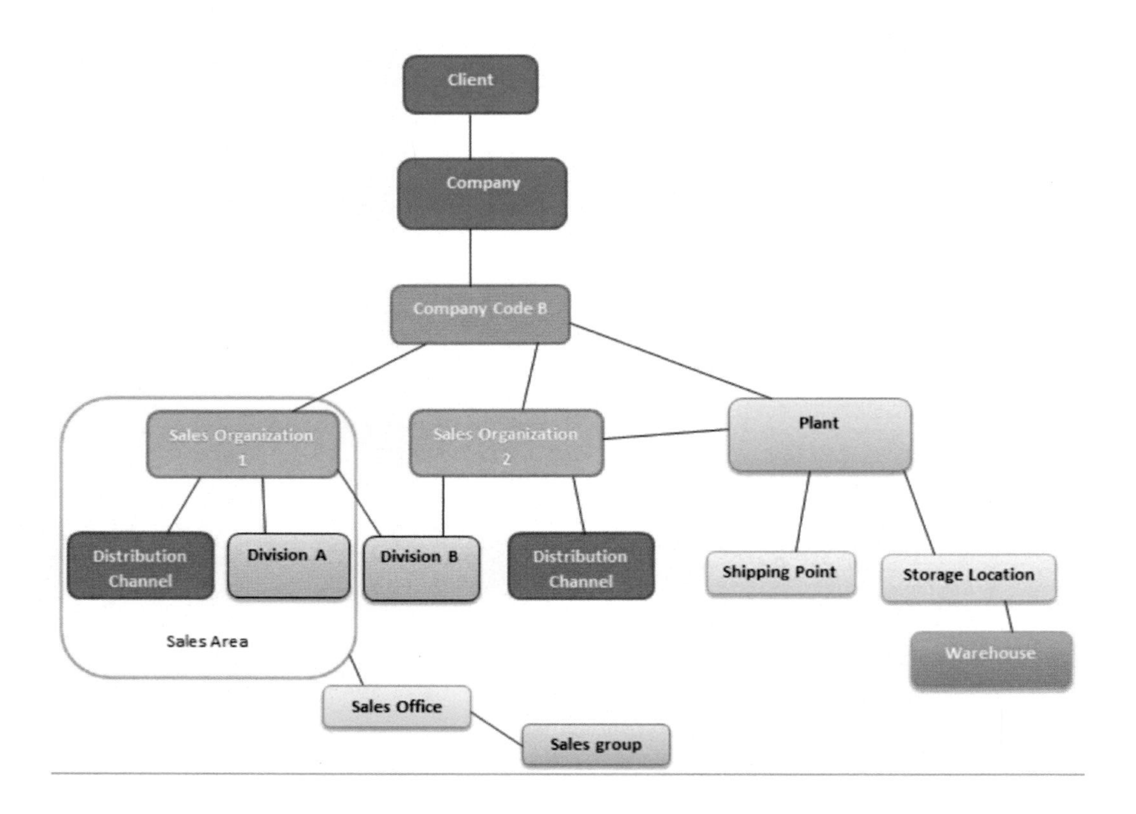

Tips:

Successful organizations don't overlook on the importance of an optimum enterprise design. Enterprise structure should be considered based on the master data and transactional data, impact analysis. If the enterprise structure setup without considerations it can create more master data and more complexity for the users. For example if one company created in multiples sales areas, then same customer have to be created with each sales area which can end up with two master data in system.

Enterprise structure figure

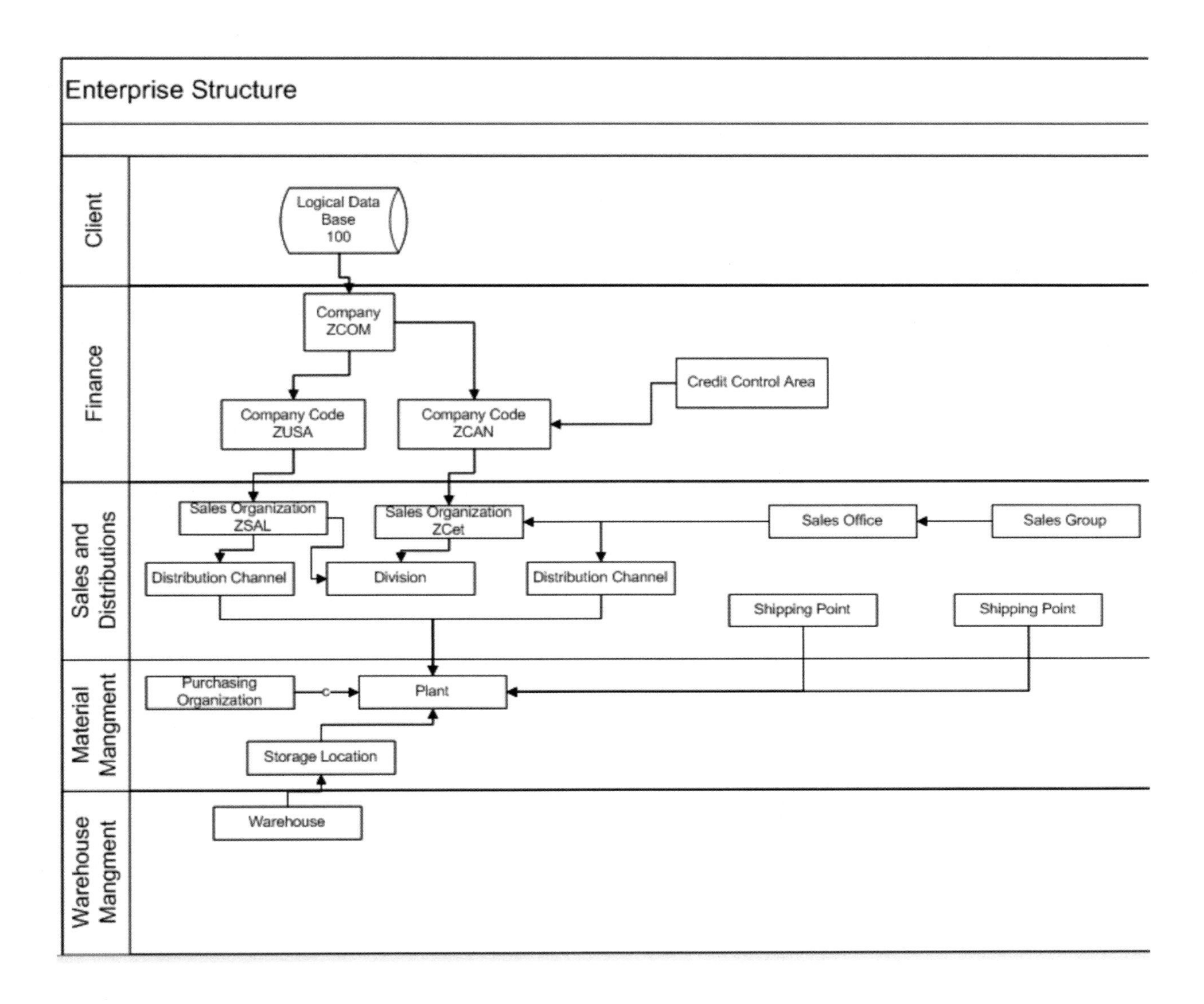

Implementation Guide Customization:

Any kind of configuration or customization can be possible with transection code SPRO. IMG refers to implementation guide customization. It is also called back end customization. Access to customization is limited to project or support team. Customization allowed in development server and then the changes are transported to quality or test system to test the changes. After all of the changes are tested in quality or test system same transport move to production system.

Easy access menu path:

SAP Menus → Tools → Customizing → IMG → Execute Project

T-code: **SPRO**

Client:

Client number concept is SAP way of creating separate database on the basis of client number identification. Client is the logical database represented in SAP with three-digit number. It is utilized for multiple instances on the same machine (server). Client's number is required for SAP GUI logon. Some customizations in SAP are specific to the client and some customizations are not client specific. When company creates a different client actually they can be on same database but identified with different client database number. When all of the clients are from same database then any change to client independent changes can affect data for all of the clients on same database. The customizations that are global in nature able to affect all clients and for this reason it supposed to done with caution, thus causing change. The development means it automatically will be in production, t. The client is single logical instances of the database.

Company:

Company represents a business, legal entity. In SAP each company able to assign multiple company codes to it. In SAP company number created with alpha or numeric characters. Company's creation in SAP is a responsibility of FICO consultant.

Example: Company "XYZ" able to have one company code from United States and one company code from Canada. Each company code will be the legal entity formed in that country and feature separate transactions specific to that company's code.

To create a Company code use T-code: **OX15**

IMG → Enterprise Structure → Definition → Financial Accounting → Defines Company

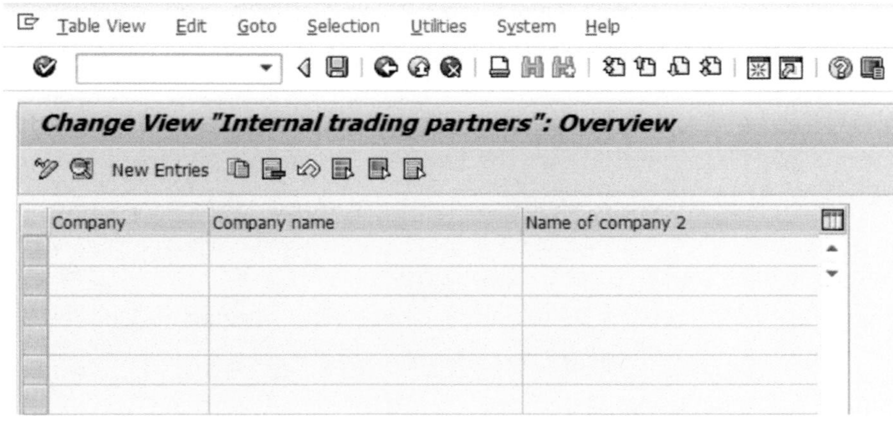

In the above screenshot, the company is defined with four characters. The company number in SAP able to define in alpha or numeric or composite value. The second field is for the company's name and the third field is for company's name 2.

Why define company in SAP?

Company code setup in SAP to represent hierarchy of a company which could have multiple company codes assigned to a company.

Company Code:

Company code represents the financial and organizational unit in SAP. Company code represents the legal entity. Company code customization is also done by a FICO consultant. Each company code maintained with address, currency, language etc.

IMG → Enterprise Structure → Definition → Financial Accounting → Define Company code

T-code: **OX02**

Credit Control Area:

Credit control area defines how customer's credit controls are setup for credit related transactions. Control area customizations able to manage independently or centrally managed. Credit control area controls the customer's credit functionality. The credit control area should have the same currency as company's code. Each company's code with one credit control assigned to it, but credit control able to have many company codes assigned to it. The credit control area also able to assign to multiple company codes. The credit control area is utilized in customer credit master creation. Credit Control Area customization is the responsibility of the SAP FI and SD modules area.

Credit Control Area Customization:

The credit control area able to set by T-code **OB45**

IMG → Enterprise Structure → Definition → Financial Accounting → Defines Credit Control Area

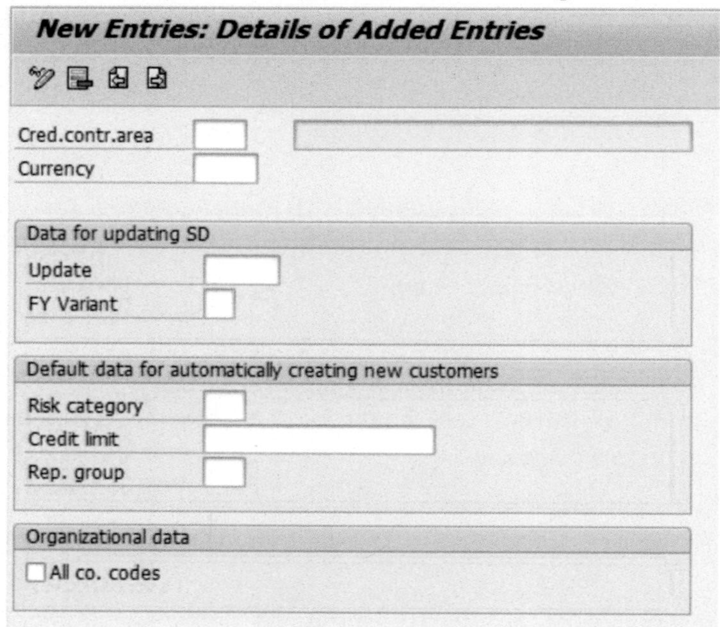

Credit control area:

Credit control area is four characters long and it could be alphanumeric combination.

Currency:

The currency must be the same as company code currency.

Data for updating SD:

In these controls two elements are relevant to sales and distribution related controls.

- **Update**
- **FY Variant**

Update:

Update customization controls uses of credit exposure will open sales documents, deliver documents and invoice documents, to be later calculated in the credit process. Three different standard values able to utilize.

- **000012**
- **000015**
- **000018**
- **000012**

This value references the sales order lines with a confirmed delivery date. For any delivery and billing it considers open delivery, along with the billing document line value that are included in the credit calculation. For any new orders and transaction processing credit gets updated.

000015

The credit exposure for this selection considers the open delivery value and open billing value. For clearing account for it consider an unclear item for credit processing.

000018

This selection is criteria for service related sales order when deliveries should not be considered. This credit exposure considers sales order, billing and financial open entries for the credit processing.

FY Variant

This is utilized to set the fiscal year period for the credit control area.

All Company Codes:

The credit control area able to activate for all company codes in which credit control area given to defined and allowed for postings.

Assigning credit Control area to Company Code:

To assign a credit control area to the company code use **T-code OB38**. Also for manual path from SPRO is
IMG → Enterprise Structure → Assignment → Financial Accounting →Assign company code to credit control area. (Select defines)
Company codes have an option to enter one credit control area to it. With the option selected overwrite the processing of the transactions, and the credit control area able to change. It will

overwrite the old credit control area.

Sales Organization:

Sales organization is an organizational unit that is responsible for sales activity. This organizational element is represented in SAP by the enterprise element of sales organization. Sales organization able to define with the alphabet and numeric values. Sales organizations are only assigned to one company code. The one company code able to have multiple sales organizations assigned to it. Sales organizations able to define based on the location or business requirements. Sales organization customization comes under the Sales and Distribution consultant.
T-code: **OVX5**

IMG → Enterprise Structure → Definition →Sales and Distribution → Define Sales Organization.

Sales Organization Business Tip:

Each sales area will generate an additional master data if a customer is created in it. To save the system resources, performance, database, complexity and efficiency, it is better to create less sales areas and utilized alternative fields for the grouping or functions of customers if possible.

⋆ Short Definition: Organizational unite that is responsible for sales.

Distribution Channel:

In SAP distribution channel represent ways of distribution. Distribution channels are utilized for different means of distributions. Some examples of the distribution channels are: direct sales, online, retail, wholesale, etc. Distribution channels able to assign to multiple sales organizations, also in sales, distribution channels assigned to the plant.

Code use T-code: **OVXI**

IMG → Enterprise Structure → Definition →Sales and Distribution → Define Distribution Channel

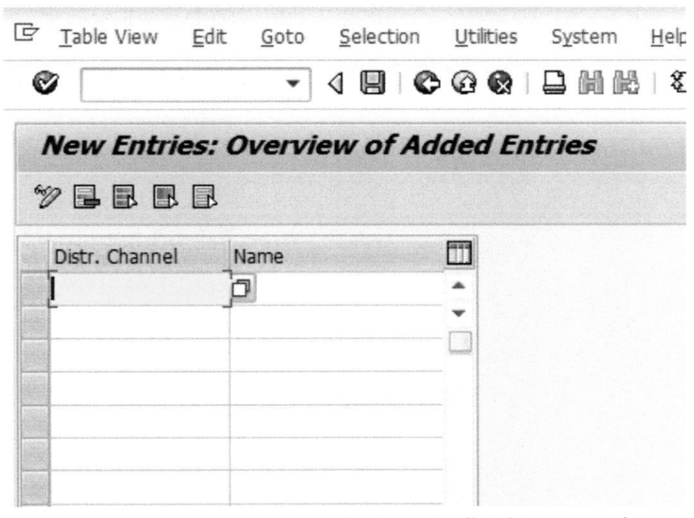

⋆ Short Definition: How products getting distributed.

Division:

Division represents the "line of products". For example, company XYZ able to have two different product lines, so that different divisions able to separate them. In SAP, the division is assigned to sales organization. The division able to assign to multiple sales organizations or utilized in the sales area setup. Division utilized in customer and material master.

Code use T-code: **OVXB**
IMG → Enterprise Structure → Definition →Logistics - General → Define Division

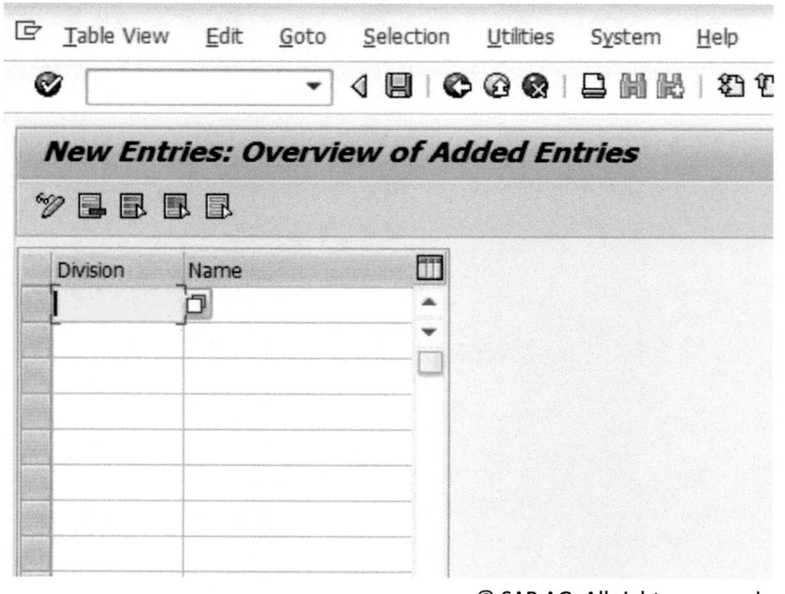

⋆ Short Definition: Line of Products

Sales Area:

Sales area represent a unique combination of sales organization, distribution, and division. The sales area utilized for the master data setup and also becomes the basis for the transactions, along with the master data creation. The sales area required for the customer master creation. In the sales area setup, the sales organization assigned with distribution channel and division with unique combinations. Sales and Distribution consultants or analyst configure sales areas for customization.

Code use T-code: **OVXG**

IMG → Enterprise Structure → Assign →Setup Sales Area

Sales Org	Distribution	Division
1200	12	92
1200	14	10

Sales area for this example will be 1200 | 12 | 92 will be considered one sales area.

Sales Office:

Sales office represent a business unit in the sales department. The sales office represent the enterprise element utilized for sales activities. In SAP, Sales office able to assign employees to a specific sales office, which sales order item levels responsibility, sales document to the sales office, selection criteria for delivering and billing due list. The sales office feature address property to the main office address. Sales office customizations come under sales and distribution consultant.

T-code: **OVX1**
IMG → Enterprise Structure → Definition →Logistics → Define Sales Organization → Define Sales Office

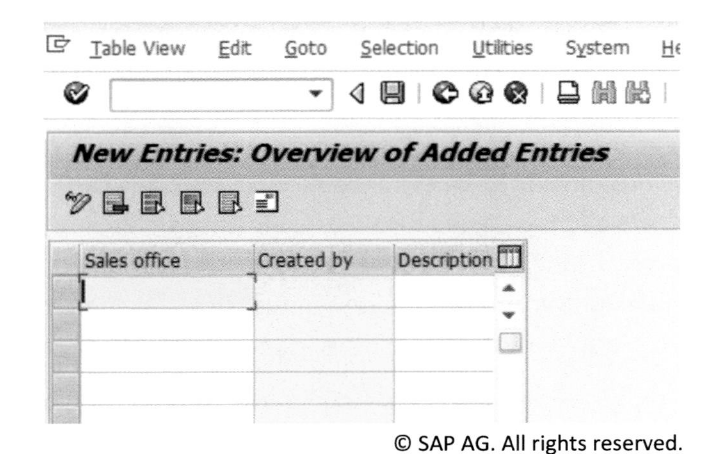

Sales Group:

SAP “sales group” represents the grouping of sales persons. The ales group utilized for assigning employees to the diverse groups for reporting of business functions. The sales group able to assign to one sales office of multiple offices. This represent one of the ways to organize different sales groups. Sales group able to be useful in reporting sales document item responsibility, and billing due list.

IMG → Enterprise Structure → Definition →Logistics → Define Sales Organization → Define Group
T-code: OVX4

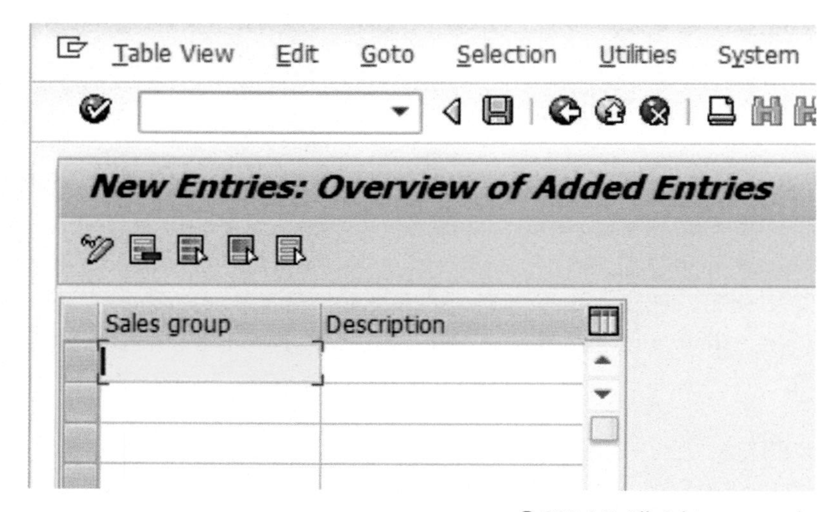

Plant:

Plant is a representation of the factory or warehouse in SAP. The plant in SAP contains warehouse and storage locations. The plant assigned to one company code and only, the company code able to have multiple plants assigned to it. The plant feature shipping points assigned to it. The shipping point represent a SAP organizational element under logistics. The plant feature an address, language, and country. The plant unite utilized for production, procurement, stock, and material planning. The plant feature finance implication. One plant able to contain multiple warehouses in it.

- The plant feature an address.
- The plant able to only be assigned to one company code.
- A company able to have many plant assigned to it.

T-code: OX10

IMG → Enterprise Structure → Definition →Logistics → Define Sales Organization → Define Plant

Change View "Plants": Details

New Entries

Plant	0786
Name 1	ABC Company Inc.
Name 2	

Detailed information

Language Key	EN	English
House number/street	110 Main STEER	
PO Box	123	
Postal Code	62226	
City	Belliville	
Country Key	US	United States
Region	IL	New York
County code	US	County in NY
City code		
Tax Jurisdiction		
Factory calendar		

Note: The address fields Name1 and Name2 are not copied from the address screen and you must maintain them separately.
All other addr. data can only be maintained in addr. screen.
The changes can only be seen in the overview and detail view after they have been saved.

Shipping Point:

Shipping point represent the location, door or docking station where goods are shipped and received from. The plant feature multiple shipping and receiving points assign to it. Shipping points are SAP enterprise elements that require customization. The shipping point assigned to the Plant. The shipping point able to assign to multiple plants. One shipping point feature multiple loading points if needed. The delivery always process from shipping point. The shipping point feature its own address and also determines in the sales order. Each plant feature at least one shipping point.

T-code: **OVXD**

IMG → Enterprise Structure → Definition →Logistics → Logistic Execution → Define Shipping Point

A shipping point factory calender defines the holiday and work days as per factory calender. Woking hours able to configured in shipping point as well. Time able to configured for loading, picking, and routing work days.

Change View "Shipping Points": Details

New Entries

Shipping Point 0564 Shipping Point - DOC1

Location

Country IN Departure Zone

Times

Factory Calendar

Working Times

Determine Times

Determine Load. Time No loading time determination

Det.Pick/Pack Time Pick/pack time not determined

Rounding Work Days

Form Text Names

Address Text Name

Letter Header Text

Text Name Foot.Lines

Text Name Greeting

Text Name SDB Sender

Print Picking List

Output Type

Message Language

Number of Messages

Send Time

Transmission Medium

Subsystem

Background Processing

Displ.info

Others

Pick confirmation

Business Area:

Business area utilized for monitoring financial segment of the business. It utilized for reporting and monitoring. The business areas are defined by financial departments.

T-code: OX03

IMG → Enterprise Structure → Definition →Financial Accounting → Define Business Area

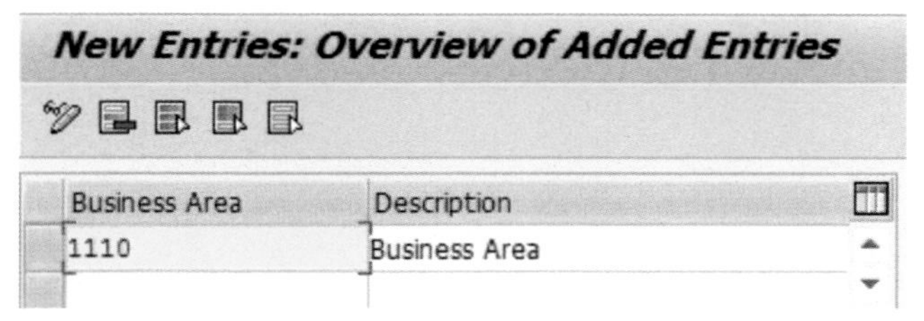

Business Area	Description
1110	Business Area

Business Area Determination Rule:

Business area determination based on the rule of the sales area. The rule governs the sales area that determines the control use, so each sales area able to have different business area determination based on this rule configuration.

Business Area Rule
T-code: OVF2

IMG → Enterprise Structure → Assignment → Sales and Distributions → Business Area Account Assignment → Assign Business Area to Plant and Division

Business Area Determination Mind Map

Business Area Determine Plant and Item Division:

In this configuration we setup, the business area is determined by plant and item division combination. This combination is based on line of product and plant.

Plant + Division = Business Area
T-code: OVF0

IMG → Enterprise Structure → Assignment → Sales and Distributions → Business Area Account Assignment → Assign Business Area to Plant and Division

Business Area Determine by Sales Area:

In this configuration we setup business area determination based on sales in each area. This setting is utilized if there are different sales area required and different business area for each sales area.

Sales Org + Distribution Channel + Division = Business Area

T-code: OVF0

IMG → Enterprise Structure → Assignment → Sales and Distributions → Business Area Account Assignment → Assign Business Area to sales area

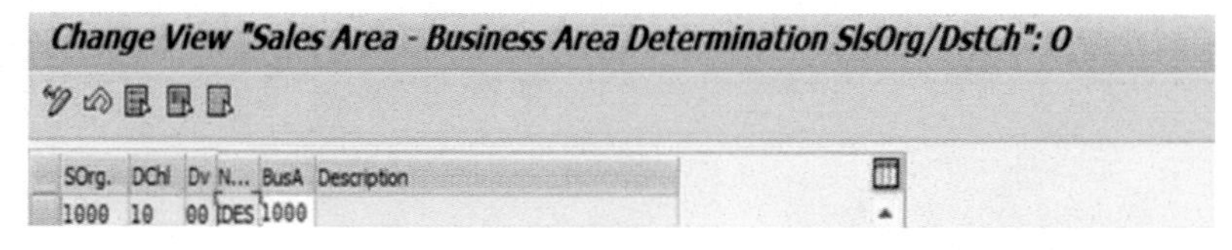

Based on this configuration, Business Area determine in sales order.
T-code: OVF2

IMG → Enterprise Structure → Assignment → Sales and Distributions → Business Area Account Assignment → Define Rule by Sales Area

Validation of Enterprise Structure:

After the enterprise structure configuration is setup, it needs to be verified. One of the ways to validate the enterprise structure and view assignments in configuration is through SAP. The assignment also shows graphically with T-code: **EC01**

First select Structure Structure then select Navigation Navigation and from the list of company code double click on the company code. Then select the company code and double click on it and view all the assignments.

Tips:

- SAP best practice is a very good source to implement effective enterprise structure.
- SAP Building Blocks is also another good source information.

Chapter 2 Summary

Enterprise structure is a very important step for the SAP ERP software setup. The enterprise structure defines functionality of the system. The enterprise structure supposed to analyze with expert consideration. Well though enterprise structures able to improve lot of business process and leverages best practices by the industry.

The following are important enterprise structure elements configuration that have been setup.

- Company
- Company Code
- Credit Control area
- Sales organization
- Distribution channel
- Division
- Sales Area
- Sales Group
- Plant
- Shipping Point
- Business Area
- Business Area Determinations
- Validation of enterprise structure

Exercise on Enterprise Structure:

1. How many company codes able to one plant be assigned to?
2. How many plants able to one company code be assigned to?
3. Can one credit control area be assigned to multiple company codes?
4. How are single or multiple sales areas setup effectively on the master data?
5. What is a "sales line"?
6. How is a validate enterprise structured?
7. In which module is plant and the division defined?
8. Can sales organization be assigned to multiple company codes?

Answers:

8) Sales organization able to only be assigned to one company code.

7) Plant and division belong to the logistic general module area of configuration.

6) To validate enterprise structure, check the links in EC01 graphically. It able to also be checked this by the enterprise structure in most places SAP provides a check, copy, and edit enterprise objects .too.

5) Combination of sales organization and distribution is called a sales line.

4) Sales are increased by the master data record and system complexity when same customer is extended too many sales areas. The sales areas able to utilize if it required but the software development and team able to achieve system efficiency performance by many other ways to maintain functionality. For example, the customer's group or, customer's industry, listing and exclusion, pricing, and much more.

3) Credit control able to assign to multiple company codes and also each company code able to have different credit control areas assigned to it, such as credit management.

2) The company code able to have many plant assigned to it.

1) The plant able to only be assigned to one company code.

Notes:

CHAPTER 3

MASTER DATA

Topics of Master Data Chapter:

- Master Data
- Transactional Data
- Customer Master (SD/FI)
- Common Division and Distribution channel
- Account Group Customization
- Customer Partner Function Customization
- Vendor Master SAP MM
- Material Type (MM)
- Customer Master Info Records (SD)
- Payment Terms (SD/FI)
- Payment Plan Customization
- Table View topics
- Table View Old (SE16)
- Table View New (SE16N)

What is in this chapter for me?

This chapter is all about master data. Learn SAP master data configuration including customer master account group. Learn SAP MM vendor master and material type configuration. In this chapter learn how payment term is setup and configured. Learn SAP SD Material determination configuration. Learn SAP SD Customer material info record.

Chapter 3 Learning Objectives:

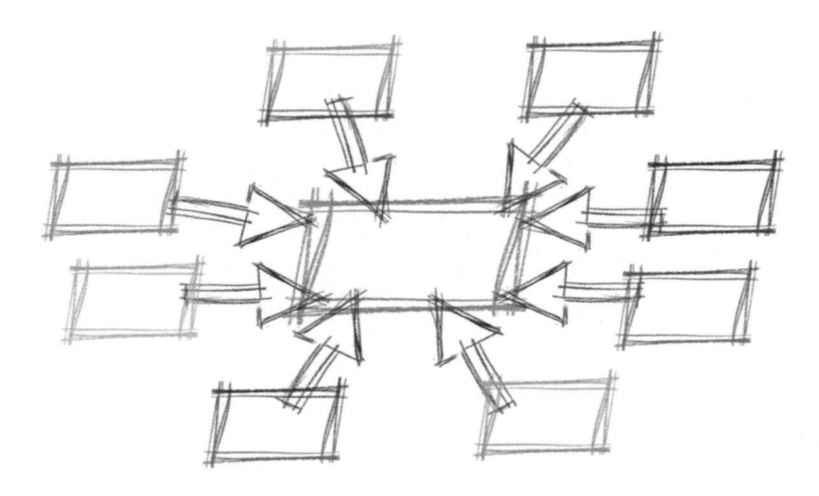

- Understand Master and Transactional Data concepts
- Learn How to create Customer Master (SD/FI)
- Learn How to create Pricing Condition Record (SD)
- Learn configuration of common distributions and common division
- Learn How to setup Vendor master
- Learn How to setup Material Master (SD/MM)
- Learn Customer Information Record Creation
- Learn Material Determination Configuration (SD)
- Learn how to create material determination condition record
- Learn how to customize Material type (MM)

Master Data:

The short description of master data is that "Master data hardly changes." Master data is the means of transactions, for example the customer and products (material) utilized for sales order creation. Master Data is required to create transections like sales orders, delivery, invoice, etc. SAP Sales and Distribution master data elements are customer Master, Material Master, and Pricing Records. The master data are based on a group of tables for each master data. To represent one master data, each table represents a unique view of the master data. In SAP Sales and Distribution Customer master, material master and condition records are important master data.

In Sales and distribution a few of master data examples that are relevant to sales order processing in general.

- Customer Master Data
- Material Master Data
- Pricing Condition Records
- Customer material Info Record

Transactional Data:

The short description of Transactional data is that "Transactional data is dynamic in nature." It changes transaction to transaction with different values. Most inquiry, sales orders, delivery, and billing documents all are example of transnational data, which constantly change the sale order representation of transactional data.

Customer Master Data:

Customer master represents is customer information in a system. Customer Master feature much functionality driven from customer master. Customer master is utilized for different business functions with different roles. Customer master is divided into three different views. In SAP customer master Data saved with three different views:

1. **General Data**
2. **Company Code Data**
3. **Sales Area Data**

> ⋆ **Short Definition:** ⋆
> **Transactional data is dynamic in nature**
> **Transactional data changes more frequently.**

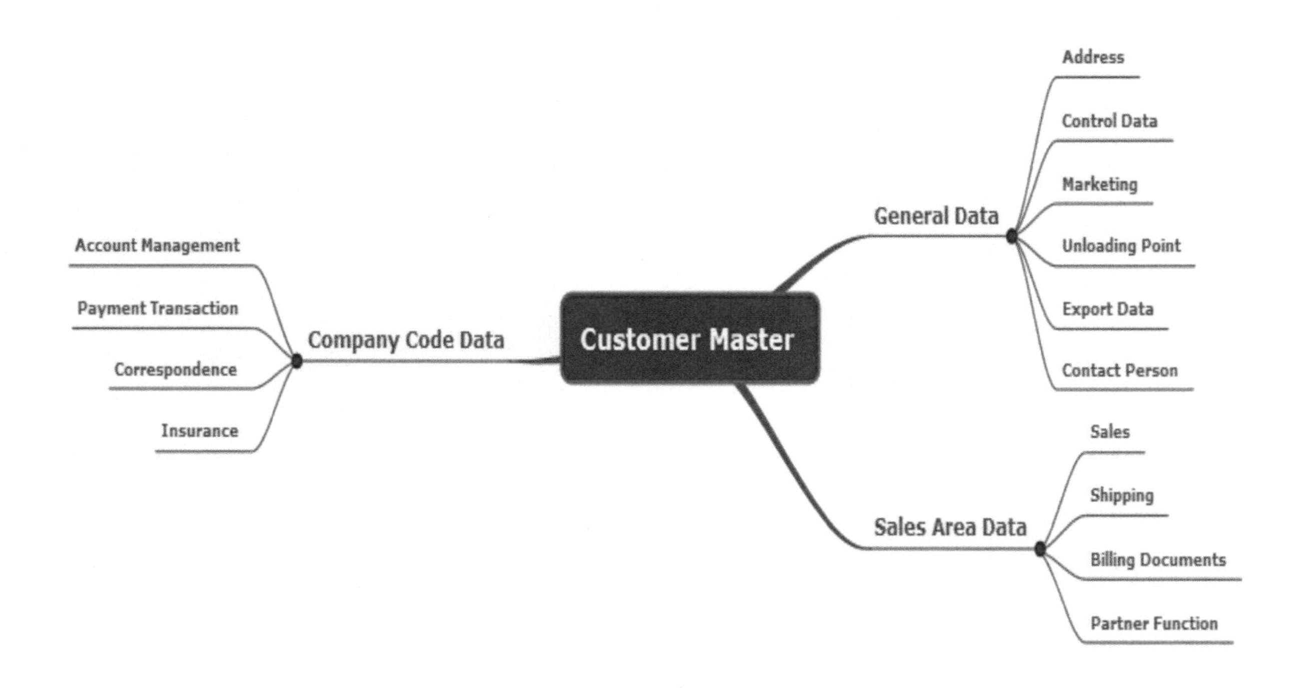

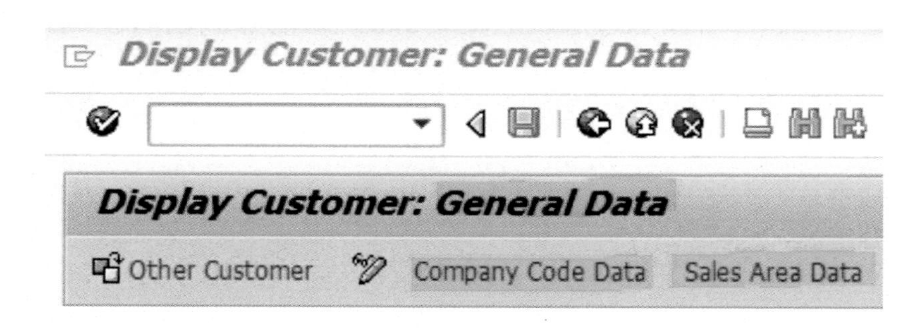

Customer Master feature three views.

Master data is required for transactional data.

Three different views are created to maintain different business sections. This view also relates to functions, or roles. A customer master able to create with two combinations: General data with Company code and data or General data with Sales area Data. The

Customer Master also able to maintain centrally with all the views. General data consists of general information such as the name, address, P.O box address, phone number, fax number, and so on. Sales Data consist of billing, shipping, pricing, related information, and partner functions. With master data and Customer Master additional data is also available for control and functionality.

General Data

In customer master general data consists of name, address, phone, and fax from the address tab. With Each tab from the Customer Master General Data feature more detail information from customer Master. To view customer T-code is utilized XD01

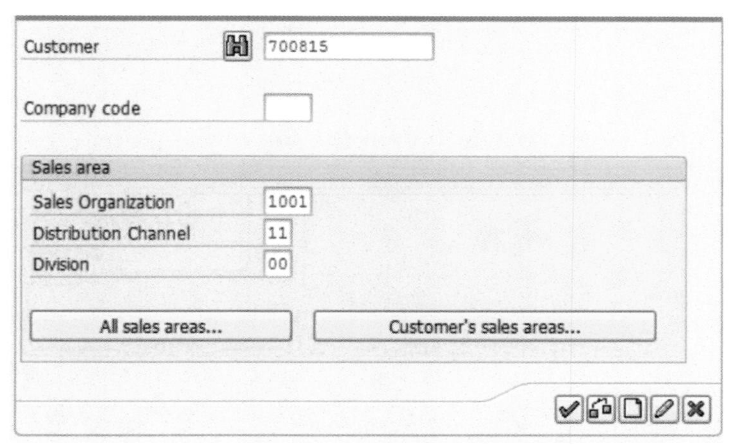

To view user should enter: customer number, company code, and sales area number.

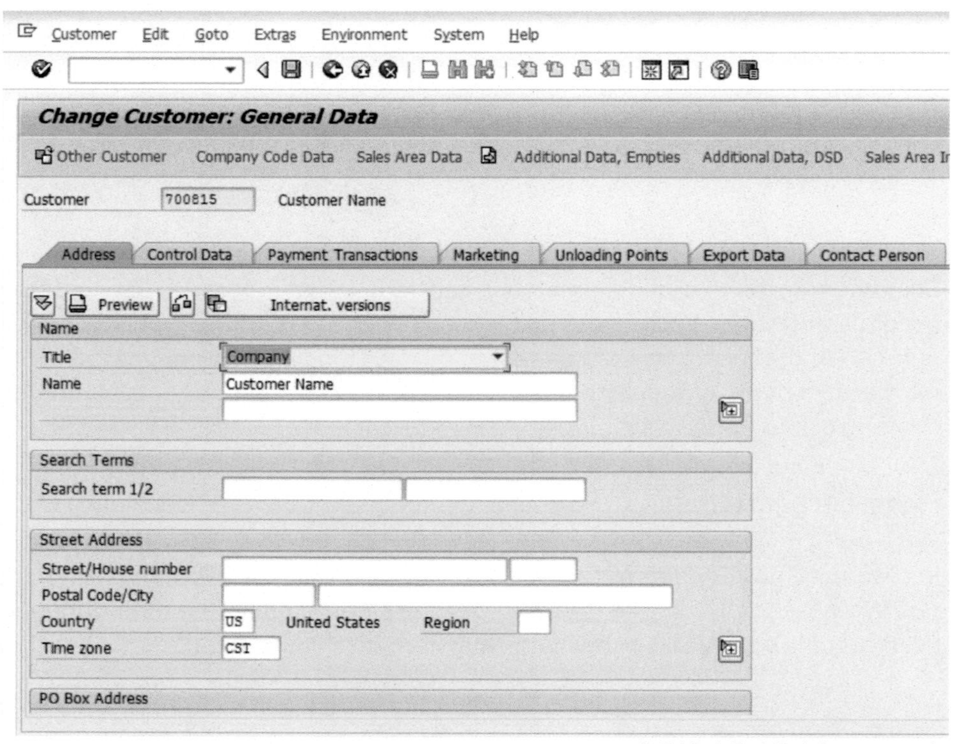

Each view feature heading on the top of the page to represent each view

2. **Company Code Data**

Company code data feature the customer financial related information. The additional information able to see in the screenshot.

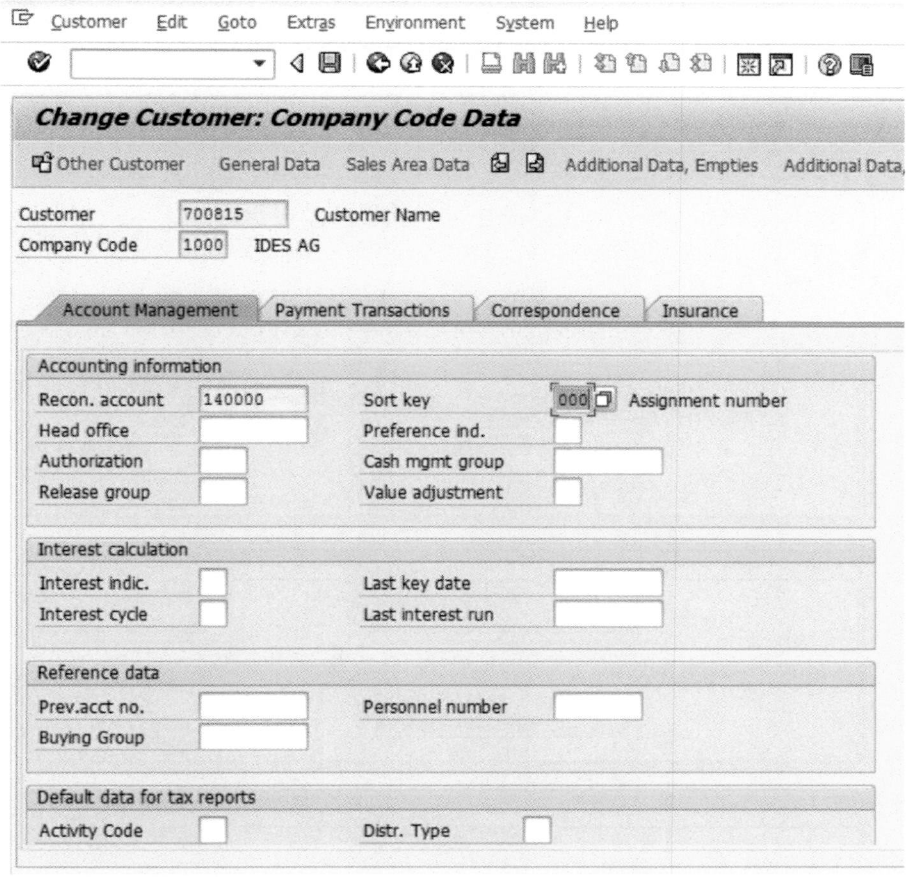

Customer Edit Goto Extras Environment System Help

Change Customer: Company Code Data

Other Customer General Data Sales Area Data Additional Data, Empties Additional Data,

Customer 700815 Customer Name
Company Code 1000 IDES AG

Account Management | Payment Transactions | Correspondence | Insurance

Accounting information

Recon. account	140000	Sort key	000 Assignment number
Head office		Preference ind.	
Authorization		Cash mgmt group	
Release group		Value adjustment	

Interest calculation

Interest indic.		Last key date	
Interest cycle		Last interest run	

Reference data

Prev.acct no.		Personnel number	
Buying Group			

Default data for tax reports

Activity Code		Distr. Type	

3. Sales Data

Sales area consists of a unique combination of sales organization, distribution channel, and division. Sales data also feature additional information related to that of the sales area like plant, partner function, shipping and billing information.

To create a customer master three different T-codes are followed.

1. XD01 Central view (all the views)
2. FD01 General and Company Code Data
3. VD01 General and Sales Data

XD01 includes all the views to be maintained. VD01 includes sales area and general area views. FD01 is only for company code view with general data to be maintained.

The following four tabs are sales or view of customer master

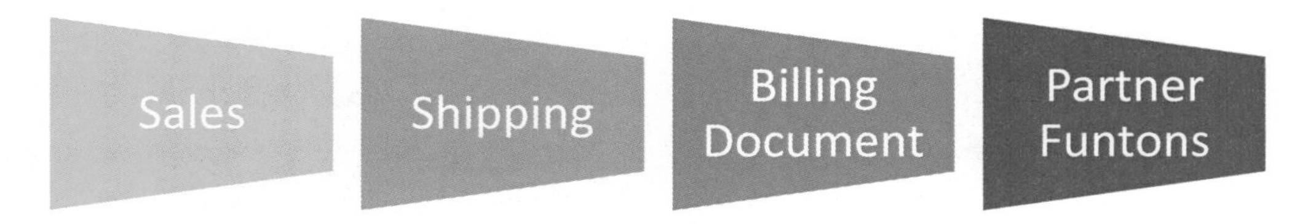

Each Sales Area Data feature many fields.

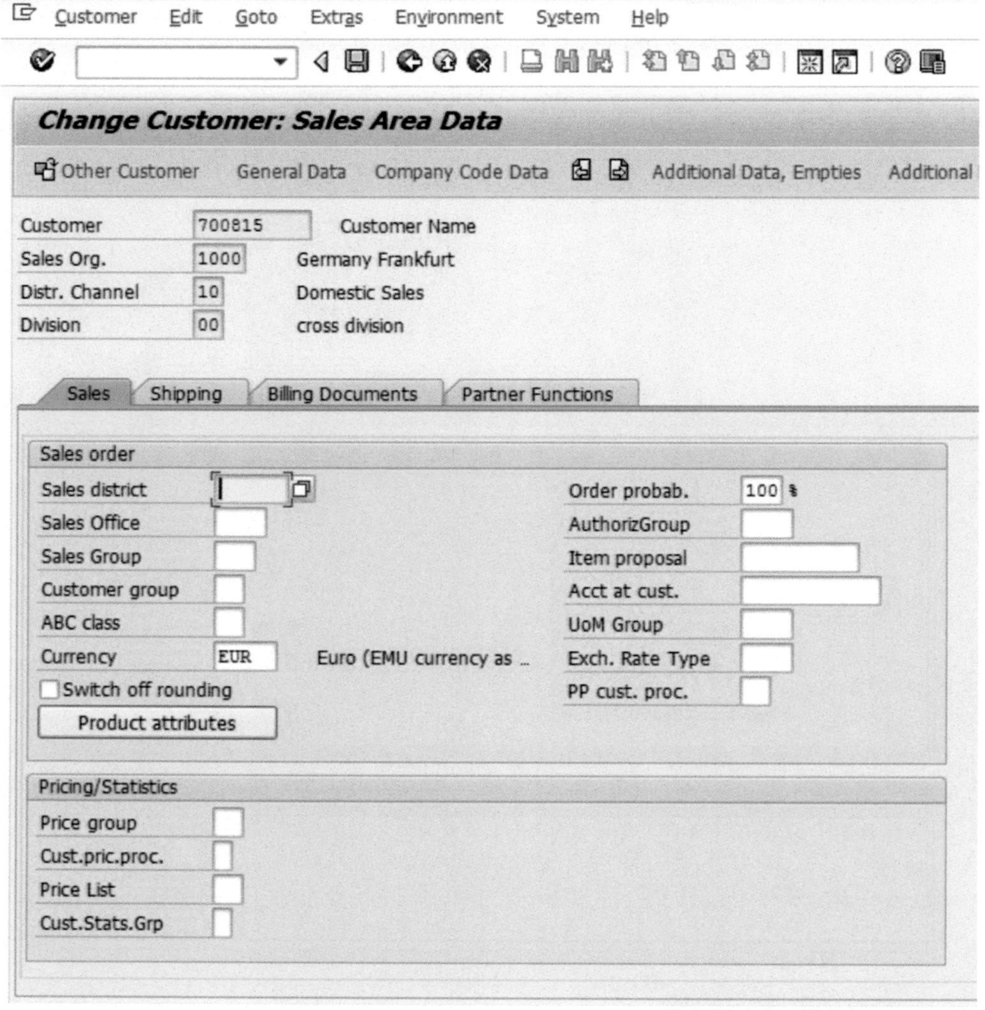

Customer Master Partner Functions:

Partner function is the role of customer in the transaction. For example, customers able to have many shipping addresses so this customer feature many ships to partner functions. In general Customer Master feature four partner functions. The "sold to" customer partner function never changes so only ship to, bill to and payer change in customer partner function changes.

1. Sold to Party
2. Ship to Party
3. Bill to Party
4. Payer

Additional partner functions able to add to the customer master. There can be multiple "bills to" and multiple payer functions able to add for one customer. For each customer the "sold to" partner function able to create only once.

Additional Partner Functions:

The following are a few of the additional partner functions that able to configure and assigned to the customer master.

- Freight forwarder
- Sales representative
- Contact person
- Sales representative

Customer Master Related T-codes:

NO	Description	T-code
1	Create Customer Master (Centrally)	XD01
2	Change Customer Master (Centrally)	XD02
3	Display Customer Master (Centrally)	XD03
4	Create Customer Master with Company Code View	FD01
5	Change Customer Master with Company Code View	FD02
6	Display Customer Master with Company Code View	FD03
7	Create Customer Master Sales View	VD01
8	Change Customer Master Sales View	VD02
9	Display Customer Master Sales View	VD03
10	Block Customers	VD05
11	Delete Customer	VD06
12	Display Change's	VD04
13	Mass update	XD99
14	Create Contact Person	VAP1

Centrally means that all the view of the customer Master is with a single t-code.
Mass updates allow multiple customers to change it at once.
Display changes show when the customer master was changed and by which user.

Customer Master Related Tables:

The following are some of the customer master tables:

Table	Description
KNA1	General Data
KNB1	Company Code Data
KNVV	Customer Sales Data
KNAT	Customer Master Tax Grouping
KNBK	Customer Master Back Detail
KNB5	Customer Master Dunning Data
KNKK	Customer Credit Management Data
KNMT	Customer Material Info Record Data
KNVI	Customer Master Tax Indicator
KNVP	Customer Master Partner Function

To view table use T-code SE16N or SE16

Creating a customer master centrally (XD01) means all required views of customers are maintained at the same time. Creating a customer master with finance view (FD01) means two views are maintained, such as General Data and Company code data. Creating a customer master with sales view means two view of customer master is maintained hence sales view and general data.

Contact Person partner function:

Master data is utilized as a business partner's function in customer master. It able to create separately or entered while creating or changing customer.

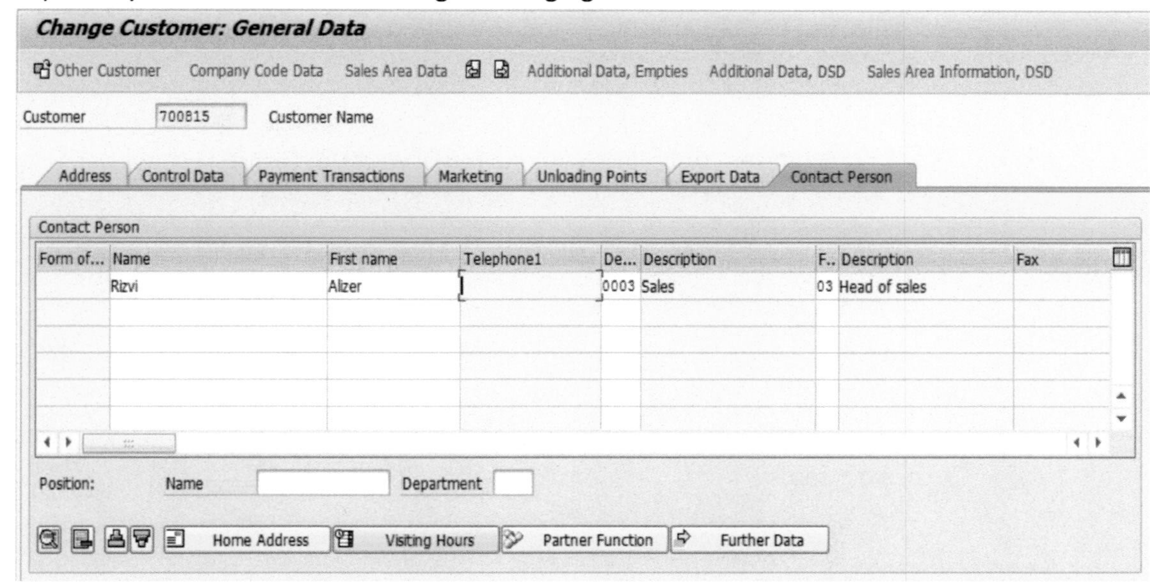

T-code for Contact person is: **VAP1**

Customer Master Customization:

The first step to customization for a customer master is the account group, this is after the account group partner functions are configured.

Account Group Customization:

Account group controls the followings:

- **Customer Number range**
- **Field status of Customer Master**
- **Partner Determination**

Define Customer Number range:

Account group number range is utilized for customer number definition. The number range able to set the internal number or external number range. In the internal number range the customer number will be picked by the system and with external number the customer number able to set manually entered at the time of customer creation. The number range able to include in transport otherwise it is a manual activity to perform in the system landscape setup.

Customization Path from SPRO T-code is

IMG →Financial Accounting → Account receivable and Account Payable → Customer Account → Master Data → Define Number Range for customer Account Group

T-code for customization: **XDN1**

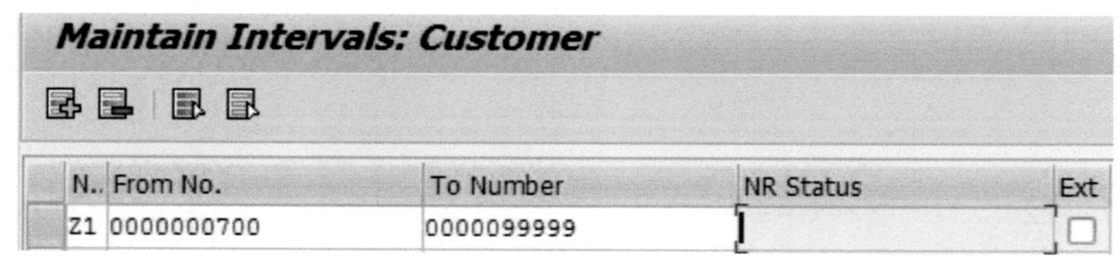

Number range: it is two letter field utilized to assign to account group. Based on the number range the customer's number are generated.

Define Account Group:

Customization Path from SPRO t-code is

IMG →Financial Accounting → Account receivable and Account Payable → Customer Account → Master Data → Define Account Group

T-code for customization: **OBD2**

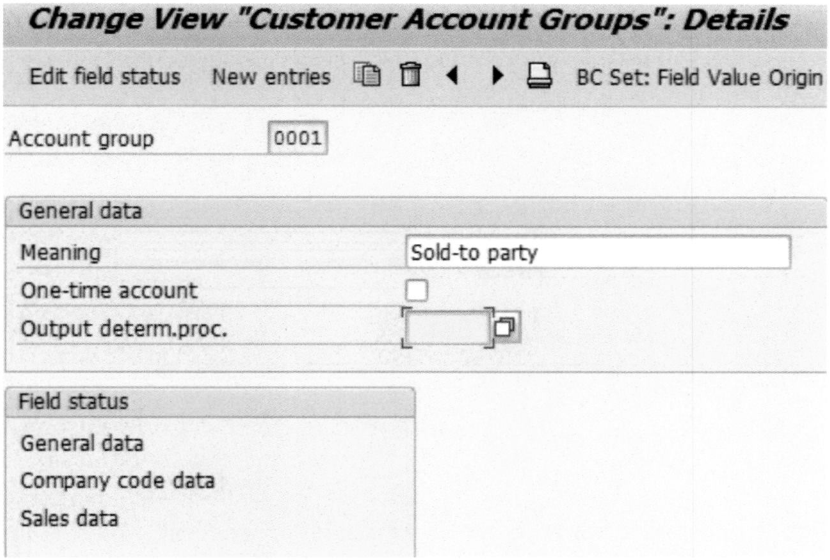

Field Status Group:

Field status group controls the status of the field in the customer master. Field status communicates the status of field in the transaction or master data. Four field statuses utilized are mandatory, hidden, display, and optional. The account group able to control the field status group. Account group controls each field status by configuration setup.

- Suppress
- Required Entry
- Optional Entry
- Display

The field status group is applied to each tab level of the customer Master.

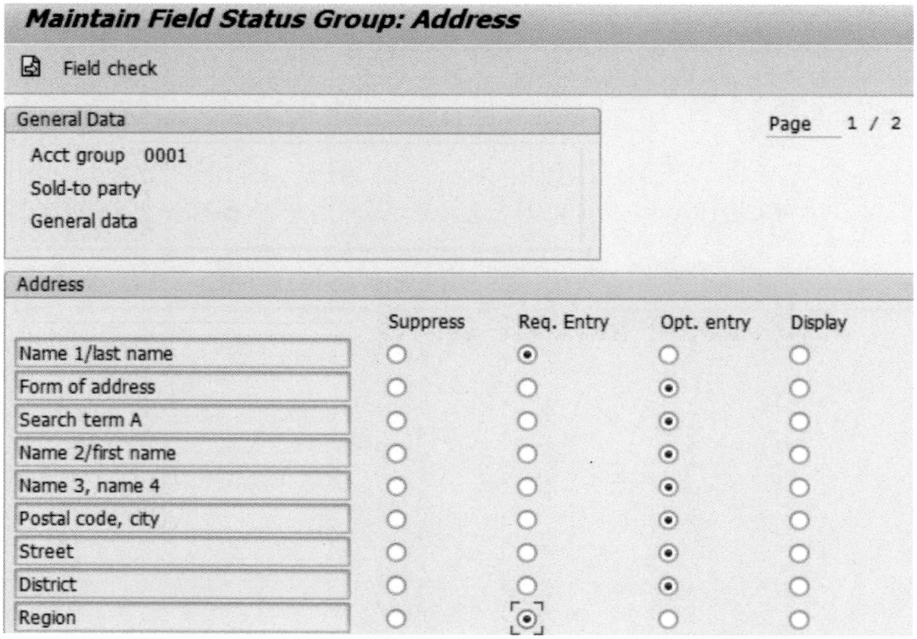

Maintain Field Status Group: Address

Field check

General Data

Acct group 0001
Sold-to party
General data

Page 1 / 2

Address

	Suppress	Req. Entry	Opt. entry	Display
Name 1/last name	○	◉	○	○
Form of address	○	○	◉	○
Search term A	○	○	◉	○
Name 2/first name	○	○	◉	○
Name 3, name 4	○	○	◉	○
Postal code, city	○	○	◉	○
Street	○	○	◉	○
District	○	○	◉	○
Region	○	◉	○	○

The above screenshot is from the customer master address tab. The first field feature “Name /last name” which require fields. Based on this customization; this field will be required at the time of customer creation.

Below is an account group screenshot.

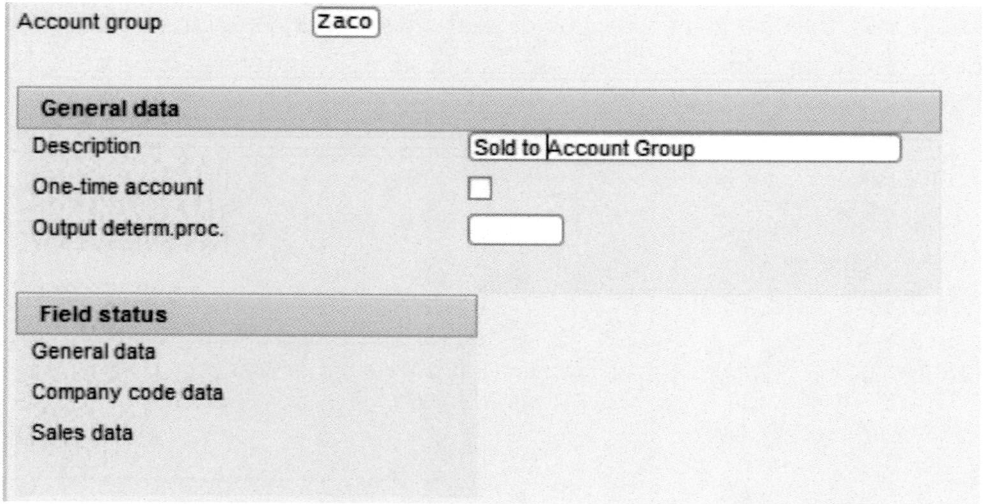

Account group Zaco

General data

Description Sold to Account Group
One-time account ☐
Output determ.proc.

Field status

General data
Company code data
Sales data

Account group controls, customer number, field’s setup and partner functions.

One Time Customer:

One-time customer only utilized once because it able to set different customer so the address changes transactional basis so it able to select here to be activated. If the account group needs to be made for a one-time customer, then the one-time customer check box needs to be checked.

Output Determination Procedure:

This field is utilized for the type of output determination. An output procedure is utilized to define what output able to set determined from the account group. Generally this field is not utilized in most cases.

Customer Partner Function Determination:

Partner function defines the customer role with many transactions. Each customer expected to have multiple partner functions. The main four partner functions are the following:

- Sold To
- Ship To
- Bill to
- Payer

Additional partner functions are customizable.

- Contact Person
- Sales Manager

The partner functions able to configure, as they are required. The partner function determination able to configure for the following transactions.

Partner Function determination at transaction level is the following:

- Partner Function Determination
- Sales order header level
- Sales order item level
- Delivery Item Level
- Delivery Header
- Shipment
- Billing Header Level
- Billing item level
- Partner Function at sales activity

All of transaction configurations are the same, so the partner function customization will be focused on standard partner function determination. It is almost same as for all of the above.

Customization Path from SPRO T-code is

IMG →Sales and Distribution → Basic Functions → Set Up Partner Determination

Steps for partner function determination are following:

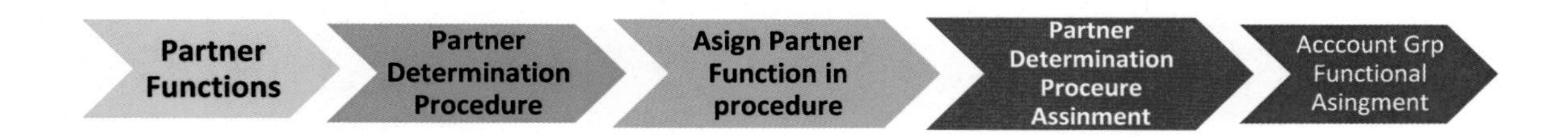

Here is a screenshot of partner function determination customization steps.

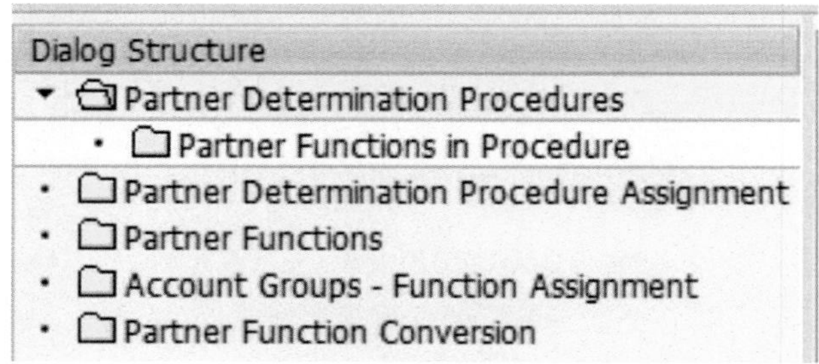

Partner Functions:

For the customization we will be focusing on standard partner functions.

- Sold To
- Ship To
- Bill To
- Payer

In this step we define partner functions with two letter-abbreviated identification.

Partner Functions						
Part...	Name	Part...	Error ...	Sup...	U...	CHT...
SP	Sold-to Party	KU	07		☑	
BP	Bill-to Party	KU	07		☐	
PY	Payer	KU	07		☐	
CR	Carrier	LI	08		☐	
TF	Freight service agt	LI	08		☐	
SH	Ship-to Party	KU	07		☐	

The partner Function field is two characters long name of the partner function. The name field description of the partner function needs to be maintained. Partner function type is the type of partner function. The following are a few examples of the partner function type.

Partner Function Type	Description
KU	Customer
AP	Contact Person
LI	Vendor
US	User

The partner function type defines what kind of partner function it is. If the partner function is a vendor, then it means we pay the vendor for the service or product vendor they provide.

Error group is an incompletion procedure and it will auto populate. A superior partner function is utilized to setup customer high-level partner function. Unique field is utilized to define the uniqueness of the partner function. For example, a hierarchy partner function and sold supposed to unique field so this function is not repeated in customer master. Field "CH Type" represents the customer hierarchy type and it is utilized to define what type of customer hierarchy is utilized.

Partner Determination Procedure:

Partner Determination Procedures	
Part.Det.Proc	Name
ZACT	Test Procedure

In this step we define the partner function procedure. The procedure expected to be two to four letter characters with descriptions of the procedure. The procedure is utilized for partner functions assignment. The partner function that is defined previously will be assigned into the procedure. We able to make partner function non-modifiable and also make the partner function mandatory with each customization.

Partner Determination Procedure Assignment:

Partner Functions in Procedure

Part....	Partn...	Name	Not Modifia...	Mandat.Funct
ZACT	PY	Payer	☐	☐
ZACT	SP	Sold-to-Party	☐	☐
ZACT	SH	Ship-to party	☐	☐
ZACT	BB	Bill to party	☐	☐

In the above screenshot ZACT is procedure next field is partner function.

In this step the account group gets assigned to the partner determination procedure. This configuration allows procedure partner function into the account group.

Accountancy Group - Function Assignment:

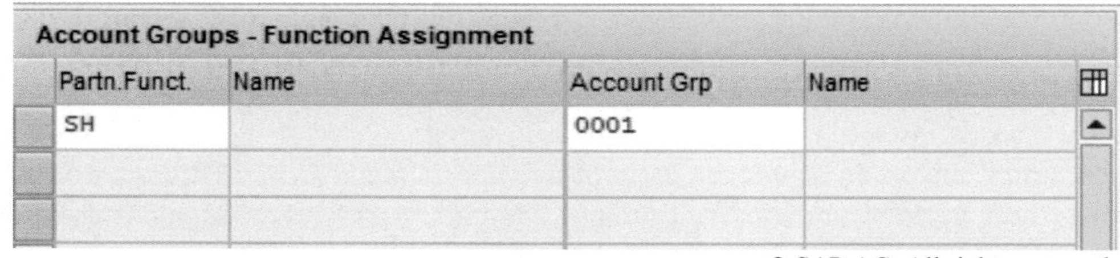

Account Groups - Function Assignment

Partn.Funct.	Name	Account Grp	Name
SH		0001	

In this configuration step all the partner function is assigned to the account group individually.

Partner Function Conversion:

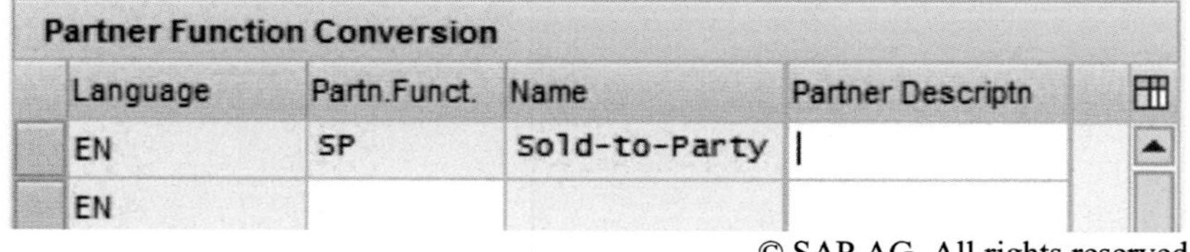

Partner Function Conversion

Language	Partn.Funct.	Name	Partner Descriptn
EN	SP	Sold-to-Party	
EN			

This customization controls the language of customer's master partner function.

Common Distribution Channel:

Common distribution channel is the customization in sales and distribution for defining common distribution channel for the master data. Based on this the sales org able to come under common distribution channel instead of extending sales that are to multiple distribution channel. This is also called referenced condition because the master data distribution channel is conditional record or grouping.

Customization T-Code: VOR1

IMG → Sales and Distribution → Master Data → Define Common Distribution Chanel

Common Division:

Common Division is utilized when grouping of division is required in the sales area into single common division. Common division streamlines the master data maintenance. While common sales are able to maintain from this function into common conditional master data for sales area use.

Customization T-Code: VOR2

IMG → Sales and Distribution → Master Data → Define Common Division

Vendor Master SAP MM:

Vendor master is the supplier or service provider for the purchasing department. Vendor Master feature three views similar to the Customer Master. Vendor master requires configuration of the partner determination account group, but vendor master belongs to a material management module and it is procurement related activities.

- General Data
- Company Code Data
- Purchasing Organization View

Moderately Important

General Data feature fields including name, address, phone number, phone number, fax, P.O Box, etc.
Purchasing Organization feature the fields of partner functions, purchasing, group pricing indicator, etc.
The company Code view feature financial related information such as reconciliation

account number, industry sector, etc.

T-code to create vendor XK01

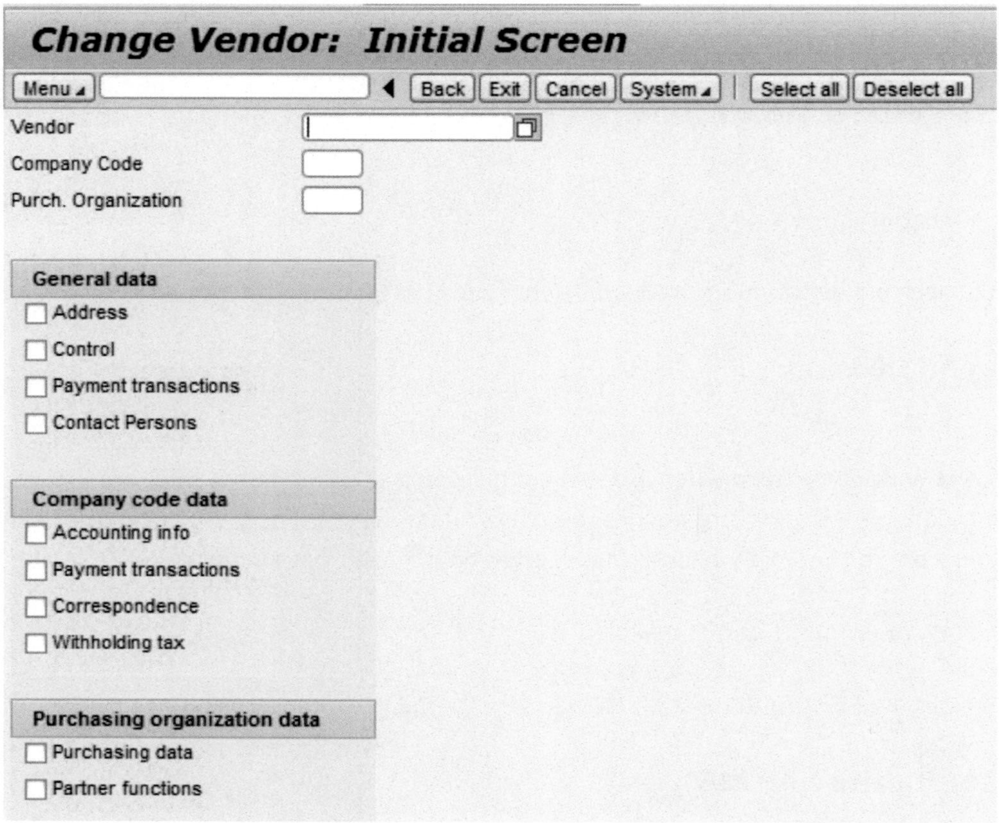

Material Master:

Material master represent product information in the system. Material master represents saleable material, raw material, services material, finished products and more. SAP Martial Master feature data information with multiple tab views. These views belong to different modules and departments e.g. Sales, procurement views, sales, and distribution's sales views, and general views. Each module feature relevant master data controls and functions. Material master views configured for Material Type.

Sales side of material master views are the following:

Basic Data 1
Basic Data 2
Sales Org. 1
Sales Org. 2

General / Plant Data
Foreign Trade: Export Data
Sales Text
Accounting 1
Accounting 2

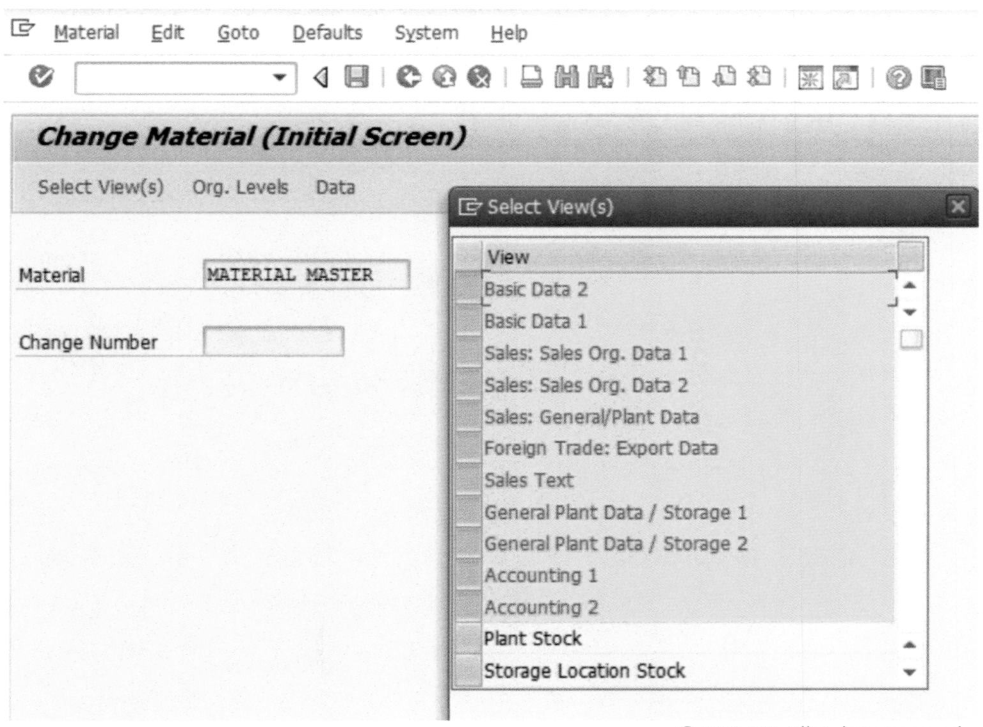

Material Type:

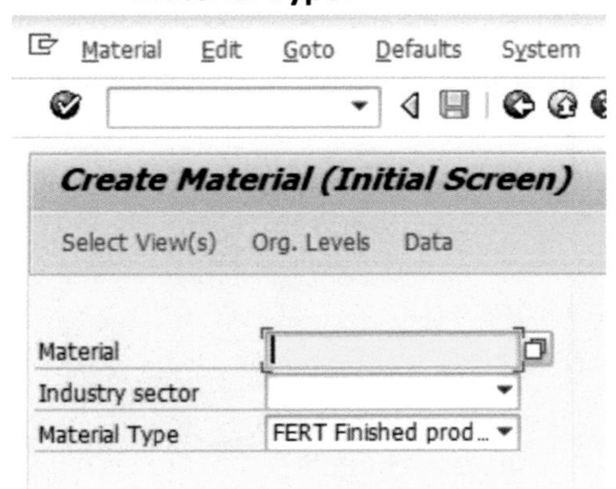

Material Type categorizes different between types of Materials. It controls material views and field status. New material types able to customize for the field status group. Here are few examples of material types.

Material Type	Description
FERT	Finish product:
HAWA	Trading good:
NLAG	Non-stock material
RAW	Raw material
VERP	Packaging material
DIEN	Services (non-stock items)

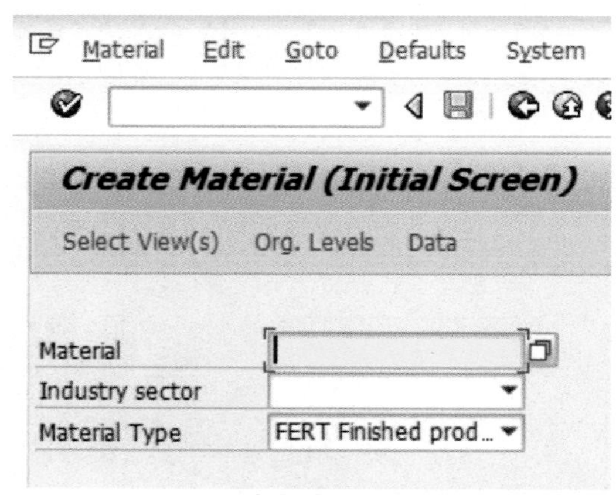

Industry sector:

Industry sector defines what kind of industry is assigned to the material master.

Material Master T-codes:

The following are some of the transaction codes for material master.

Transaction Code	Description
MM01	Creating Material Master
MM02	Change Material Master
MM03	View Material Master
MM12	Material Master Change on schedule
MM06	Flag for deletion
MM17	Mass maintenance
MMAM	Change Material Type

MMBE	Stock overview
MMPV	Close Period

The following are some of the tables for Materiel Master.

Table Name	Description
MARA	General Material Data
MARC	Plant Data for Material
MVKE	Sales Data for Material
MAKT	Material Master Description
MBEW	Material valuation (accounting)
MLAN	Tax classification
T179	Product Hierarchies
STXH	STXD SAP script text file header
STXL	STXD SAP script text file lines

Material Type:

Material Type able to customize for views that allowed for the material and field status group. Material type configuration does not belong to general logistics. The scope of this topic is covered limited for better understanding of how the material type controls material master related filed and functions.

T-code: **OMS2**

IMG → Logistics General → Material Master → Basic Setting → Material Types → Define Attribute of Material Types

The following areas are at Material Type controls:

- Special Material Type
- General data
- User Departments
- Internal and internal Purchase Order
- Classification
- Valuation
- Quantity / Value Updating
- Retail Specific fields

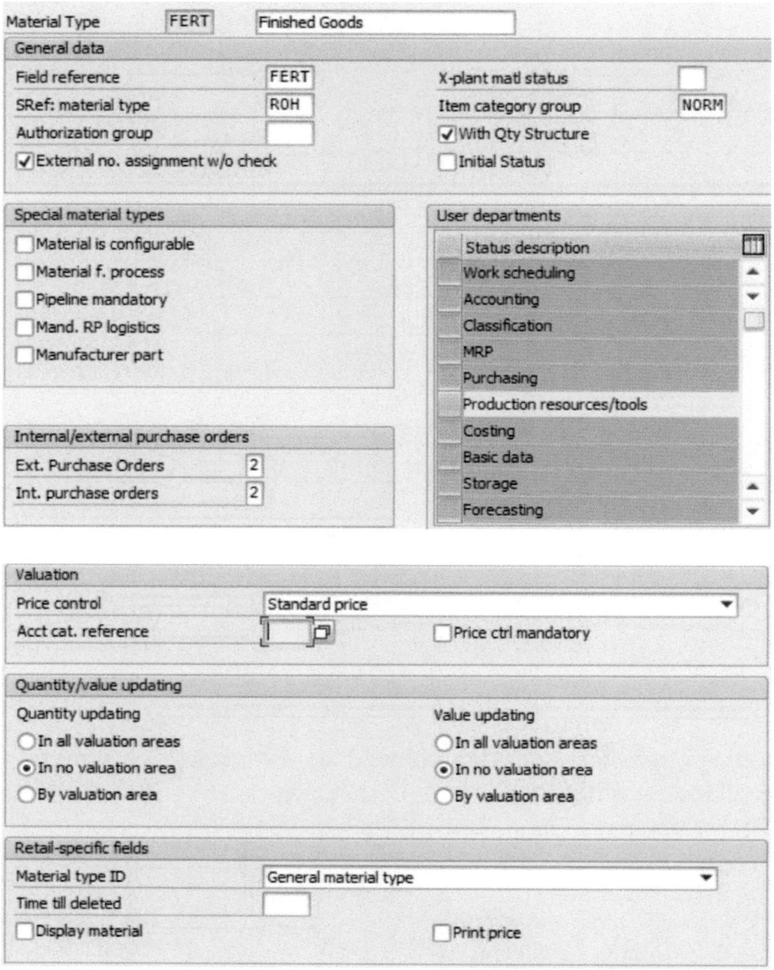

Material Type FERT Finished Goods

General data

Field reference FERT

SRef: material type ROH

Authorization group

External no. assignment w/o check

X-plant matl status

Item category group NORM

With Qty Structure

Initial Status

Special material types

Material is configurable

Material f. process

Pipeline mandatory

Mand. RP logistics

Manufacturer part

Internal/external purchase orders

Ext. Purchase Orders 2

Int. purchase orders 2

User departments

Status description

Work scheduling

Accounting

Classification

MRP

Purchasing

Production resources/tools

Costing

Basic data

Storage

Forecasting

Valuation

Price control Standard price

Acct cat. reference

Price ctrl mandatory

Quantity/value updating

Quantity updating

In all valuation areas

In no valuation area

By valuation area

Value updating

In all valuation areas

In no valuation area

By valuation area

Retail-specific fields

Material type ID General material type

Time till deleted

Display material

Print price

Customer Material Info Records

Customer material info record is a master data. CMIR is utilized for customer material number to SAP material master number reference. CMIR is also utilized for defaulting some of the values into sales orders. For example, if a customer feature its own material number then the system will substitute values from customer material info record into sales orders. Customer material info record also able to override values from Unite of measure, Plant data, rounding profile, and delivery priority. These values are maintained in master data, but preferences come from the Customer material info record.

T-code to create a Customer material info record is the following:

Create: VD51
Change: VD52
Display: VD53

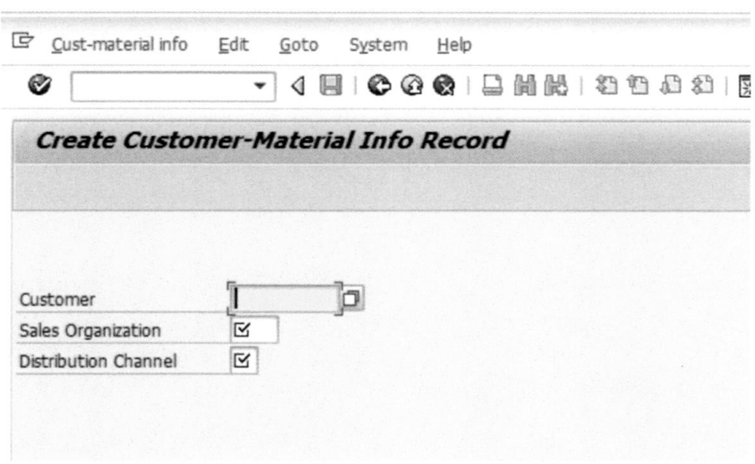

Customer Material info record able to base on customer number + sales organization + distribution channel.

Tables for CMIR is KNMT

Payment Terms:

The payment term defines the term of payments in transection. Payment terms are utilized in transaction like sales order, invoice etc. If payment terms is net thirty, it means the net is due upon thirty discounts is offered for early payment. If payment is delayed, then the customer will be dunned and issued a letter based on the business process and procedure of the organization.

IN SAP payment term able to assign to the customer master so that the customer specific payment term automatically copy into sales order. The payment term able to change in sale order creation and entered if not maintained for the customer master.

Payment term configuration is marked for customer and vendor. Payment term also able to have an installment plan assigned to it too.

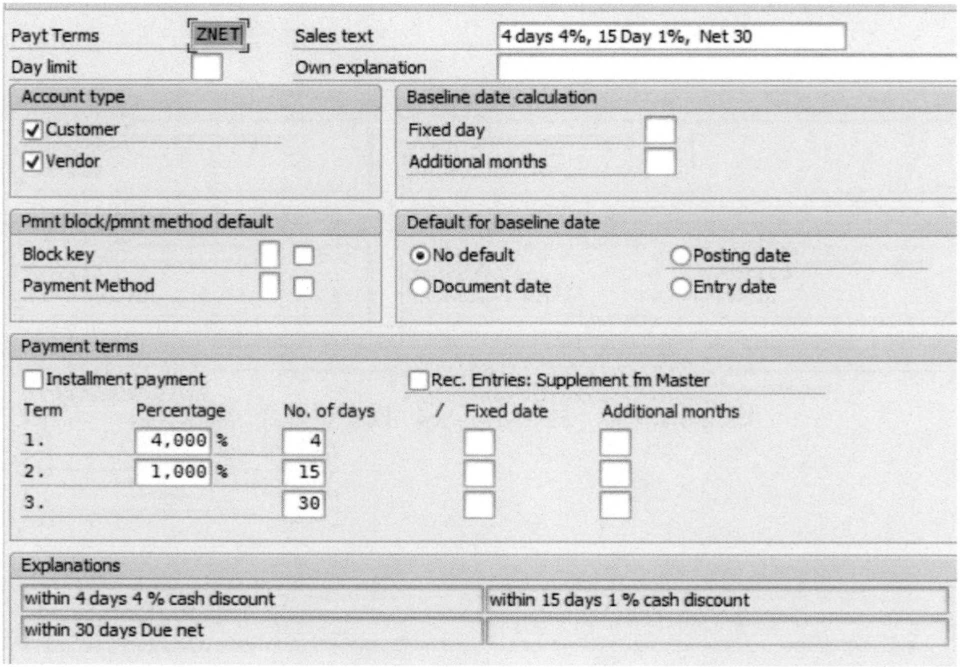

Payt Terms ZNET Sales text 4 days 4%, 15 Day 1%, Net 30
Day limit Own explanation

Account type
- [x] Customer
- [x] Vendor

Baseline date calculation
Fixed day
Additional months

Pmnt block/pmnt method default
Block key
Payment Method

Default for baseline date
(•) No default ( ) Posting date
( ) Document date ( ) Entry date

Payment terms
- [ ] Installment payment
- [ ] Rec. Entries: Supplement fm Master

Term	Percentage	No. of days	/ Fixed date	Additional months
1.	4,000 %	4		
2.	1,000 %	15		
3.		30		

Explanations
within 4 days 4 % cash discount
within 15 days 1 % cash discount
within 30 days Due net

In the screenshot the payment term feature discounted four percent if dues are paid in four days, one percent discount if the payment is received within fifteen days and total are due in thirty days. This payment term is without a payment plan.

Configuration for Payment Term:

Implementation Guide path from SPRO

IMG → Financial Accounting → Account receivable account payable → Outgoing Invoice/Credit Memo → Maintain Term of Payment

T-code: OBB8

Payment Plan of Payment Term:

The payment plan is utilized in payment term with the payment installments. The installments equal out to the total invoice due and payment the term needs to be marked in the configuration for the installments and the system will carry out the payment term for each payment.

Configuration for Payment Term:

Implementation Guide path from SPRO

IMG → Financial Accounting → Account receivable account payable → Outgoing Invoice/Credit Memo → Define Terms of Payment for Installment Payment

T-code: OBB9

Terms of Paymen	Inst	Percent	Pmnt term
I20	1	50.000	A003
I20	2	50.000	A004
I30	1	33.333	A003
I30	2	33.333	A004
I30	3	33.334	A005

The terms of payment have installments that define how many installments this term of payment feature and percentage. For each percentage is in payment term so the invoice able to divide into payment installment.

SAP SD Material Determination:

Material determination is product substitution of newer product or when the old product is outdated. The new product or similar products able to replace or subtitle in the sales order. When a business offers newer model of product similar to the previous product, it able to automate with material determination configuration.

For example: a black, blue-ray player able to replace with a white, blue ray player. That examples of last year's model able to replace this year's product. Another example is a material determination. Material determination is utilized if the company comes up with a new model of phone and new ones replace old phone becoming obsolete so that material determination able to utilize for parts. The same product with different packaging also able to replace with material determination.

The benefit of this functionality is that when business is out of materials or products, it then manually researches replaceable product, this process able to streamline the sales process.

Customization:

The material determination configuration is based on the principle of condition technique. After the configuration condition record it needs to be created from material substituted for determining material in the sales order.

Maintain Table for Material Substitution:

Customization Path: from T-code SPRO
IMG → Sales and Distribution → Basic Functions → Material Determination → Maintain Prerequisites for Material determination (from the selection box select "Create Condition Tables").

T-code: OV16

Condition table is created for fields that material need being substituted. The standard tables are two in the system "001 material entered" and "002 sales area + material entered" The new table entry able to create as per requirements.

Maintain Access Sequence:

T-code SPRO

IMG → Sales and Distribution → Basic Functions → Material Determination → Maintain Prerequisites for Material determination (from the selection box select "Maintain Access Sequence").

Access sequence is a search limit with the table fields. In the access sequence, we enter tables.

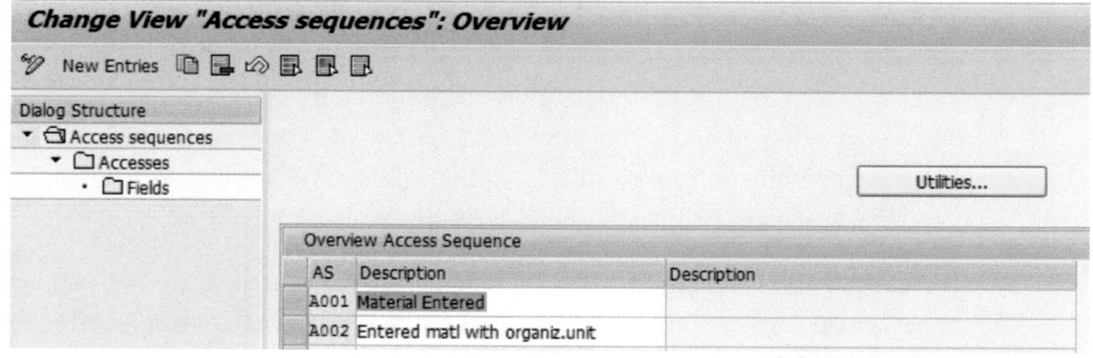

In access sequence A001 access it shows the table entry.

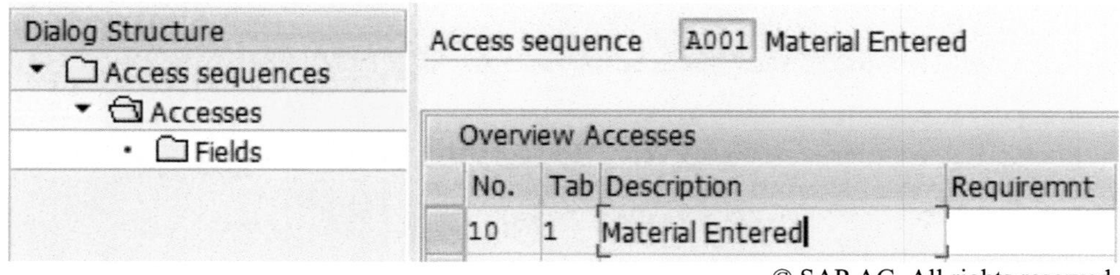

In the above screenshot it is displaying Accesses (as folder icon is open) in this field the “No” field represents the sequence number of access sequence and fled “Tab” represent a table entry in access sequence.

Condition Type:

T-code SPRO

IMG → Sales and Distribution → Basic Functions → Material Determination → Maintain Prerequisites for Material determination (from the selection box select “Condition Type”).

Condition type A001 would be assigned to access sequence A001 in screen shot. It also feature validity function valid from and to dates.

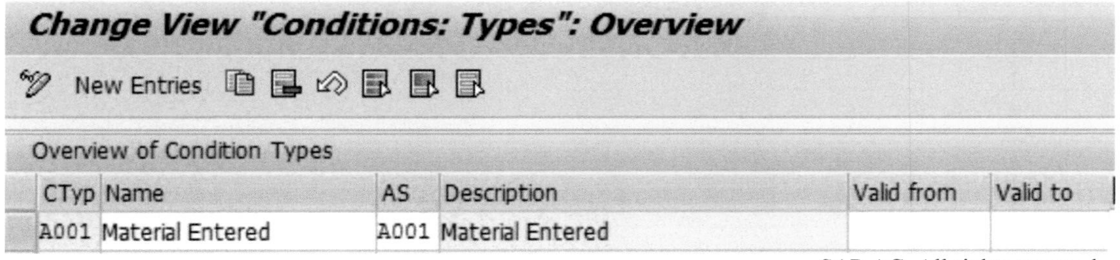

Material Determination Procedure:

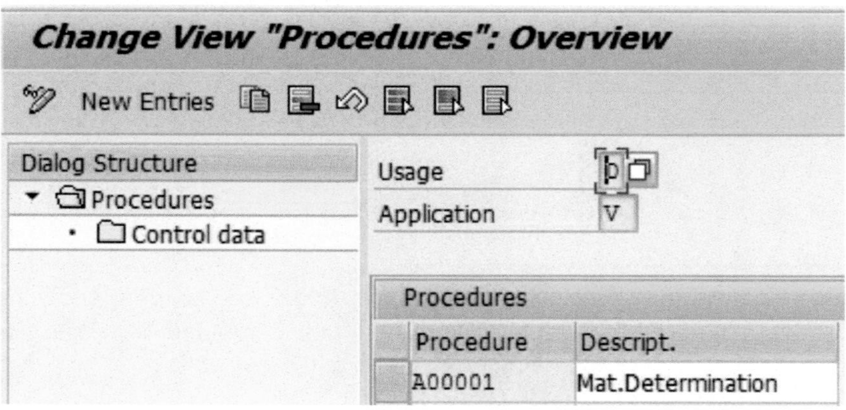

Material determination procedure is defined in the above screenshot and in the next step by selecting the procedure it goes into Control data for further controls in the procedure.

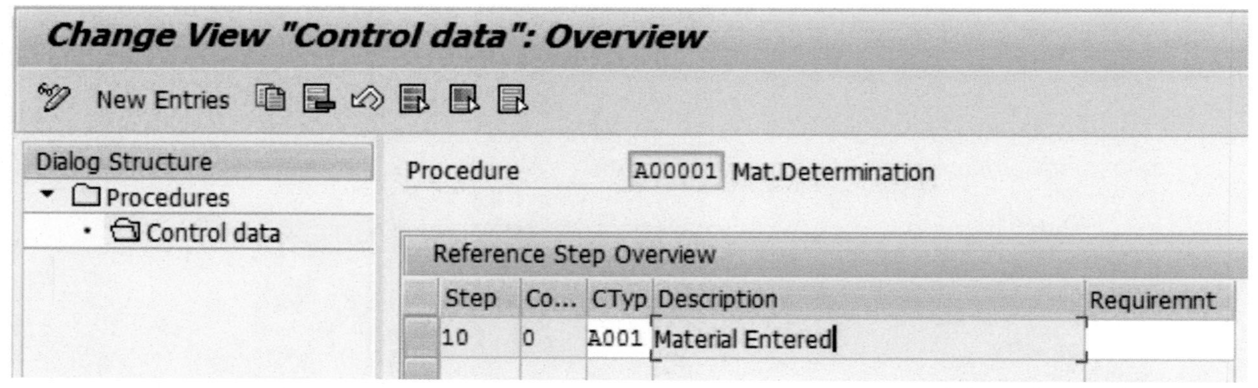

Material determination feature four fields for customization.

- Step
- Counter
- Condition Type
- Requirement Type

Step: Step is the counter in the material determination procedure. It is utilized to indicate system the in which step supposed to processed first. The step starts with 10 and the second step feature 20, so if additional steps are required then it able to add in-between.

Counter: Counter is utilized if the same step is repeated and feature had additional process then it able to add to count to process it in counter sequence.

Condition Type: Condition Type is the customized in this field, the step and a counter field is related to the condition type for the process of condition type.

Requirement Type: Requirement Type is a program that able to customize to process additional functions for material determination. The standard requirement type able to utilize, but additional requirement types require customization of ABAP development.

Material Substitution Reason:

Material substitution also able to customize based on the substitution reason.

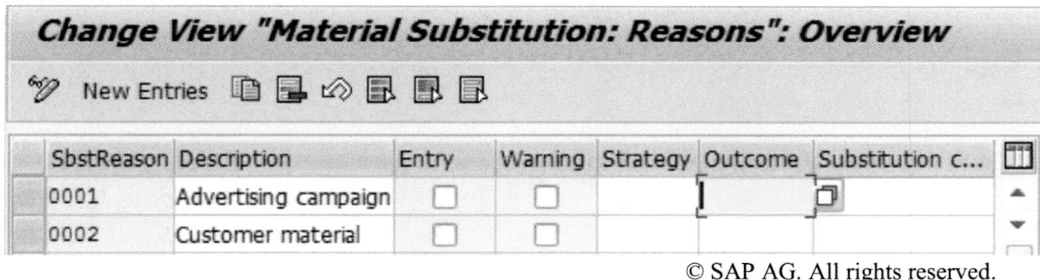

Substitution Reason:

The automatic substitution reason is the first field to configuring the automatic substitution to be determined.

Entry:

Entry is the second control in substitution reason controls, if this option is selected the original entry will be printed. Based on the requirements, if the original material needs to be printed or not, this option able to utilize accordingly.

Warning:

Warning field is the third option in substitution reason controls. If this option is selected the system will issue warning message before material substitution. This option able to utilize if warning message is needed for the user to be aware that new material is determined.

Strategy:

Strategy is the fourth control in substitution reason customization. It controls material if it needs to be selected automatically in back ground or if they require to be selected manually.

Outcome:

The Outcome is the fifth option for customization in substitution reason controls. This field value control is a substitution that supposed to carry out. The substitution items will show in sub items or only in relevant sales order creation process with the option of showing in sub items.

Substitution Category:

Substitution Category is sixth customization in substitution reason controls. It controls service related functions. The service item able to categorize for substitution.

Material Deamination Condition Record:

The mater determination condition record is a master data. The T-code is utilized for the materiel determination is VB11.

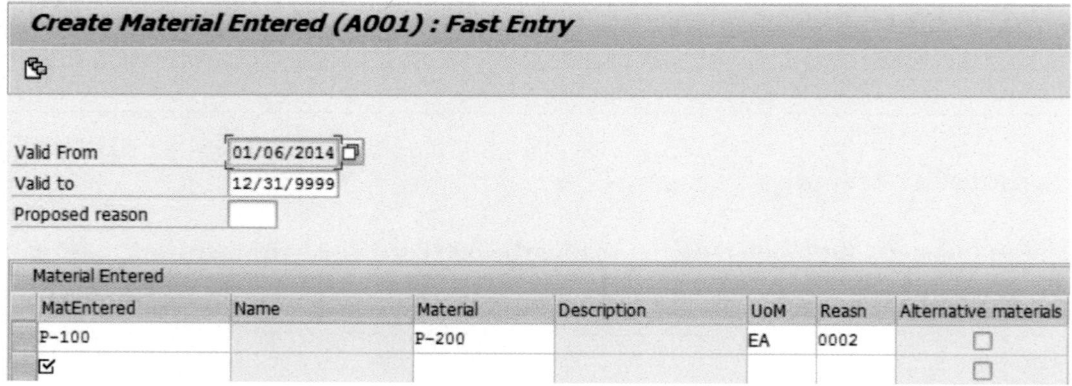

Validity from and Valid To:

The material determination feature validity period controls.

Chapter 3 Summary:

The following topics have been covered in the chapter:

- Introduction to Master Data
- Transactional Data
- Customer Master Data and related topics
- Customer Master customization
- Account Group customization
- Partner Function Determination
- Introduction to Material Master
- Material Type Configuration
- Introduction to Customer Material Information Record

Notes

CHAPTER 4

ORDER MANGMENT & CONTRACTS

- Contracts and rebate Agreement
- Quantity Contracts
- Value Contract
- Service Contract
- Master Contract
- Scheduling Agreement
- Sales Order Customization
- Item Category Customization
- Item Category Determination
- Plant Determination
- Route determination Customization
- Dynamic Item Proposal Customization
- Schedule line customization
- Schedule Line determination
- Rebate Agreement
- Quantity Contract
- Sales Document Block
- Sales Order Customizing

What is in this chapter for me?

This chapter focused on sales order and contract customization. Addition to sales order this chapter also include contract type, inquiry and quotation documentation customization. This chapter also cover topics including item category and schedule line configuration. This chapter also include scheduling agreement customization.

A contract represent a legal agreement between the buyer and

Contract

Contract is a legal agreement. It is a written document and agreed upon binding document. The contract feature validity date. It feature term and conditions. Sales and Distribution have four types of contracts that are available. Schedule agreement is also considering a type of contract. The contract is one of the first steps, but not all-sales processes require contracts, it depends on the requirements. In Sales and Distribution the contract type customization and sales order customization is same.

Contract Types:

The following are four types of contracts.

1. Quantity Contract
2. Value Contract
3. Service Contract
4. Master Contract

Quantity Contract:

Quantity Contract is based on quantity. If the quantity contract exists, it will issue a warning in the sales order. With customization as it is it also able to have references that are made mandatory, so that the sales process will require quantity contract type reference made mandatory. Example: If the customer able to bound to buy 100 pieces per each sales order.

To create contract, the T-code is **VA41**
the quantity contract order type is utilized **QT**

Value Contract:

Value contract is based on value. Value contract calculates the value with an assortment or selected product. There are two kinds of value contracts in the system, one with assortments and one with fix products. Unlike quantity contract, it depends on the value of the sales order. For example, if a customer places an order, regardless of quantity of material, the value should match contract value.

To create contract, the T-code is **VA41**
Value contract order type: **WK1**
Value contract order type: **WK2** (Material Related)

Contracts are presales activity document.

Service Contract:

Service contracts are a based-on service for example if the customer creates a service contract with a wireless company provider for one year of service.

To create contract, the T-code is: **VA41**
Service and Maintenance contract order type: **SC**

Master Contract:

Master contract is a combination of quantity contract, value, contract, and service contract. For example, if the customer feature multiple contracts they able to combine into one master contract. The master contract expected to only contain only two types of contracts.

To create contract, the T-code is **VA41**
Master contract order type: **GK**

Scheduling Agreement:

Scheduling agreement is a type of a contract, but functions like a sales document. The scheduling agreement is created with periodic delivery schedules and the billing is based on delivery of goods. If the customer makes a bulk order, but wants recurring shipments periodically, then scheduling the agreement able to help the process. It helps with repeated orders or demand with a schedule of periodic deliveries.

To create Scheduling Agreement the T-code is: VA31
Order type: CO
Many other types of scheduling agreement available: LZ, CO, LZM and etc.

Scheduling agreement is a sales document that has periodic delivery scheduling.

Rebate Agreement:

The rebate is a type of a discount with accrual. When a customer buys a product and condition get fulfills, then the customer receives credit back. The only difference between a regular discount and rebate, is that the credit is given back to the customer after the purchased sales order and when the discount is given to the customer at the time of sales order or invoice.

Rebate condition able to base on the customer purchase volume, product rebate or other basis. Once the first rebate agreement is setup, it will contain a percentage or fix price, or discount, and it feature a validity period on the conditions. Rebate agreements are created before the rebate process starts from the sales order. It is accrual process and its credit gets accrued at the end of the process. SAP standard rebate agreement able to create based on Customer, Material, group rebate, and hierarchy types. Additional rebate agreements able to create with t-code, "VB(2 ". A rebate agreement feature a start date and an end date. Rebate pricing is accrual with pricing condition types.

Rebate is type of discount that is issued after invoice process.

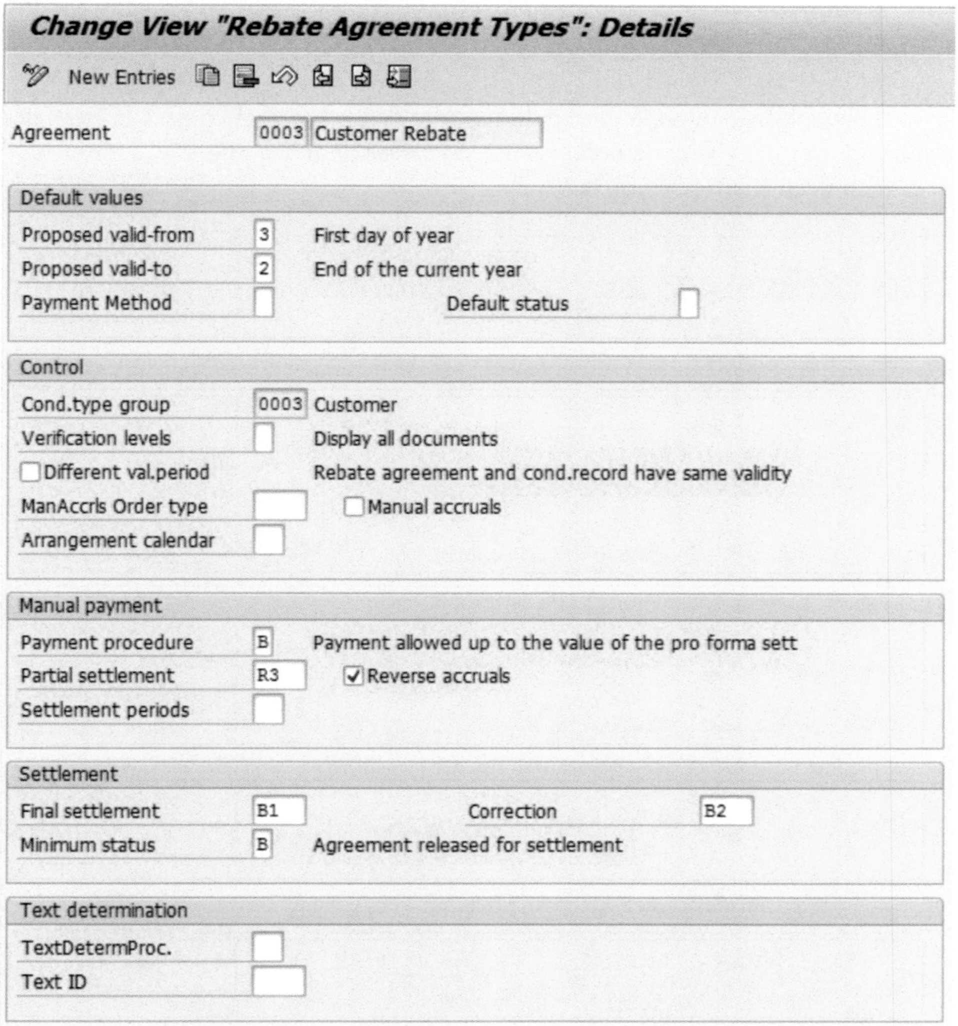

Change View "Rebate Agreement Types": Details

New Entries

Agreement 0003 Customer Rebate

Default values

Proposed valid-from 3 First day of year
Proposed valid-to 2 End of the current year
Payment Method Default status

Control

Cond.type group 0003 Customer
Verification levels Display all documents
Different val.period Rebate agreement and cond.record have same validity
ManAccrls Order type Manual accruals
Arrangement calendar

Manual payment

Payment procedure B Payment allowed up to the value of the pro forma sett
Partial settlement R3 Reverse accruals
Settlement periods

Settlement

Final settlement B1 Correction B2
Minimum status B Agreement released for settlement

Text determination

TextDetermProc.
Text ID

Sales Order Configuration:

Order type controls the sales document header level. Order type configuration is configured with T-code VOV8. The customization for contracts, scheduling agreements, sales orders, and credit/debit memo also use the same configuration. This section able to utilize as a configuration guide for all sales documents, including, sales orders, contract, scheduling agreements, credit and debit memo, Inquiry, and quotation. It's the best practice to copy from start order type so that the customization doesn't require recreating the whole order type. However, it is critical to understand the controls so they able to set utilized per requirements.

Header level Sales document type customization

This section will be covering quantity contact type customization.

Contract type QC is standard contract type.

Document category:

Document category defines what kind of document it is. It is the first control in sales document customization, so it categorizes the document type based on this value.
Document category for Contract type is “G“.

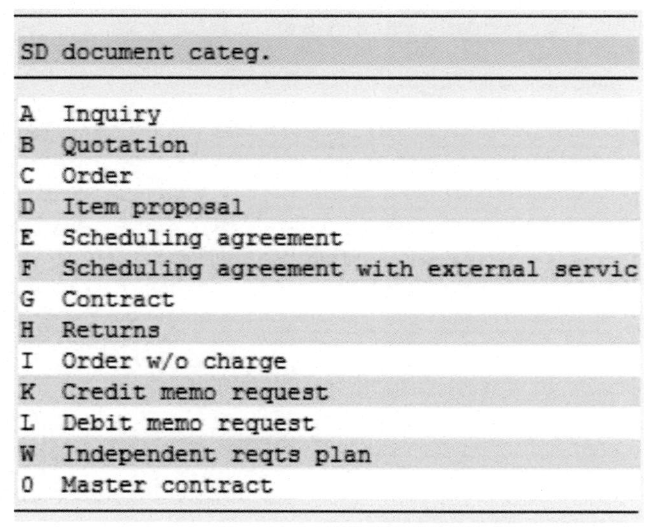

SD document categ.	
A	Inquiry
B	Quotation
C	Order
D	Item proposal
E	Scheduling agreement
F	Scheduling agreement with external servic
G	Contract
H	Returns
I	Order w/o charge
K	Credit memo request
L	Debit memo request
W	Independent reqts plan
0	Master contract

These values control the document type.

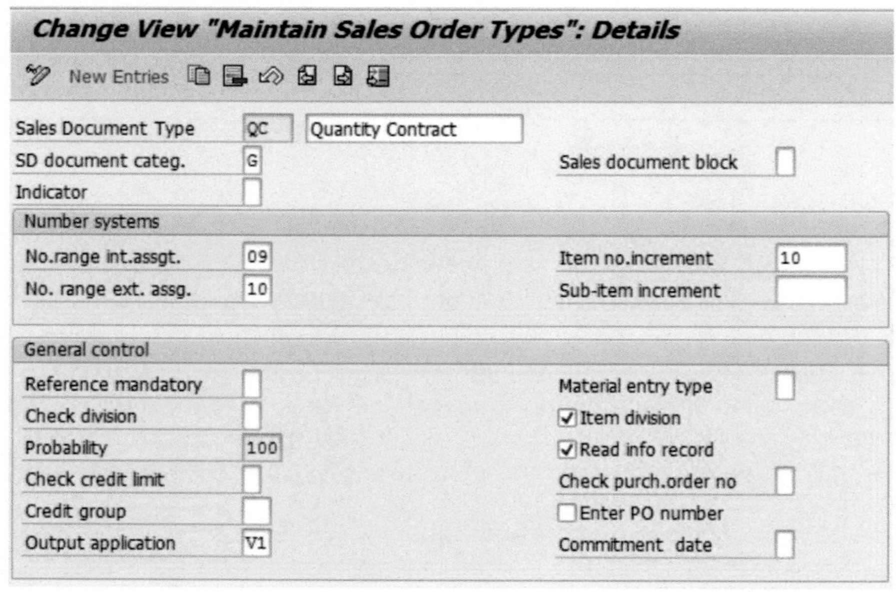

To Configure Sales Document the document category determines the sales document type.

Please follow the Figure "Sales Document Type".

SD document categ.
A Inquiry
B Quotation
C Order
D Item proposal
E Scheduling agreement
F Scheduling agreement with external servic
G Contract
H Returns
I Order w/o charge
K Credit memo request
L Debit memo request
W Independent reqts plan
0 Master contract

Sales Document Types for other document controlled with an element of the configuration.

Sales Document Block:

Sales document Block able to set by this field options. It able to set for credit notes in the process of approvals.

Indicator:

The Indicator field able to set to control the document indication of the process. It classifies further controls of sales of the document type.

Indica...	Short Descript.
	No classification
B	Delivery order
C	Scheduling agreement with delivery order
D	Invoice correction request
E	Delivery order correction
F	Repair processing: Leading serviceable material
G	Repair processing: Leading service product
H	Scheduling agreement with external service agent processing
I	Consignment issue by external service agent
K	Correct consignment issue by external service agent
R	Order for Billing Between Company Codes (RRICB)

Number Range:

Number systems			
No.range int.assgt.	09	Item no.increment	10
No. range ext. assg.	10	Sub-item increment	

The number range determines the sequence document number at the time of sales order creation. To able to identify between document types it is appropriate to assign different number ranges, so it able to help with the identification of document with different numbers. Examples of the service contract able to start with 2000 and sales order able to start with 3000 numbers, so it is easy to identify just looking at document number and it also able to help in reporting.

Two types of number ranges able to maintain in sales document customization: internal number range and external number range. The internal number range will auto populate, and external number range is manually entered into a sales document. Item increment is for what next number supposed to inclement of the next number. For example if the order feature increment, the first order is 20010 and second order is 20020.

General Control:

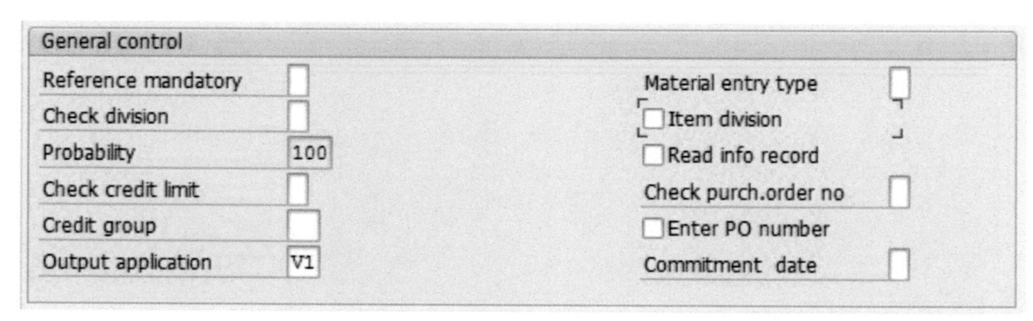

In "General Control" section 9 option for controls and three selection options.

Reference mandatory:

The reference mandatory controls the reference document which is required for preceding document and for the reference before going forward to create a sales order.

Check Division:

Check division error able to set to issue error at the time of creation of sales from warring, dialog, or no dialog display.

Probability:

This field is utilized for the planning of consumption based on probability set in the sales order header type. It is utilized for inquiry and quotation to value the probability that will be confirmed to be a sales order.

Check Credit Limit: Credit limit checks the controls for sales order level that able to set here.

Credit Group: Documents able to assign to different credit groups in this field.

Output Application: This selection field is utilized for outputs application identification.

Material entry control: This Selection field controls product catalog related controls if they want to activate product catalog in the sales order.

Check boxes:

Item division: This check is required before saving or creating sales order.

Read Info Record: check for the Customer Material Info record, so with this selection sales order will check CMIR.

Enter PO Number: If this check is set, it will make Purchase order fields required in the sales order document.

Check, Purchase Order Number:

This function checks if any purchase order already exists to avoid duplication of same purchase order in the system.

Commitment Date:

A number of factors are involved with different combination options. If the user selects the data, then system checks for the stock and calculates the delivery time, according to selected value system schedule commitment dates.

Transaction Flow:

Transaction flow				
Screen sequence grp.	LP	Outline agreement	Display Range	UALL
Incompl.proced.	12	Outline Agreement	FCode for overv.scr.	UER1
Transaction group	4	Contract	Quotation messages	
Doc. pric. procedure	Ö		Outline agrmt mess.	
Status profile			Message: Mast.contr.	A
Alt.sales doc. type1			ProdAttr.messages	
Alt.sales doc. type2			☑ Incomplet.messages	
Variant				

Transaction flow feature controls on the sales document processing with required filed. Such as pricing, alternative sales order types, messages, transaction group, open contract check, document completeness messages, and more.

Document Pricing Procedure:

It is utilized for pricing determination from sales document controls then the document pricing indicator helps pricing determination procedure to get determine in sales document.

Alternative Sales Order Type:

Two or more alternative sales order types able to configure. The users able to specify alternative sales order types in these fields if an order is required to be saved with different sales order type. With this, sales order type able to change after the sales order sales.

F-code default for overview screen:

This able to set to display sales order header tab screen as a default screen to start the order entry. If a user wants to start the order with "ordering party" tab, then the value needs to be set here to get the "Ordering tab" as a first screen.

Message: Master Contract:

This feature is utilized to enable if the system needs to check if the master contract exist.

Outline Agreement Message:

This feature is utilized to enable if the system needs to check if an open contract exist at the time of sales order creation and display a message.

Quotation Message:

This feature is utilized for displaying a message if the system needs to check if an open quotation exist at the time of sales order creation.

Incomplete Procedure:

Incomplete procedure uses "incompletion log" configuration settings here for the sales document. Incompletion log setup is a separate configuration; it able to set to make fields in the sales document required and optional.

Screen Sequence Group:

Screen sequence group selection controls the display, which the screen needs to be displayed and what sequence they will be displayed. It able to identify with appropriate sales orders categories.

Transaction Group:

The transaction group identifies or separates a document from categories like: Contract, scheduling agreement, sales order, and item proposal.

Scheduling Agreement:

This section of sales order controls is for scheduling agreement. The sales document type feature four customizations.

- Correction Delivery Type
- Usage
- MRP for Delivery schedule type
- Delivery Block

Correction delivery type specifies which delivery order type will be utilized to correct delivery for the scheduling agreement. Usage is utilized for material usage for order type at header level and it will be determined in all the line items. Material requirement planning is a set active MRP requirement for delivery date confirmation with agreement dates. Delivery block are utilized to set delivery block initially at the time of the creation of the scheduling agreement.

Shipping:

Shipping

Delivery type

Delivery block

Shipping conditions

ShipCostInfoProfile

Immediate delivery

This customization of sales order controls deliveries and shipments. Shipping controls the shipping relevant delivery types. If an order needs to be on the delivery block and shipping condition, set at header lever. The following are controls in shipping control tab.

- Delivery Type
- Delivery Block
- Shipping Conditions
- Shipping cost info profile
- Immediate delivery

Delivery Type:

This specifies type of delivery able to create against sales order and additional configuration may be required for copy control setup.

Delivery Block:

Delivery block sets delivery block in the sales order. If the delivery block feature set the sales order then it will create a delivery block, and delivery cannot be created until this block is removed.

Shipping Conditions:

Shipping Point able to assign at a sales order header level.

Shipping cost info profile:

The profile setup pricing is the determination in delivery from sales order.

Immediate Delivery:

If this option is selected, then the delivery will be created at the time feature the sales order creation. Example: Rush order requires immediate delivery, and with this option selected delivery document will be created as soon as sales order is created.

Billing:

Billing feature controlling elements similar to order type-controlling elements. Additional sales order headers controls orders and delivery related billing options.

Billing	
Dlv-rel.billing type	CndType line items
Order-rel.bill.type	Billing plan type
Intercomp.bill.type	Paymt guarant. proc.
Billing block	Paymt card plan type
	Checking group

Delivery related Billing Type:

This option makes a sales order for delivery related billing. The delivery type will be entered in this field.

Order Related Billing:

Order related billing controls the billing as soon as sales order is created.

Intercompany Billing type:

Intercompany billing type control is utilized for intercompany sales order processes.

Billing Block:

This function controls the billing block in sales order at the time of sales order creation.

Condition Type Line Item:

The pricing condition is utilized for the pricing in sales order and billing document.

Billing Plan Type / Payment Card Plan type:

Billing plan is the kind of billing plan that will be utilized from for sales orders. Billing plans able to set milestone billing or periodic billing or customized billing plan able to utilize here as well.

Payment Guarantee Procedure:

Payment Guarantee is utilized from order types that guarantee payment determination from it.

Checking Group:

Checking group determines the payment card type processing functionality.

Requested Delivery Date / Pricing Date / Purchase Order Date:

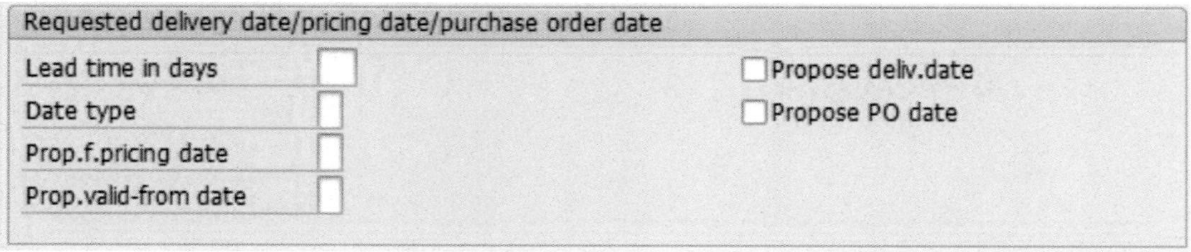

Requested delivery date/pricing date/purchase order date		
Lead time in days		☐ Propose deliv.date
Date type		☐ Propose PO date
Prop.f.pricing date		
Prop.valid-from date		

Here we configure parameters to set date in sales order which are relevant in pricing and related functions.

Lead Time in days:

The number of days is proposed in the sales order for the lead-time. The number values utilized to define days needed to be calculated.

Date Type:

Date type is a selection option. Data types expected to be in days, weeks, months, posting period and year.

Purposed Pricing Data:

Price validity able to set on the following:

- Contract Data
- Valid from data
- Required delivery date

If no values maintains then price effective date will be from toadying, meaning sales order creation date.

Purpose validity of data:

In this field if no values is maintaining then the date effective date will be from toady, meaning the sales order creation date. Validity date is set for quotation data, that validity data will be effective for sales order processing.

Purpose delivery date / Purpose PO data:

For delivery dates, the proposal check box is selected. Then the system will populate today's date in the sales order. If the Purpose PO check box is selected, then the system will carry out todays date in the sales order.

> The important configuration in this section is **pricing date**.

Contract:

Following the contract section will be covered in detail with field level descriptions. Contract screenshot is the following.

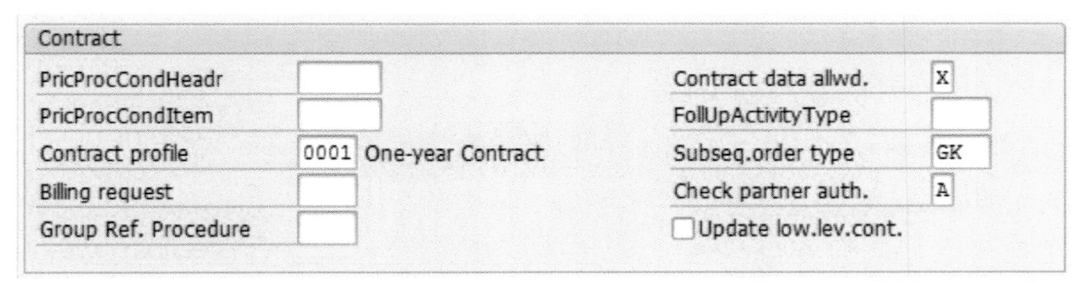

Pricing procedure condition Header:

Pricing procedure is purposed from "Pricing procedure condition header" field selection options.

Pricing procedure condition Item:

Pricing condition type is for contract purposed from "Pricing procedure condition item" field selection options.

Contract Profile:

This profile selection is utilized for valid date of the contract, while start and end dates are part of profile setup.

Billing Request:

Billing request types are selected, for example, credit memo.

Group Reference procedure:

Group reference procedure is utilized in the master contract. This procedure required that identical field, copy field and configuration between contract type with master data setup.

Contract Data Allowed:

If this selection is selected, then the contract date able to set manually entered in the sales order.

Follow-up Activity Type:

Customization set-ups follow the document procedure after this contract is created.

Subsequent Order Type:

The subsequent order type identifies with what is the next document supposed to utilized for in the contract.

Check Partner Authorization:

This will check for valid partner uses of the contract.

Update Low-level Contract:

This checked box controls the high-level contract that should change the low-level contract. If it is selected in the master contract, then it will carry out changes in all the contracts that are under it.

Availability Check:

This setting is relevant for the APO availability check.

The sales order configuration will be very similar to contracts order type configuration but with different variations according to order type. Order type feature header level controls and any customization will affect all of the lines in sales documents. For additional and secondary level control items the category customization will affect the line level based on item category group. Order type customization with t-code VOV8.

Some of Standard Order types are:

Order Type	Description
OR	Standard Order type
RE	Return order
CR	Credit Request
DR	Debit Request
FOD	Free of Delivery
RO	Rush Order

Sales Order Related T-Code:

T-code	**Description**
VA01	Create Sales Order
VA02	Change Sales Order
VA03	Display Sales Order
VA05	Sales Order Report
SD01	Sales order report with date range
V.02	Incomplete Sales Orders (Report)
V.15	Backorder report

Sales Order Screenshots:

The following screenshot of sales order is without customer master and material master information. Customer Master is utilized in Sold to field and Ship to field.

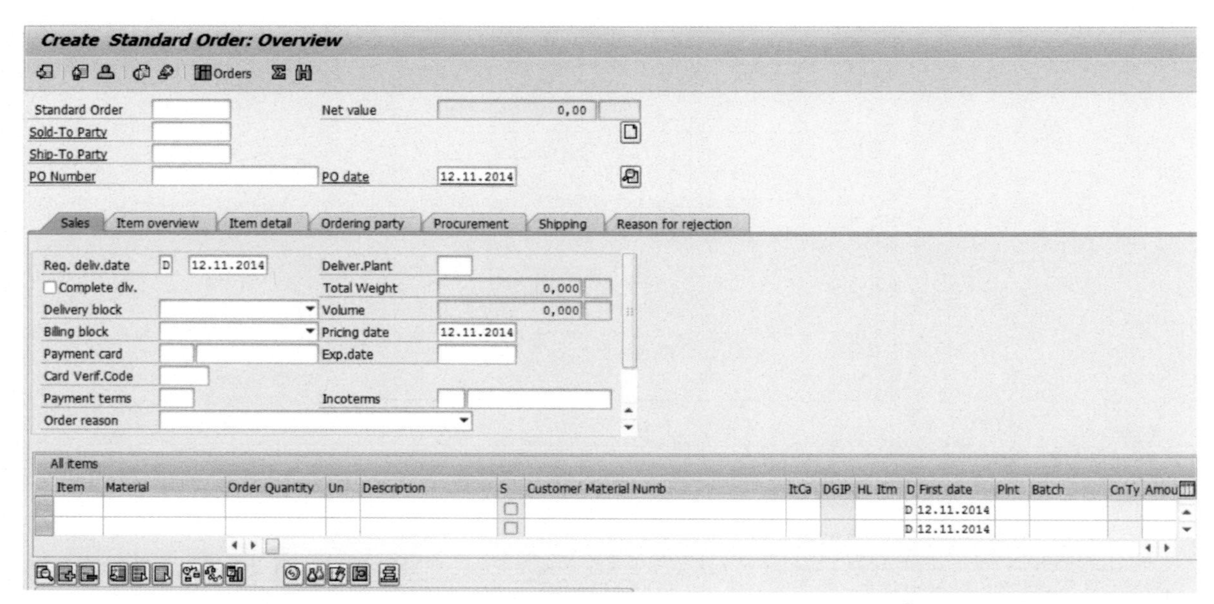

Sales Order Structure:

Sales Order feature many controls from header, Item and schedule line. The following figure represents the high-level overview of the sales order.

- Sales order header information flow into sales order item information and schedule line.
- Header information applied to all the lines but at line level information able to change.
- Schedule lines able to set changed separately

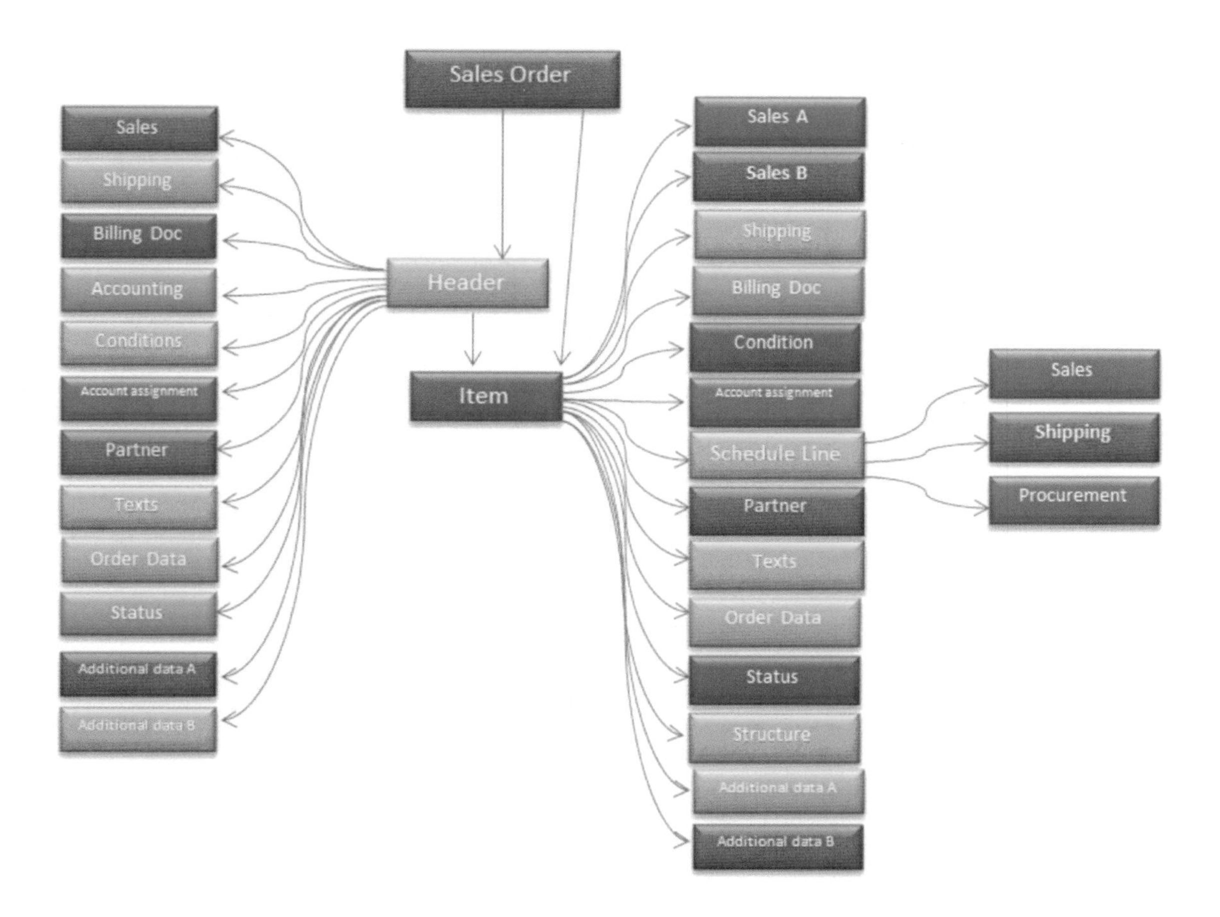

The screenshot represents how the header information drives down to the item level and how it effects item and schedule lines. Additionally the functionality at the item level item category and schedule line category able to differ from the header. These items also receives direct input for material independent of the header.

Sales Order

Sales order header and item information are available from t-code VA01 or VA03:

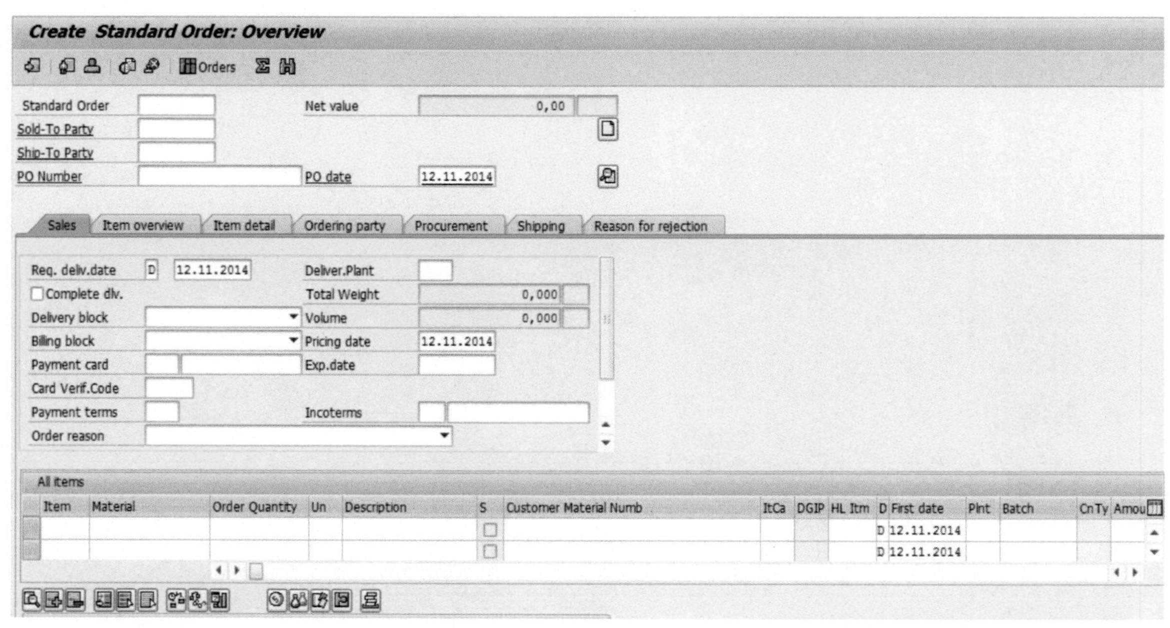

Sales Order Header with Tabs:

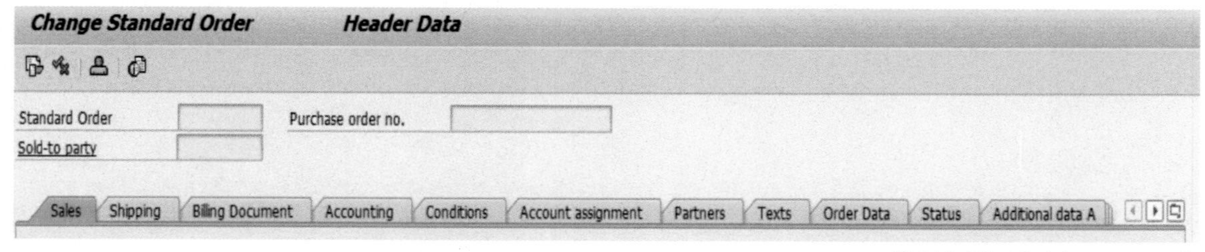

Sales Order able to view in detail via clicking this button 

Sales Order with Item Tabs:

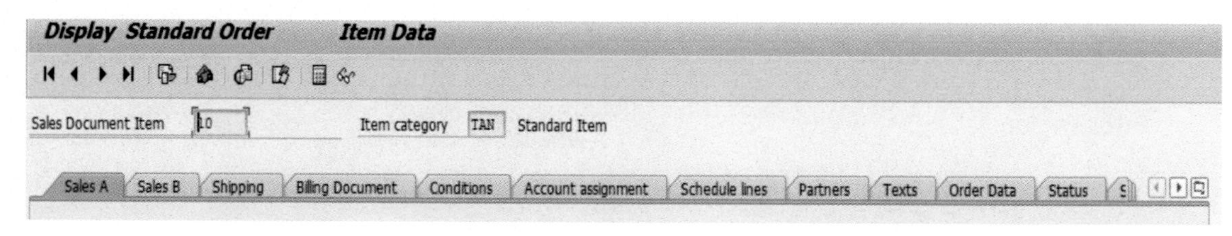

Item Category Customization:

Item Category controls the behavior of sales order line level. Line Items are mini sales order line levels, and it is dictated by the order type then item category. Item category customized with T-code VOV7.

IMG → Sales and Distribution → Sales → Sales Document → Sales documents Item → Define Item Category T-code: VOV7

Change View "Maintain Item Categories": Details

New Entries

Item category TAN Standard Item

Business Data

Field	Value		Checkbox
Item Type			☑ Business Item
Completion Rule			☑ Sched.Line Allowed
Special Stock			☐ Item Relev.for Dlv
Billing Relevance	A		☐ Returns
Billing Plan Type			☑ Wght/Vol.Relevant
Billing Block			☐ Credit active
Pricing	X		☑ Determine Cost
Statistical value			
Revenue Recognition			
Delimit. Start Date			

General Control

☐ Autom.batch determ. ☐ Rounding permitted ☐ Order qty = 1

Transaction Flow

Incompletion Proced.	20	Standard Item	Screen Seq.Grp	N
PartnerDetermProced.	N	Standard Item		
TextDetermProcedure	01	Sales Item	Status Profile	
Item Cat.Stats.Group	1	Order, Debit Memo	☐ Create PO Automatic.	

Bill of Material/Configuration

Field	Value	Checkbox
Config. Strategy		
Mat. Variant Action		☐ Variant Matching
ATP material variant		
Structure scope		☐ Create Delivery Group
Application		☐ Manual Alternative
		☐ Param. effectivities

Value Contract

Value contract matl

Contract Release Ctrl

Service Management

Repair proced.

Control of Resource-related Billing and Creation of Quotations

Billing form DIP Prof.

- Item category controls billing type, (if item is for billing relevant or not)
- Item category customization utilized for line item controls.

- Pricing relevant
- Type of Item
- Incompletion rule
- Stock type
- Relevant for delivery
- Credit control
- Resource related billing controls
- Control for variant
- Bill of Material controls
- Item relevant for return
- Variant Configuration material

Item Type:

Item type is a first customization object in the item category configuration.

Item ty...	Short Descript.
	Standard Item
A	Value Item
B	Text item
C	Packing item (will be generated)
D	Material not relevant
E	Packaging Item (External)

If the value maintained as "B", then the system is considered as a text item. Packaging material Item type is C. With this customization transaction process ,changes and system behavior changes.

Completion Rule:

Item category able to find at the sales order level. It creates a sales order and the line there for supposed to an item category field. Item category may affect many processes and control items and schedule line determination.

Item category types:

Description	Item Category
The standard	TAN
Free Item category	TANN
Consignment fills up	KBN
Consignment issue	KEN
Consignment returns	KRN
Consignment picks up	KAN
Inquiry item	AFN
Quotation item	AGN
Scheduling agreement	LPN
Service item	TAD
Debit Memo Request	L2N
Credit Memo Request	G2N
Value contract item	WKN

Each of Item categories feature different controls. These item categories supposed to utilize as a template to copy to a new item category.

Item Category Group:

Item category group is the classification of material master grouping. Item category grouping used in item category determination. Item category group is assigned to the material master. Item category group is assigned to material master basic and the sales org views.

E.g.
Standard Item Category Group: NORM
Services and non-stock material. DIEN
Third party ordering Item Category Group: BARNS
for service contracts we need Material with Item Category DIEN,

Item Category Determination:

Item category determines the sales order automatically based on following configuration:

IMG → Sales and Distribution → Sales → Sales Document → Sales documents Item → Assign Item Category

Item category is determining by four things:

- Order Type
- Item category group
- Usage
- Higher level Item category

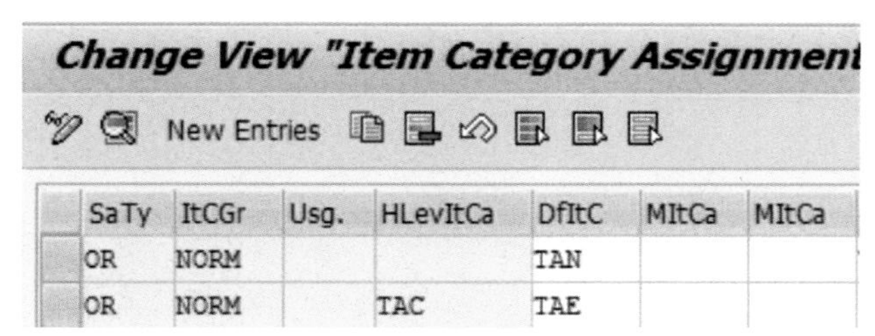

Change View "Item Category Assignment

SaTy	ItCGr	Usg.	HLevItCa	DfItC	MItCa	MItCa
OR	NORM			TAN		
OR	NORM		TAC	TAE		

1. Order type comes from order creation.
2. Item category group comes from material Master.

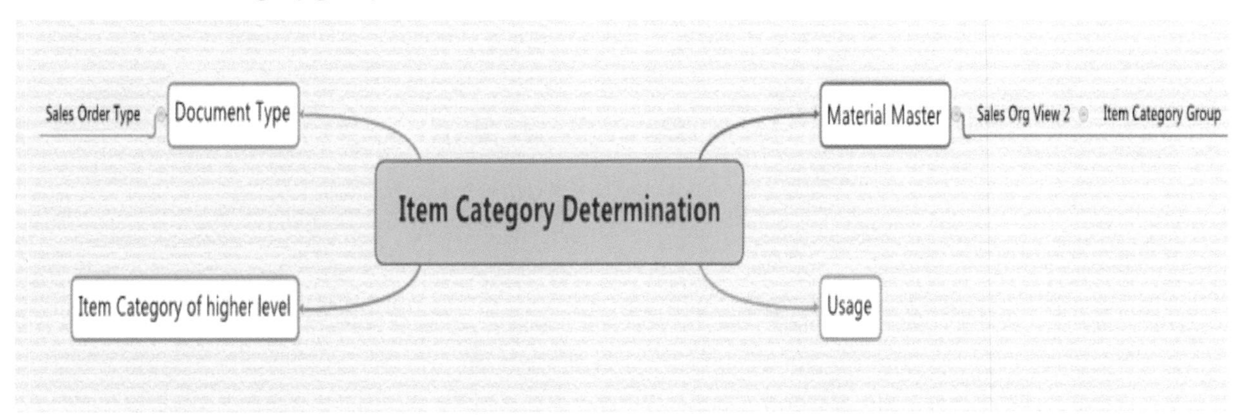

3. Default item category gets populated based on this and while manually these item categories able to allow in additional fields, as in the above screenshot.

Usage: It able to indicate the usage of an item if it is a text item and return process.

Higher level Item category: Higher-level item category is utilized for Bill of material higher level item category or free good higher-level item category.

Figure of item category determination:

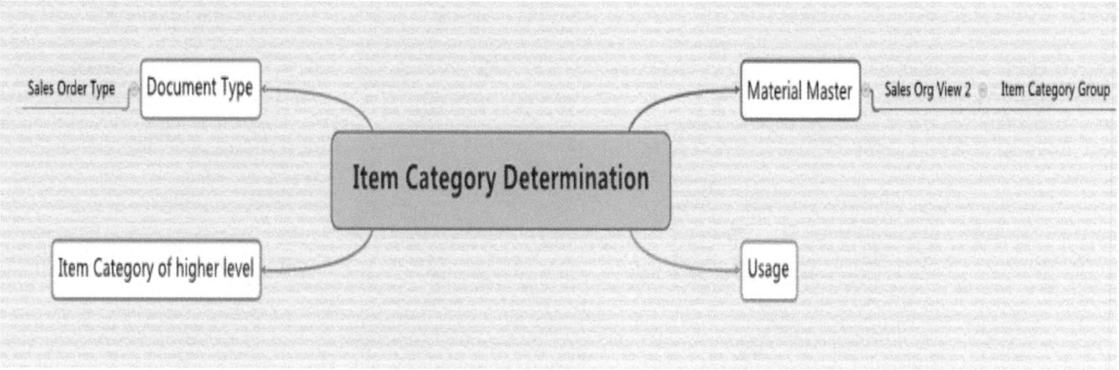

As it is shown in the figure, the item category is determined by four things in sales order, but two of them are required to determine the item category: order type and item category group. In the figure it shows the order type comes from the sales order header and item category group comes from material master.

Schedule Line:

Schedule line control, scheduling and MRP related element in the sales order.

IMG → Sales and Distribution → Sales → Sales Document → Sales documents Item → Assign Define Schedule Line category

Schedule line controls the following element:

- Delivery Block
- Movement type
- Relevant for delivery
- Required / Assembly-relevant
- Availability-relevant
- Product allocation
- Third-party order Purchase Requisition

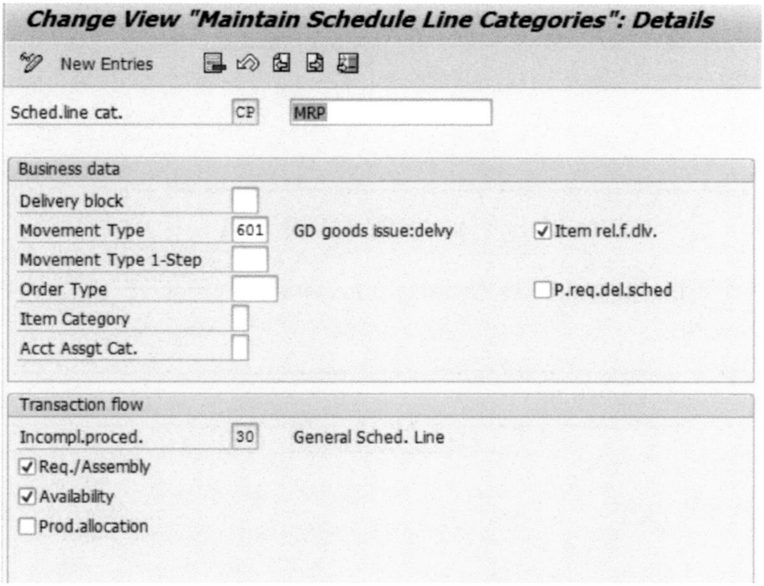

Change View "Maintain Schedule Line Categories": Details

New Entries

Sched.line cat.	CP	MRP	

Business data

Delivery block			
Movement Type	601	GD goods issue:delvy	☑ Item rel.f.dlv.
Movement Type 1-Step			
Order Type			☐ P.req.del.sched
Item Category			
Acct Assgt Cat.			

Transaction flow

Incompl.proced.	30	General Sched. Line

☑ Req./Assembly
☑ Availability
☐ Prod.allocation

Delivery Block:

Delivery block able to set for the customized schedule line category. If this is set every line created with the schedule line will be created with a delivery block.

Movement Type:

Movement type control system postings for each movement type, it effect debit and credit entries. Movement of good expected to be receiving, transfers, or goods are issued. Each movement type feature postings set for it. In general, few movement types are utilized with schedule lines.

601 Good Issues for Delivery
651 Delivery Return
631 Consignment Lending

Relevant for Delivery It controls the item relevancy for delivery so the schedule line is scheduled.

Availability Relevant: It controls if the schedule lines that should pass requirements for availability check.

Product Allocation: This check box controls if this schedule line needs to be relevant for the product allocation.

Schedule Line Determination:

IMG → Sales and Distribution → Sales → Sales Document → Sales documents Item → Assign Schedule Line category

Schedule line is based on two things:

1. Item category
2. MRP type

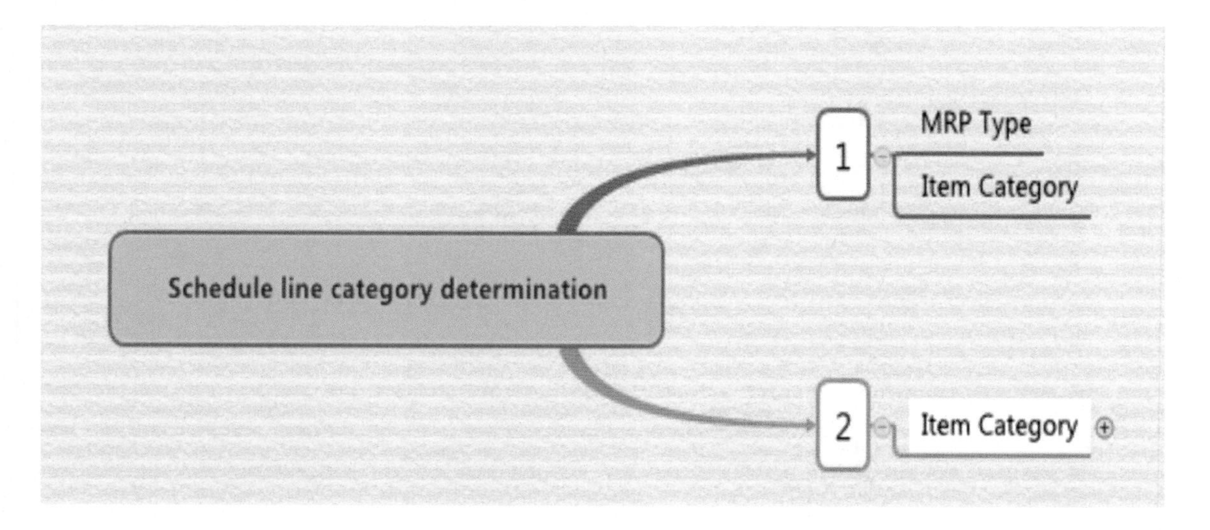

Item category and MRP determine the item category determination. The system looks for item category and MRP type combination first. If it's not found, then the system only able to consider the item category. MRP type determines from material master MRP 1 view. MRP type determines what kind of planning is utilized for the material.

IMG → Sales and Distribution → Sales → Sales Document → Sales documents Item → Assign Schedule Line category

T-code: VOV5

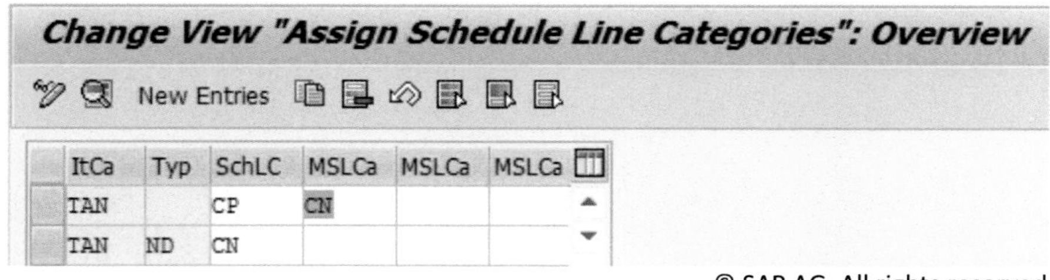

ItCa	Typ	SchLC	MSLCa	MSLCa	MSLCa
TAN		CP	CN		
TAN	ND	CN			

SAP Return Process RMA

- Introduction
- Business Process
- SAP process and Configuration
- Summary
- T-codes, Tip and issues on RMA

Introduction:

RMA stands for Return Merchandise Authorization. RMA process starts from when a customer wants to return an item. A return order is created if the sales order exists. The RMA process able to set differently based on business requirements and business process. Some business process requires that a return authorization approval before customer return the merchandise.

Business Process:

The return authorization process is mainly based on how the business operates. It depends how they would like to keep the process with their terms and conditions. When returning initiated, then customer contact customer service before returning and they issue an RMA approval number to the customer and return label. When returning shipment is received back at the warehouse, it goes through the quality inspection and then it will be added back in inventory. After the return order is good, then credit will be issued to the customer.

SAP Process:

In the SAP RMA process starts with creation of return sales order. After returning the sales order, a return delivery will be created, and a delivery document will be given to the customer as an RMA approval number. An few factors need to be considered such as what item categories are allowed and what other copy control settings are needed for the return process. RMA returns should have a sales order to reference to the return order, this is also called RMA return material approval. For RMA some restrictions may apply according to the terms of customer and business. The return RMA is a sales order RE created with t-code va01 and then return delivery is created and then a credit memo is issued to the customer.

Summary

The RMA process is a combination of business process and how it will translate into SAP. RMA is business process where the return process is utilized from SAP.

T-codes

T-codes are utilized in RMA process are:

T-code for returns is VA01
Item Category Group: NORM
Item Category: REN

Consignment Process:

In consignment process, companies move their inventory to customer locations, but ownership stay with the company and it will be counted in company stock. The stock is moved on the basis of condition, if the customer sells the product then only it able to charge to the customer. If the customer did not sell, then they will be picked back to the company's plant or warehouse.

The Consignment Fill-Up

Consignment stock transfer to customer location is called a consignment Fill-up. In consignment fill-up, sales order process material belongs to the company transferred at customer location. Consignment fill-up order type follows up with delivery document. In the system the customer's number will assign the stock so the customer stock levels able to track.

Order type: CF

Item Category: KBN

Controls for Item Category: KBN

- Relevant for pricing: No
- Business Item: Yes
- Schedule Line allowed: Yes
- Weight/Volume Related: Yes

- Credit Check: No
- Cost: No
- Relevant for Billing: No

The schedule line states the item is relevant for deliveries. When the delivery is processed with movement type is "631" at the time of goods issue, it posts the stock into a special consignment category.

The Consignment Issue:

This transaction is processed when customer sells the materials. After the customer is informed about the product being sold, then consignment issue order type is processed. With consignment issue processed the liability transfers to the customer and in system invoice able to generate to the customer.

Order type: CI
Item Category: KEN

Controls for Item Category: KEN

- Relevant for pricing: Yes
- Business Item: Yes
- Schedule Line allowed: Yes
- Weight/Volume Related: Yes
- Credit Check: Yes
- Cost: Yes

Relevant for Billing: Delivery Related

The Consignment Returns:

In this process consignment stock able to return. Returning the process is based on when a customer wants to return the product at their location in the reference to consignment issue.

Order type: CONR

Item cat: KRN

Consignment Pickup

Consignment pickup is the process when the stock from customer site is taken back to the company, this process called consignment pickup. It's followed by inbound delivery and stock that will reflect in the regular stock category.

Order type: CP

In Consignment process, stock is led to the customer; if customer sells then we charge, otherwise it will be returned.

Plant Determination in Sales Order

The plant gets determination in sales order from following elements, plant gets to determine in sales order if these entries have value maintained in them. The system starts with following priority.

1. Customer Material Info Record
2. Customer Master
3. Material Master

Plant Determination logic figure:

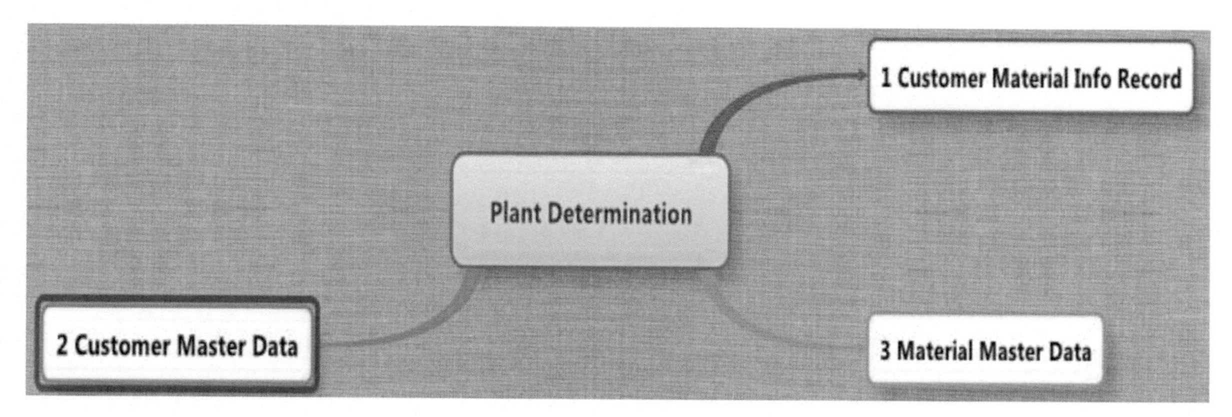

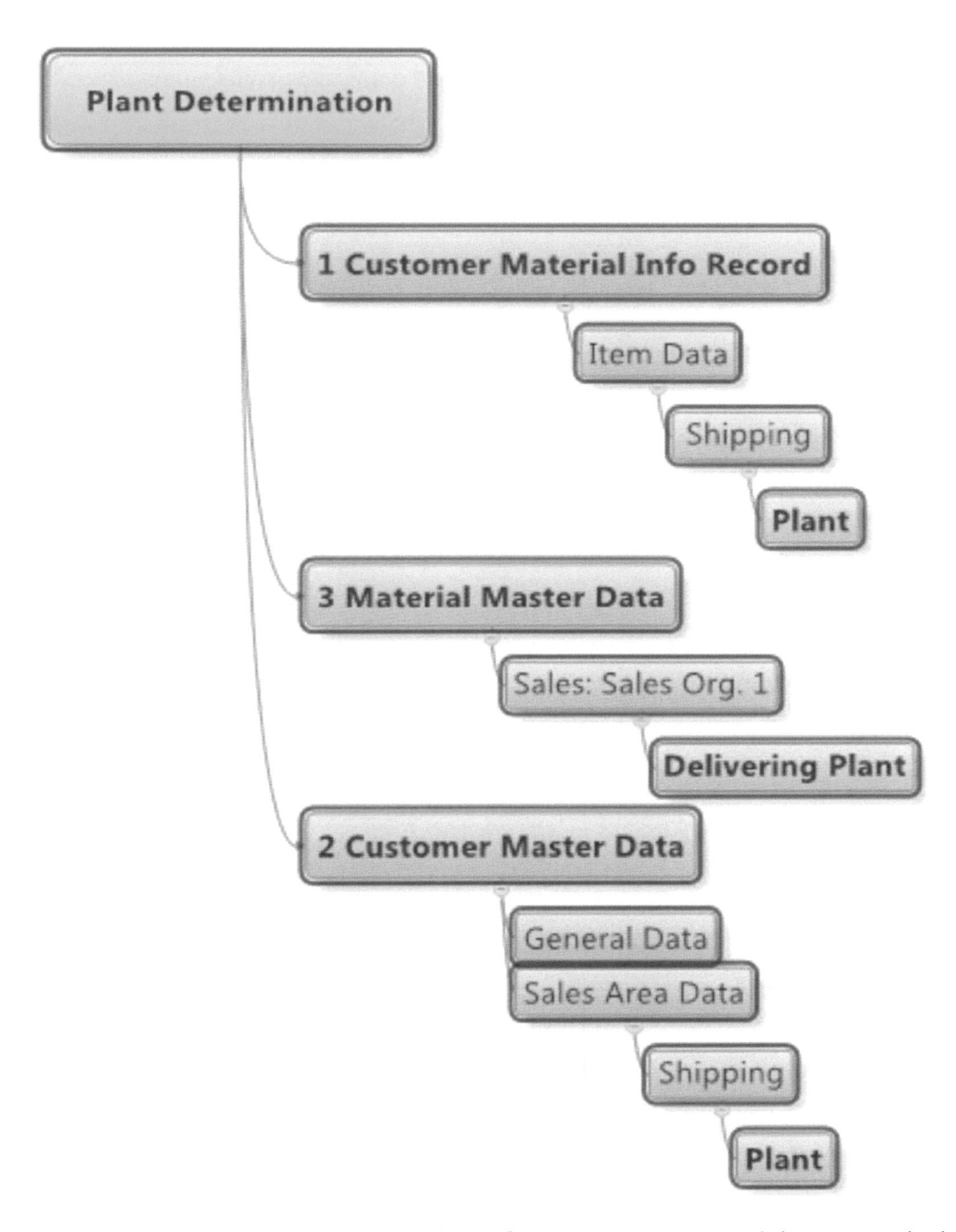

The system will check CMIR first if it contains Plant, of CMIR is not maintained then system look up the customer master if it is not maintained there if not then finally system will take a field value from material master.

Customer Material Info Record

Customer material info record is maintained by t-code VD51. Customer Material Information record overwrites the values from master data and present the most up to date information for sales document processing. The plant is maintained in the Customer Material Info Record at item level.

Customer Master

If the field value is maintained in customer maser sales view, then the default plant will reflect in the sales order.

Customer Master Screenshot (plant field)

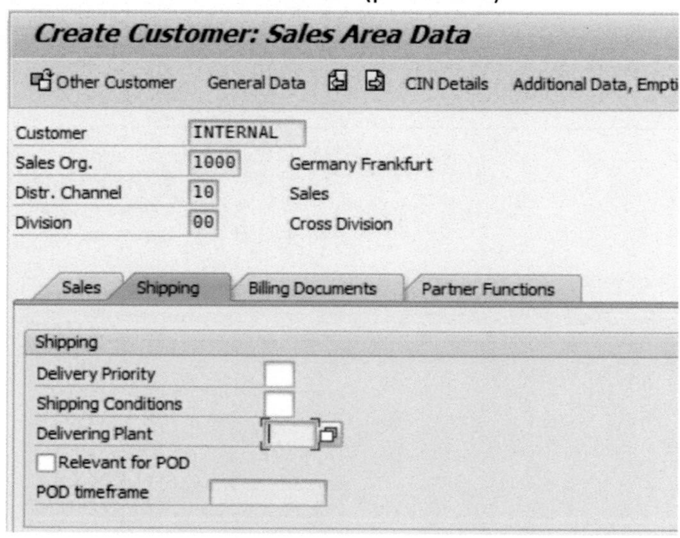

Material Master

If the field value of “delivering plant” from the material Master view of “Sales: Sales Org 1” is available, then the plant value will reflect in the sales order from Material Master.

Material master screenshot.

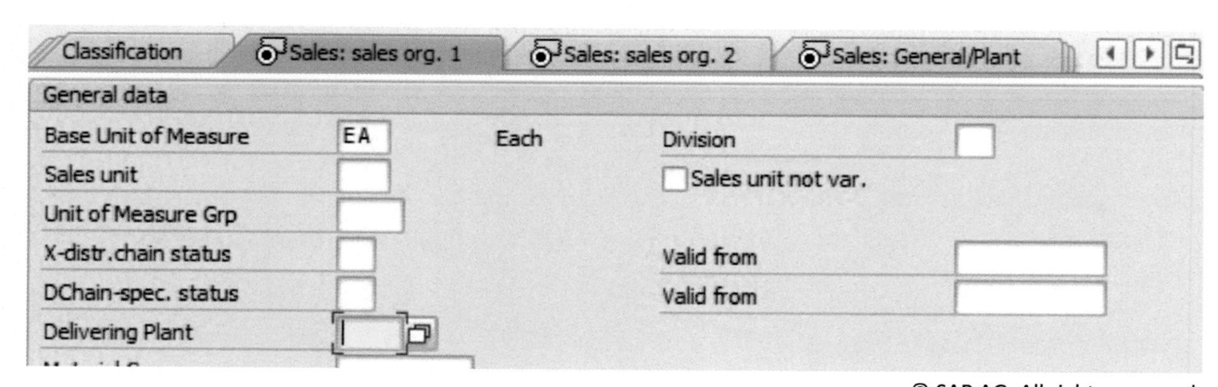

Dynamic Item Proposal:

Dynamic Item Proposal purpose is to automatically base the order history, listing and exclusion material, item proposal, customer material information record, and customer-specific master data.

The dynamic item proposal configuration is based on the condition technique principle. The following are high-level configuration elements:

- Define customer item proposal procedure
- Define document item proposal procedure
- Assign document procedure to sales document type.
- Table for Origin of product proposal
- Define a product proposal procedure
- Assign access sequence to the procedure
- Procedure determination for Background processing
- Procedure determination for online processing

IMG Customizing Path for Dynamic item proposal is
IMG → Sales and Distribution → Basic Functions → Dynamic Item Proposal

Customer Item Proposal Procedure:

Here we define customer item product proposal procedure that gets assigned to the customer master and utilized in dynamic item proposal determination. The customer item proposal procedure is one of the elements that help automatic dynamic item proposal determination.

Customizing IMG path is
IMG → Sales and Distribution → Basic Functions → Dynamic Item Proposal → Define Customer Procedure for Product Proposal

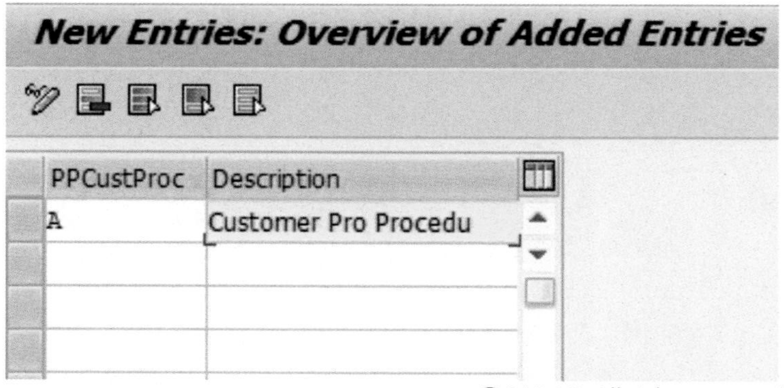

In above picture we able to define product proposal customer procedure with alpha numeric with description.

Customer Product Proposal Procedure Assignment:

The customer product proposal procedure able to assign in customer master sales area data, which is under the sales tab. It able to assign with XD01 or XD02.

Document Item Proposal Procedure:

The customizing path for Document Item Product Procedure is the following:

IMG → Sales and Distribution → Basic Functions → Dynamic Item Proposal → Define Document Procedure for Product Proposal

The Document Product Proposal Procedure able to create with a length of two characters, it could be alphabetic or numeric or a combination of both with the description.

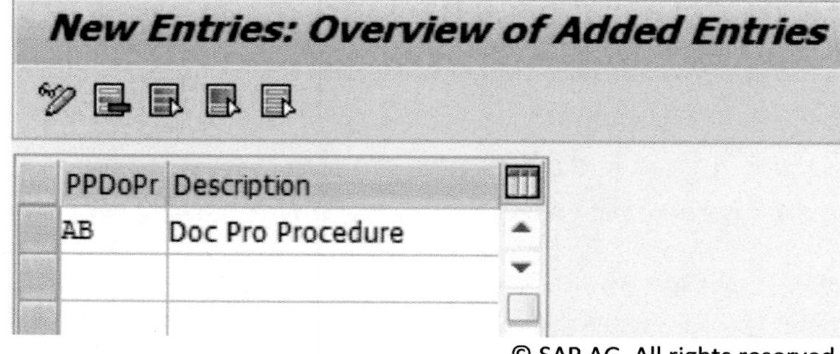

Assignment of Document Procedure of Sales Document Type:

Assignment of the document procedure for sales document type able to assign by the following IMG path. IMG → Sales and Distribution → Basic Functions → Dynamic Item Proposal → Assign document procedure for Product Proposal to sales Document Type.

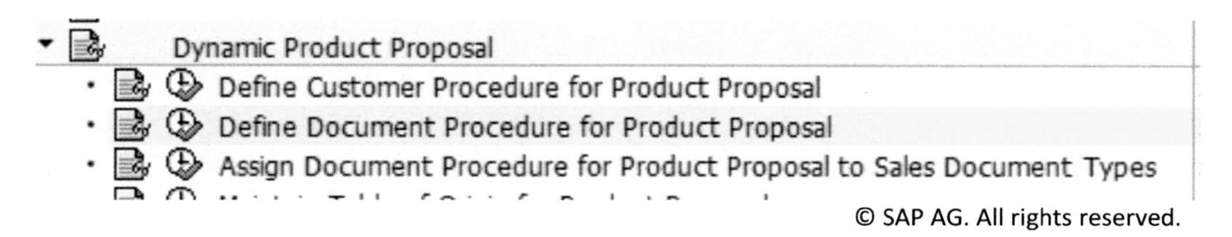

With this defined document procedure for product proposal, it will be assigned to the sales document type.

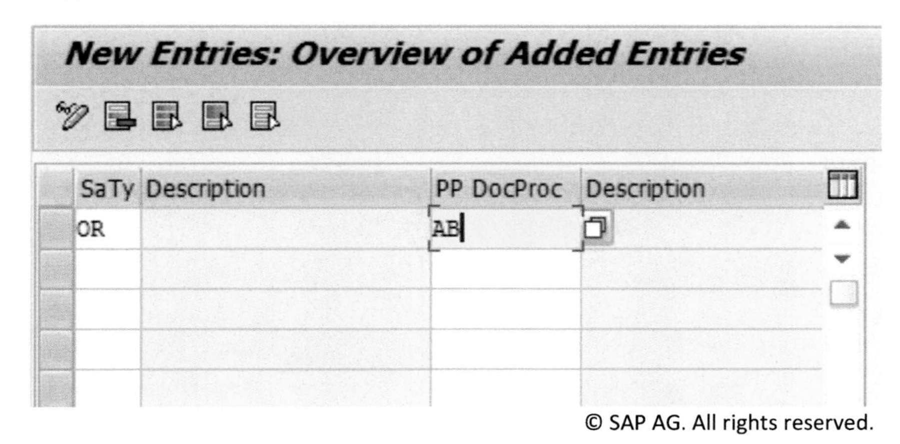

The above screenshot of the sales document type is getting assigned to document product proposal procedure. With the assignment of the document product, procedure in the sales document, it will be one of the elements to automatically determine dynamic item proposal.

Maintain Table of Origin for Product Proposal:

Customization for the table of origin of the product proposal is the following a path:
IMG → Sales and Distribution → Basic Functions → Dynamic Item Proposal → Maintain Table of Origin for Product Proposal

With the selection of the table, we are defining what source supposed to utilized for product to be proposed for. The following are predefining table entries that able to utilize for the primary source for the origin of product proposal.

- Order History
- Listed Material

- Excluded Material
- Item Proposal
- Customer Material Info Record
- Customer-Specific data source

These sources utilized in sequence are in priority needed for the requirements in access sequence.

Define Product Proposal Procedure:

We start with the procedure because the access sequence is assigned to the product proposal procedure, so we need the procedure first. To customize procedure is the following IMG guide path.
IMG → Sales and Distribution → Basic Functions → Dynamic Item Proposal → Define Product Proposal Procedure

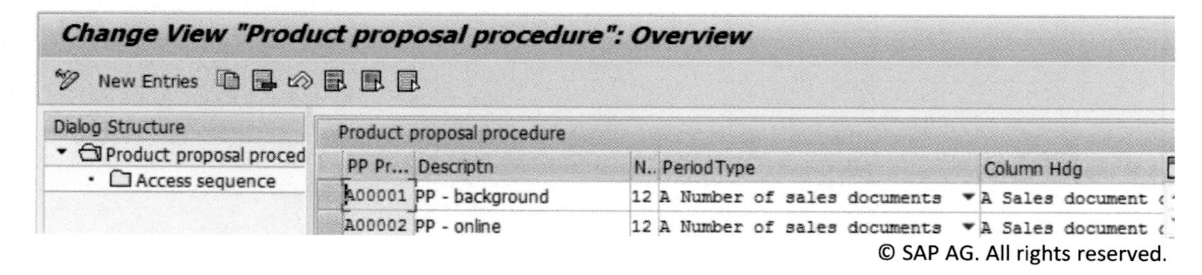

A00001 is the standard Product Proposal Procedure; it's a copy over for customization. The first field control is "No. Of Per." **Number of Period** utilized is for the history level, if it requires looking back 12 months or less, the 12TH month is maximum period that able to select. **Period Type:** feature a limit of the period needed to be checked: number of documents, days, weeks, and month. **Column Header** also feature the same values as Period Type. Assign Access Sequence to Procedure is the next step from the same customization. Assigning access sequence is needed to function the module "SD_DPP_HISTORY"

> Dynamic item proposal will automatically display relevant item(s) or list of items(s) in sales order creation.

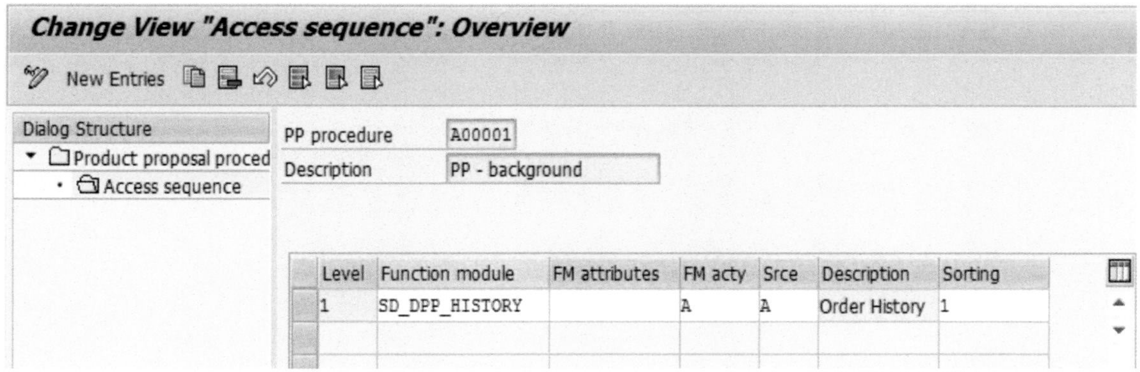

Access sequence able to run with multiple sorting options. Source are from table sales order history, listing, and exclusion as they are defined in table entries. Functional module is utilized to look at the object history as per table entry. For Online the function module is SD_DPP_READ.

Procedure Determination for Background Processing:

Background processing determination IMG customization is the following:
IMG → Sales and Distribution → Basic Functions → Dynamic Item Proposal → Maintain Procedure Determination (In Background)

Background product proposal procedure determination is based on the sales area with Product proposal customer procedure combination and it will determine background procedure based on it.

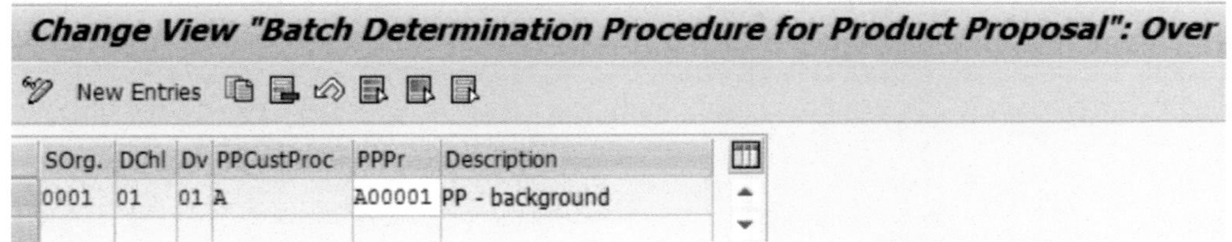

The above figure displays the sales area and product proposal determination for back product proposal ground.

Procedure Determination for Online Processing:

Online processing determination IMG customization is the following:
IMG → Sales and Distribution → Basic Functions → Dynamic Item Proposal → Maintain Procedure Determination (online)

Online product proposal procedure determination is based on sales area with Product proposal customer procedure combination and it will determine background procedure based on it.

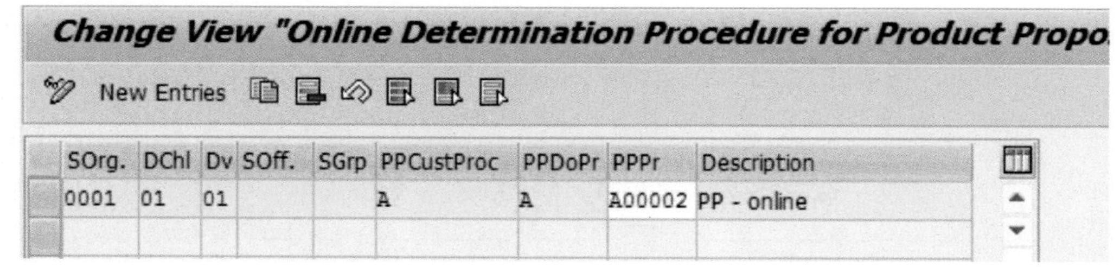
Change View "Online Determination Procedure for Product Propo

New Entries

SOrg.	DChl	Dv	SOff.	SGrp	PPCustProc	PPDoPr	PPPr	Description
0001	01	01			A	A	A00002	PP - online

In above figure online product proposal determination is based on sales area sales, sales office, sales group, product proposal customer procedure and product proposal document procedure.

Item Proposal

Item proposal is utilized when a customer uses the same set of products in sales order repeatedly. Item proposal able to copy the same quantity and able to only copy materials in new sales order.
It able to utilize for the sales order fast entry, so that is saves time. The item proposal feature validity start and end date. Its proposal able to create with reference to sales order. Item proposal able to assign to the customer master so the same item proposal will automatically propose for the sales order entry process.

T-code VA51 to create Item Proposal
T-code VA52 to change Item Proposal
T-code VA53 to Display Item Proposal
T-code VA55 Item proposal report

Create Item Proposal: Overview

Item proposals

Item Proposal
Description
Valid-from date Valid-to date

Item	Material	Target quantity	U...	Description

Item proposal Customization:

Item Proposal order type is "PV" to customize order type use t-code VOV8.

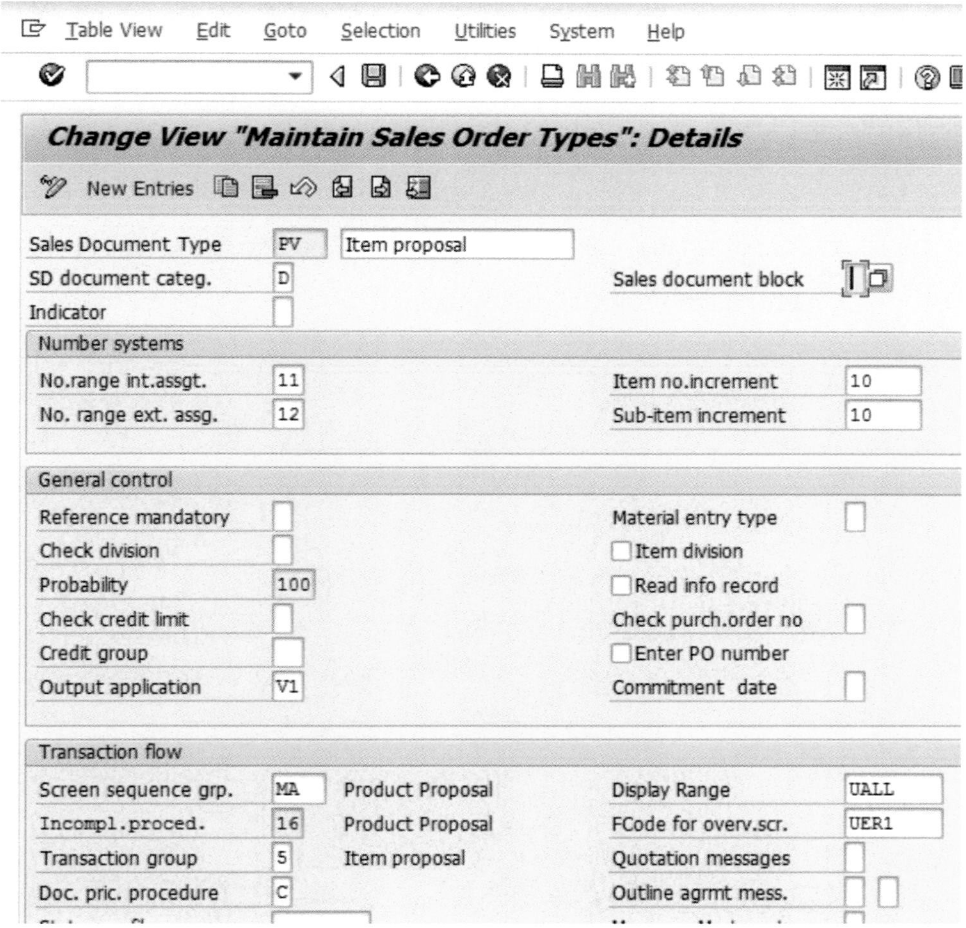

Table View Edit Goto Selection Utilities System Help

Change View "Maintain Sales Order Types": Details

New Entries

Sales Document Type	PV	Item proposal		
SD document categ.	D		Sales document block	
Indicator				

Number systems

No.range int.assgt.	11	Item no.increment	10
No. range ext. assg.	12	Sub-item increment	10

General control

Reference mandatory		Material entry type	
Check division		Item division	
Probability	100	Read info record	
Check credit limit		Check purch.order no	
Credit group		Enter PO number	
Output application	V1	Commitment date	

Transaction flow

Screen sequence grp.	MA	Product Proposal	Display Range	UALL
Incompl.proced.	16	Product Proposal	FCode for overv.scr.	UER1
Transaction group	5	Item proposal	Quotation messages	
Doc. pric. procedure	C		Outline agrmt mess.	

The following are customization fields that are utilized in same as order type customization.

- Sales and distribution document category is "D" which is for item proposal.
- The number range is set accordingly to distinguish item proposal document type.
- Document pricing procedure is standard C.

Additional order type's related to customization able to utilize for the item proposal order type.

Chapter 4 summary

- Learn about contracts and customization
- Learn about order type customization
- Contract Order type customization
- Learn about item category and schedule line determination
- Dynamic Item proposal customization
- Item proposal customization
- Plant determination
- Learn about different return process

CHAPTER 5

DELIVERY & ROUTES

- Delivery Customization
- Route Determination
- Mode of transport
- Mode of Transport
- Shipment Type
- Route Determination
- Transportation Zone
- Delivery Reports
- Shipping Point determination

Objectives:

- Learn how to configure Delivery order type
- Learn how to setup routes in SAP
- Learn Shipment configuration
- Learn shipping point determination
- Learn delivery worklist and delivery reports

Delivery Customization

Delivery is a process where warehouse or plant issues good to end customer. Delivery can be result of sales delivery or from company internal stock transfer order. Delivery processed is integrated with warehouse process of picking, packing and good issue. Sales delivery processed after scheduling and confirmation of stock. Delivery from sales order determine by order type customization. As we able to see in the screenshot, the delivery is part of logistic execution module.

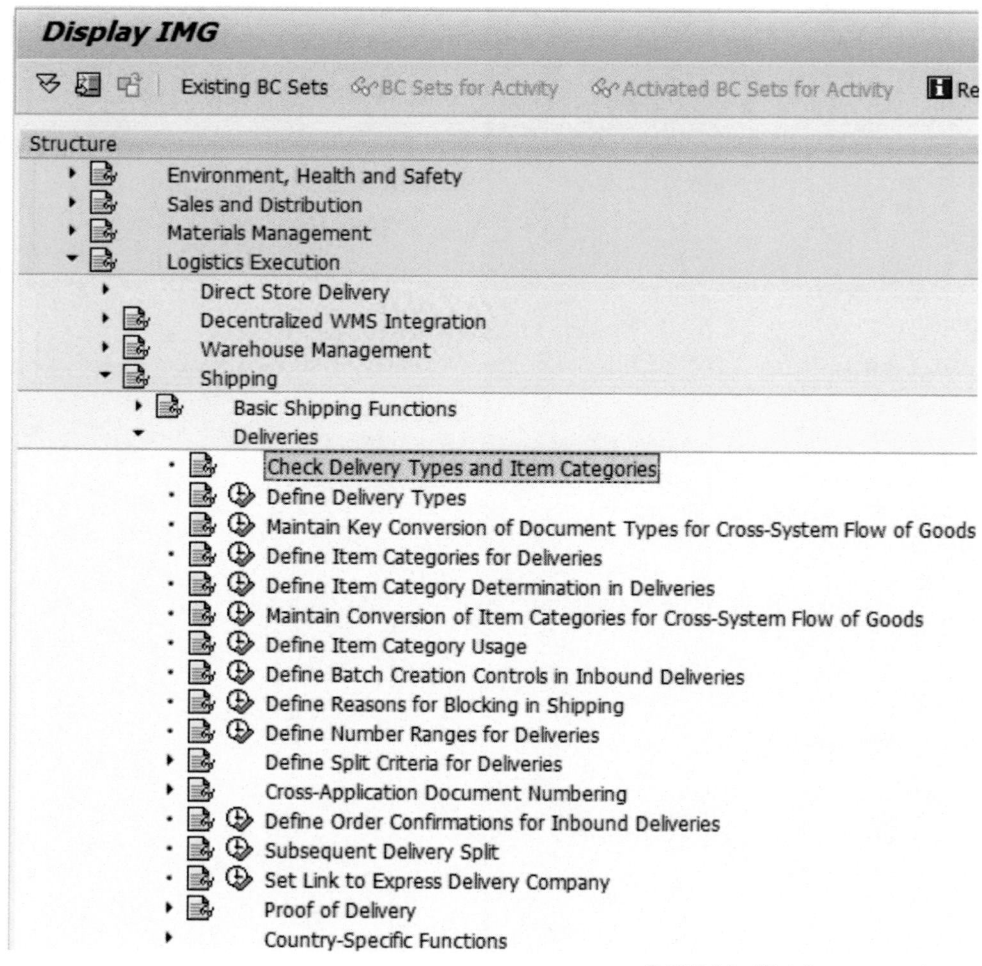

Delivery Type

Delivery type controls the delivery document behavior. Delivery type determines from sales order customization. In sales order it feature delivery type defined in it. The standard delivery type is LF.

T-code: **OVLK**
Customization Path:
IMG → Logistics Execution → Shipping → Deliveries → Define Delivery Type

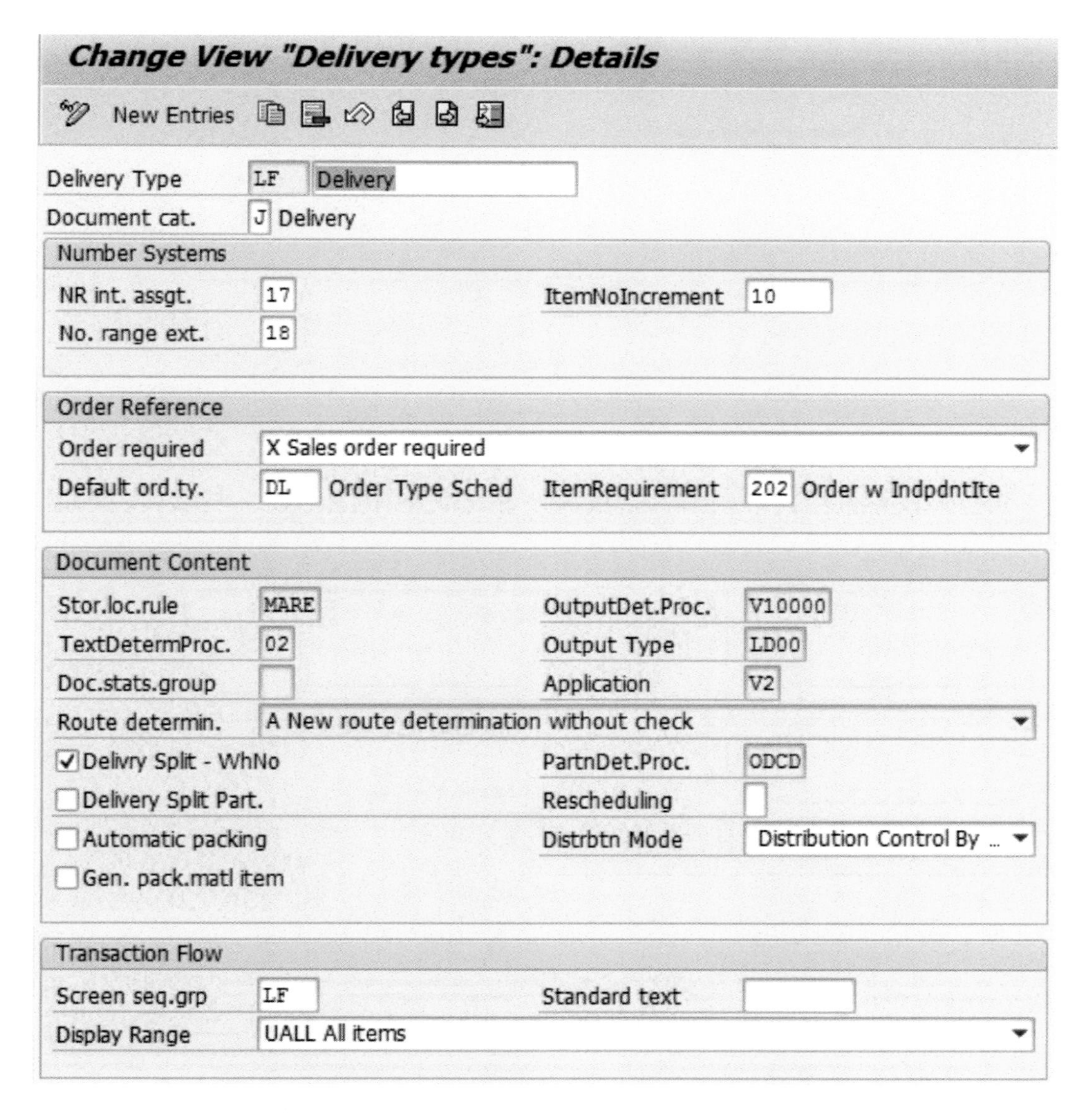

Document category:

Document category is defined as a type of delivery.

Order Reference:

This section of customization is customized if the order required reference or if the returnable packaging required to be calculated.

Route Determination

Routes are setup for delivery, starting from the sales order. The mode of transport could be Air, Rail, Ground, Road, by Sea, or others. The routes able to maintain for different type of products based on source, destination, priority, and weight group. The route time able to save in SAP to be utilized for estimate routes in the sales order process for transportation.

Mode of Transport:

Mode of transport represents the type of transport. The type of transport expected to be Air, Sea, Train or more.

Customization Path from SPRO t-code is

IMG →Sales and Distribution → Basic Functions → Routes → Define Routes → Define Modes of Transport

T-code for customization: 0VTB

Screenshot:

Mode of Transport

ShTy	Description	SType	Description
02	Train		
03	Sea		
05	Air		

"S Ty" is a representational mode of transportation system number and followed by a description of it.

S Type Field represents a dangerous good mode of good category.

Define Shipment Type:

In this customization we are defining the shipment type to be included as a mode of transportation and also a transportation group.

Customization Path from SPRO t-code is:

IMG →Sales and Distribution → Basic Functions → Routes → Define Routes → Define Shipping Type, T-code for customization: 0VTA

Screenshot:

Shipping types

PT	Description	MdTr	Description	STPG
01	Truck	01	Street	
02	Mail	06	Postal Service	
03	Train	02	Train	

Define Transportation Connection Point:

Transportation Connection point brides when product transfers from one shipment type to another shipment. The connection point expected to represent an airport or border. The connection point able to also uphold the custom office description information.

Customization Path from SPRO t-code is:

IMG →Sales and Distribution → Basic Functions → Routes → Define Routes → Define Transportation Connection Point

T-code for customization: 0VTD

Screenshot:

Transportation connection point

Points	Description	Cust.off.descr.
LOU	LOUISVILLE	
LVS	LAS VEGAS	

Define Routes and stages:

Customization Path from SPRO t-code is"

IMG →Sales and Distribution → Basic Functions → Routes → Define Routes → Define Transportation Connection Point

T-code for customization: 0VTC

Screenshot:

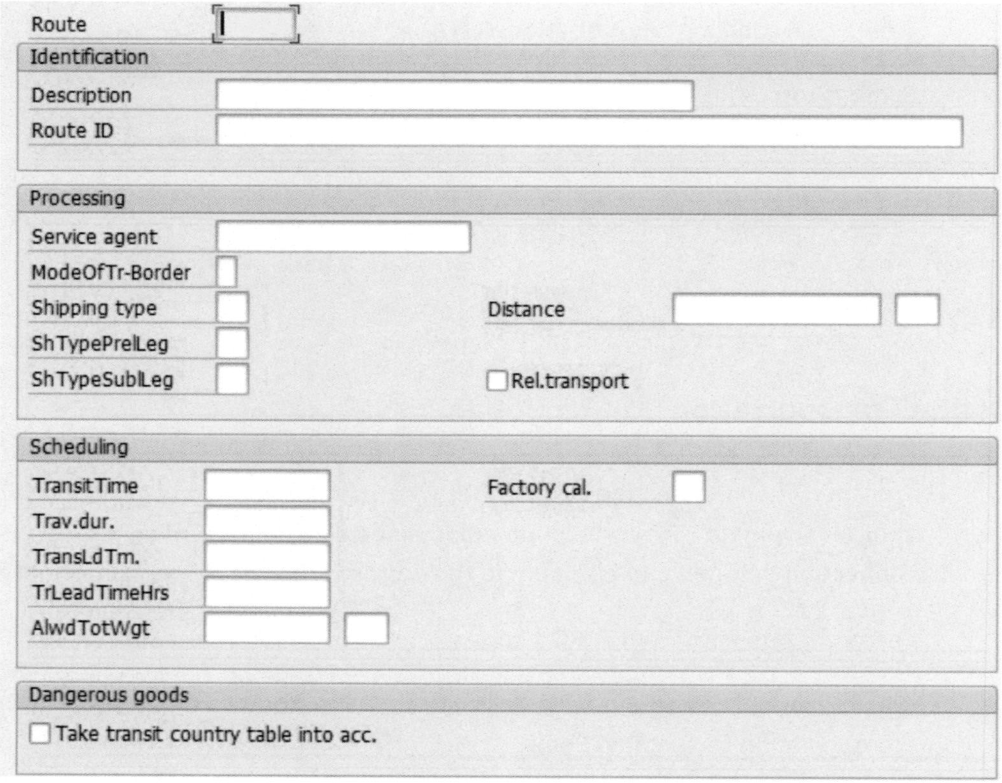

Route

Identification

Description

Route ID

Processing

Service agent

ModeOfTr-Border

Shipping type

Distance

ShTypePrelLeg

ShTypeSublLeg

Rel.transport

Scheduling

TransitTime

Factory cal.

Trav.dur.

TransLdTm.

TrLeadTimeHrs

AlwdTotWgt

Dangerous goods

Take transit country table into acc.

Route: The route field defines the name of the route that is maintained by the Z or Y field so that the route stays with system upgrade.

Description: In this field, we describe description and route.

Route ID: This is an additional field where routes able to categorize for processing and description.

Processing: The processing control is the first field in-service **agent**. The service agent field is utilized to define the freight that is forwarding to where the facilitator's shipment is. The service agent is defined as a vendor in the system for shipment related services. The second field is utilized for processing controls is mode of transportation in which it is already being discussed in customization. The values are maintained in the mode of transport that able to utilize here. The third field is utilized for the processing of shipment **type**, this field's value feature already been defined earlier in routing configuration and the values are utilized for the route. The fourth and fifth field is the primary and secondary shipment type legs of the route. The distance filed able to maintain its distance of the route and the unit of measure able to also be maintained.

The last field in the processing section is the "Rel. Transport". This control allows for delivery if it is relevant to the shipment. If this is not selected, then the route will determine the delivery, but these deliveries cannot be utilized in shipment.

Scheduling: Scheduling is the control duration and times part of the route. The first field is utilized in scheduling controls, which is called the "Transit Time". The transit time is in days and is considered the shipping point factory calendar for the calculation of transit time. The second field is utilized in scheduling the control in the travel duration, in this field. To maintain the actual time in hours and in the field value, it must not be utilized in the delivery scheduling calculation. The third field is transportation lead-time based on the leading group and picking time. The value able to maintain with the consideration of the shipping point time, and the transportation time in hours is the fourth field. The fifth option allows for the total weight of shipment. The last value maintained is a factory calendar for the route.

Stages: Staging is utilized for the shipments, which are additional steps like a border crossing. It is also additional steps in the configuration of the initial route definition. If it's in between shipments, an additional stage is required so that it able to configure in the router.

Define Stages for All Routes:

Customization Path from SPRO t-code is the following

IMG →Sales and Distribution → Basic Functions → Routes → Define Routes → Define Stages for All Routes

T-code for customization: 0VTE

Based on this configuration control it puts together many stages into routes based on the selection criteria.

Route Determination

Route determination feature four elements in the sales order

- Country of departure / departure zone
- Country of Destination / Receiving Zone
- Shipping Conditions
- Transportation Group

Route determination is same delivery but is also considered weight group for determining routes.

Customization Path from SPRO t-code is the following:
IMG →Sales and Distribution → Basic Functions → Routes → Route Determination

T-code for customization: OVRF

Screenshot:

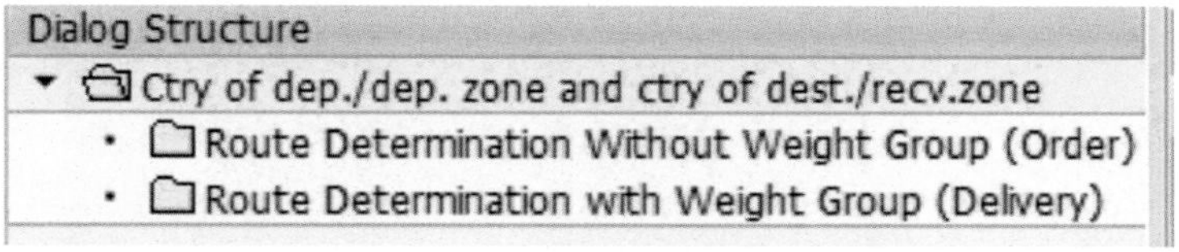

Dialog Structure
- Ctry of dep./dep. zone and ctry of dest./recv.zone
  - Route Determination Without Weight Group (Order)
  - Route Determination with Weight Group (Delivery)

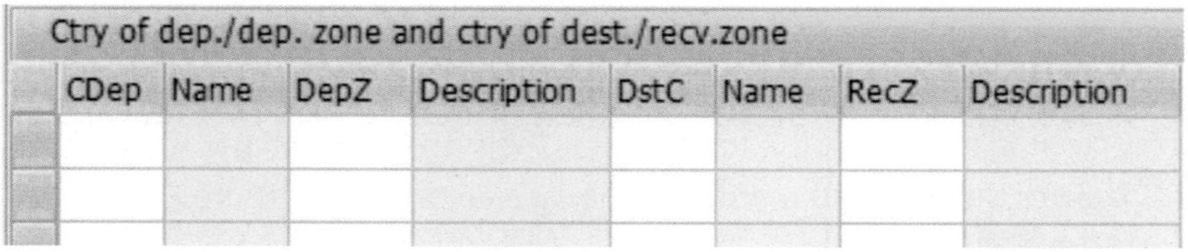

Ctry of dep./dep. zone and ctry of dest./recv.zone

CDep	Name	DepZ	Description	DstC	Name	RecZ	Description

Field	Description
CDep	In the above screenshot the first field is "CDep", this represents the country of departure.
DepZ	"DepZ" field represents departure zone.
DstC	Destination Country
RecZ	This field is utilized for Receiving Zone

Tip to remember:

The Departure Zone of Delivering Plant + Shipping Condition of the Sold to + Transportation Group + Transportation Zone of the Ship to

Define Transportation Zone

Transportation zone is defined and assigned to the customer master. This field value determines the route with a combination of other fields.

Customization Path from SPRO t-code is the following

IMG →Sales and Distribution → Basic Functions → Routes → Route Determination → Define Transportation Zone

T-code for customization: OVR1

Screenshot:

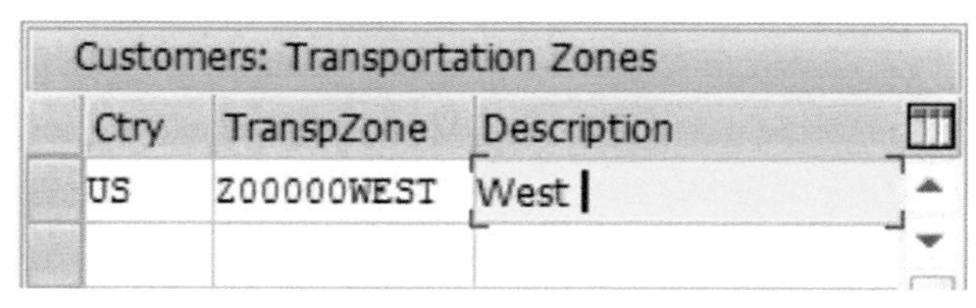
Customers: Transportation Zones

Ctry	TranspZone	Description
US	Z00000WEST	West

Define Transportation Zone for shipping point & country.

Customization Path from SPRO t-code is the following:

IMG →Sales and Distribution → Basic Functions → Routes → Route Determination → Define Transportation Zone

T-code for customization: OVR1

Screenshot:

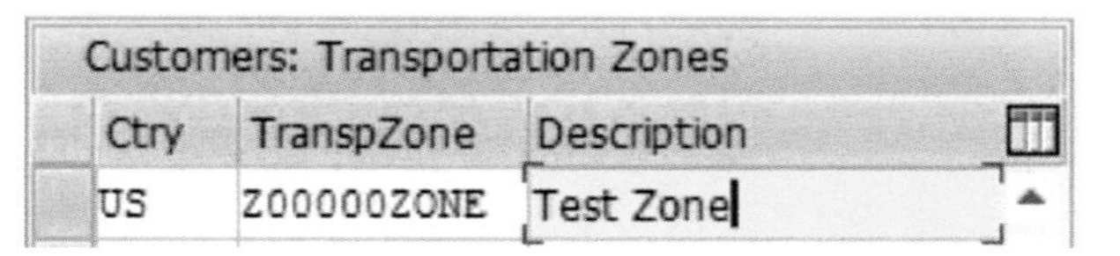
Customers: Transportation Zones

Ctry	TranspZone	Description
US	Z00000ZONE	Test Zone

In the above screenshot we select the country and enter the Transportation Zone and the description of it.

Route determination figure:

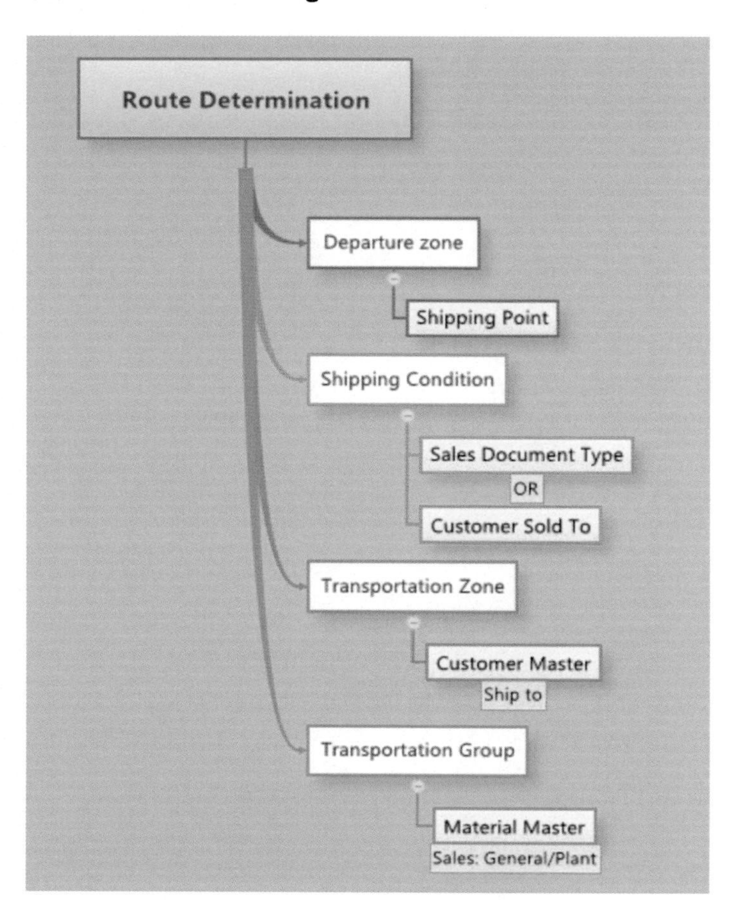

SAP SD Sales order Requirement Monitoring

The material master feature MRP views that indicate the functions of ATP and the availability to check. MRP controls the material that is in stock to order or make to an order. If MRP is maintained to create requirements then it able to tigers forecasting, production order, or create requirements to fill the order quantity. MRP able to activate by a scheduled line category. The production order is related to the production-planning module. Business production planning able to pass the requirement to the respective module with system MRP planning. Production orders are subjected to MRP master data maintenance.

Delivery Worklist and Reports on Delivery

Delivery is part of the general logistic execution module and is shared across by logistics modules. The delivery feature a different status based on the processing of delivery and what stage the delivery is at. Partial delivery means that the sales order of each line item or group of line items able to ship separately. It able to a business requirement or customer requirement. In both cases, the sales order could have different ship to with separate lines to have different deliveries. Partial delivery able to select by the sales order header option, which will complete the ship or partial ship. Delivery split happens due to different shipping point. Delivery due work list is utilized as report and monitor deliveries. Delivery monitor is one of the very useful tools utilized to check the status of deliveries.

Shipping Delivery Monitoring T-code: VL06O

This is a work list and report for user to review different stages of deliveries, picking, packing, good issue etc.

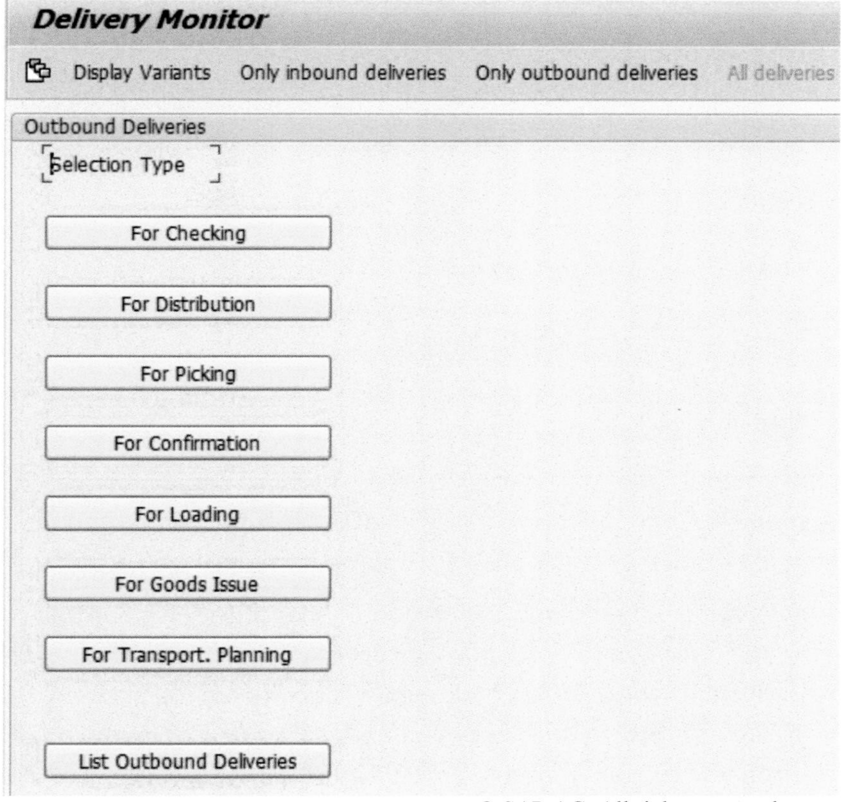

Delivery T-codes:

Description	Transaction Code
Create Outbound delivery	VL01N
Change Outbound delivery	VL02N
Display Outbound Delivery	VL03N
View Changes in delivery document	VL22
Delivery monitors	VL06O
Create In bound delivery	VL31N

Tip: The old t-codes do not contain "N" front of them, example: VL01

Delivery Related Tables

Description	Table
Delivery Header table	LIKP
Delivery Item Level table	LIPS
Delivery Note header	VBLK

Shipping Point Determination:

The shipping point determines where the product will ship from (Plant). The shipping point determines the sales order line level. The shipping point determination if an automatic process is based on three elements: Plant, Loading Group, and Shipping Conditions. The plant able to determine in sales order based on customer master or material master. The shipping condition comes on sales order line from the customer master. Loading group element comes into a sales order line level from the Material Master.

T-code: OVL2
IMG→ logistic Execution → Shipping →Basic Shipping Functions → Assign Shipping Points

Configuration, customization:

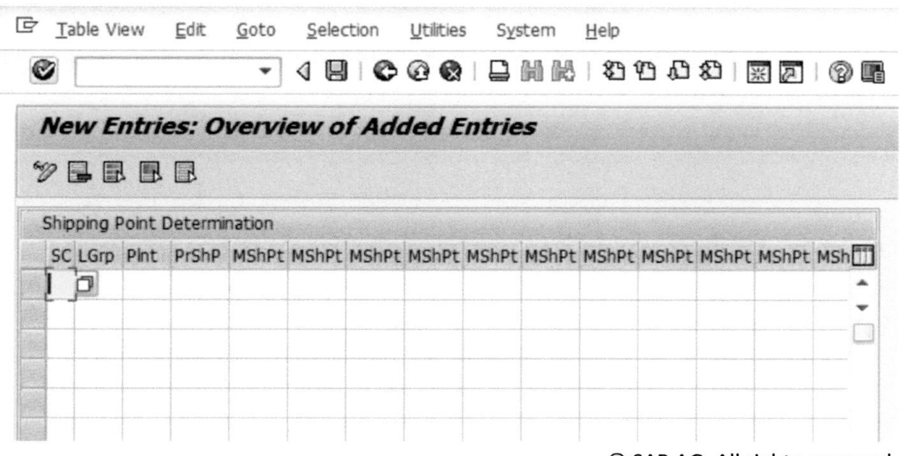

Shipping point is determine based on following:
Shipping Condition + Loading Group + Plant = Shipping point

Shipping Condition: is a copy from customer master into the sales orders.
Loading group: determines from Material Master.
The plant able to determine from multiple locations, but mostly from material master.
Also the shipping point needed to be customized in the plant to process the transaction.

Shipping point determination *mind map*

Shipping point determination is based on plant determination and that able to determine based on Customer, material, CMIR or ATP from APO.

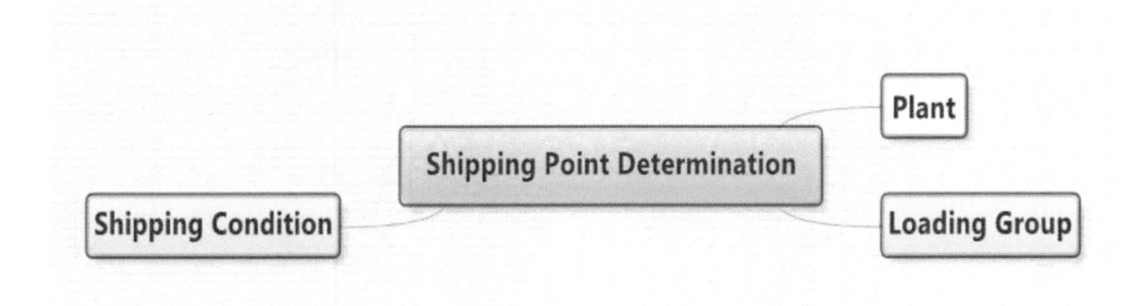

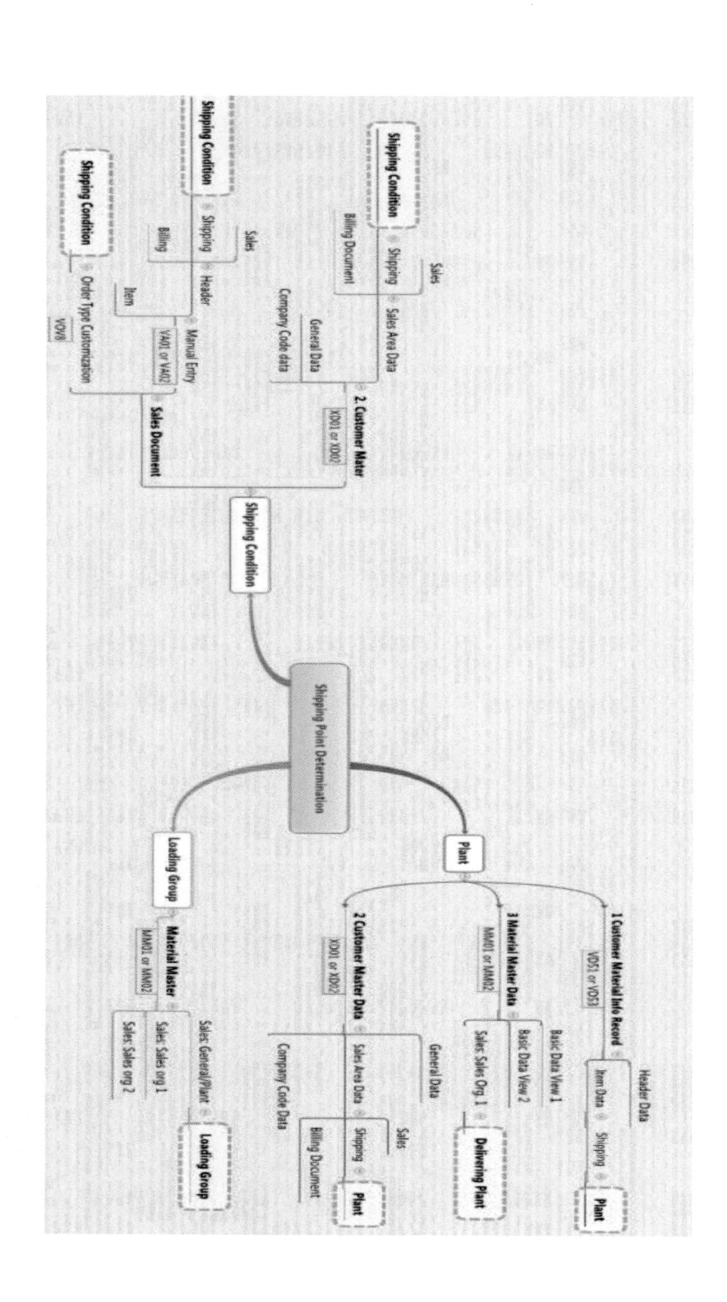
Shipping Point Determination
Shipping Condition
2. Customer Mater
XD01 or XD02
Sales Area Data
Sales
Shipping
Shipping Condition
Billing Document
General Data
Company Code data
Sales Document
Manual Entry
VA01 or VA02
Header
Sales
Shipping
Shipping Condition
Billing
Item
Order Type Customization
VOV8
Shipping Condition
Plant
1 Customer Material Info Record
VD51 or VD53
Header Data
Item Data
Shipping
Plant
3 Material Master Data
MM01 or MM02
Basic Data View 1
Basic Data View 2
Sales: Sales Org. 1
Delivering Plant
2 Customer Master Data
XD01 or XD02
General Data
Sales Area Data
Sales
Shipping
Plant
Billing Document
Company Code Data
Loading Group
Material Master
MM01 or MM02
Sales: General/Plant
Loading Group
Sales: Sales org 1
Sales: Sales org 2

Chapter 5 summary

- Learn about contracts and customization
- Learn about order type customization
- Contract order type customization
- Learn about item category and schedule line determination
- Dynamic Item proposal customization
- Item proposal customization
- Plant determination
- Shipping point determination
- Learn about different return process
- Rebate agreement customization
- Delivery related report
- Shipping point determination

Notes

CHAPTER 6

PRICING

Chapter 6 overview

- Pricing Fundamentals introduction
- Pricing Condition Technique
- Pricing Customization
- Customization of Pricing Table
- Customization of Access Sequence
- Customization of Condition Type (In detail)
- Customization of Pricing Procedure Deamination
- Introduction to Master Data Condition record
- Introduction to pricing routine
- Condition Record
- Listing / Exclusion Customization

Objectives:

- Learn SAP SD Sales Pricing Configuration
- Learn how to configure Pricing Table
- Learn how to configure access sequence
- Learn how to configure Condition Type
- Learn how to configure Pricing Procedure
- Learn how to configure pricing procedure determination
- Learn how to setup Pricing Condition Record

What is in this chapter for me?

This chapter include pricing configuration. Learn pricing condition record creation. Learn how pricing effect from sales order to cash.

SAP SD Pricing Fundamentals:

Introduction:

The price is utilized in sales, delivery, rebate, tax and billing processes. The price able to change often due to the market cost of goods sold. Pricing is a very critical part of any business. SAP pricing functions are based on condition technique customization. We need to start to understand the fundaments of pricing and background in order to understand how it works before us able to start the customization. The pricing is a critical part of the sales order. Pricing effect the account determination and revenue recognition. Pricing customization is also utilized in billing, inquiry, quotation, and delivery. Pricing configuration able to also be set-up with third party applications interfaces.

Sales and Distribution's pricing is capable enough to handle simple and much more complex scenarios. The standard pricing functionality is very flexible to handle many scenarios. There are third party tools and applications available to integrate with the pricing area to accommodate the complexity of pricing. In this chapter, we will focus on standard pricing configuration.

Condition Technique

Condition technique is utilized in Sales and Distribution for various customizations. The condition technique provides conditional options to be given to the transactions for results based on the fields. In condition technique we create a table, then create an access sequence and assign the table to access sequence. Then we assign an access sequence to condition, type, then put the condition types in procedure and after that we create a condition record. The pricing configuration is based on the configuration technique. There are additional configuration requirement for advance pricing configuration and for account determination, which is covered, in billing chapter.

The high-level objects of configuration are the following:

1. Table
2. Access sequence
3. Condition type
4. Procedures
5. Condition Record (condition type)

Condition Technique:

Table:

Any business condition able to convert into the field value. Condition technique is based on field or group of fields. The first step in the condition technique processing is to create a table. A table expected to have one field in it or multiple fields. It is recommended to use existing tables if it is available if not then create a new table.

Access Sequence:

Access sequence is the place where multiple tables able to store in it for access. To improve the system performance, use minimum tables in access sequence and select exclusive option.

Condition Type:

The pricing Condition type is utilized to setup pricing. The pricing Condition type is utilized for following type categories: Price, discount, freight, surcharge, and tax. The condition type feature condition records with validity period. Many selection options are available to choose from, such as how the condition type able to utilize.

Pricing Procedure:

Pricing procedure controls the condition types in calculations and totals. It feature 16 steps of configuration and able to control with combination of complexity.

Pricing Customization

Pricing configuration elements are the followed:

- Pricing Table
- Access Sequence
- Condition Type
- Pricing Procedure
- Pricing Procedure determination

Pricing Table:

The SAP standard system already feature around 600 entries of table that able to utilize. A table consists of a single or multiple group of fields. For customization tables to be created, it must be after 600 because first the 600 are reserved for standard table entries.

T-code for customization V/03

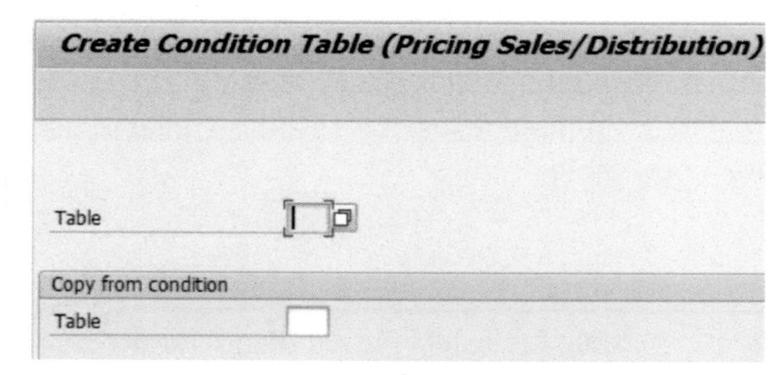

The table number is required to create a new table, and the new table able to copy from the existing tale to begin with the changes.

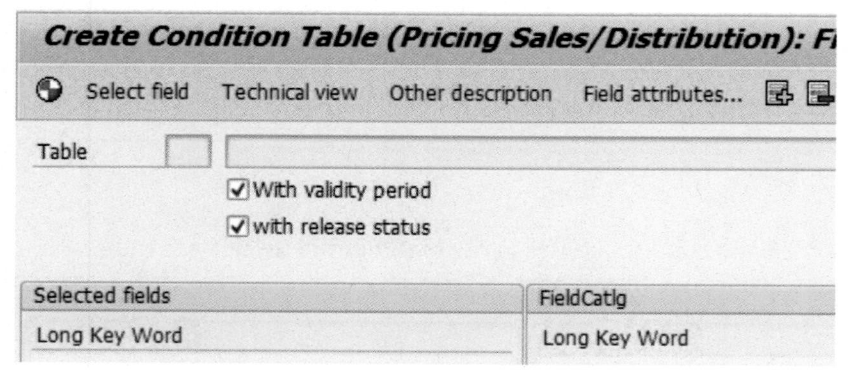

In the above screenshot, red and white buttons able to utilize to generate tables.

Access Sequence:

Access sequence is considered a search criterion and the access sequence contain tables. Access sequence feature a condition in tables so the field able to search with the table combination of fields. The access table entry able to set for exclusivity for system performance to stop searching based on found combined condition. Requirements are also utilized in the access sequence for free goods, payer, currency, domestics, exports, and many other business processes.

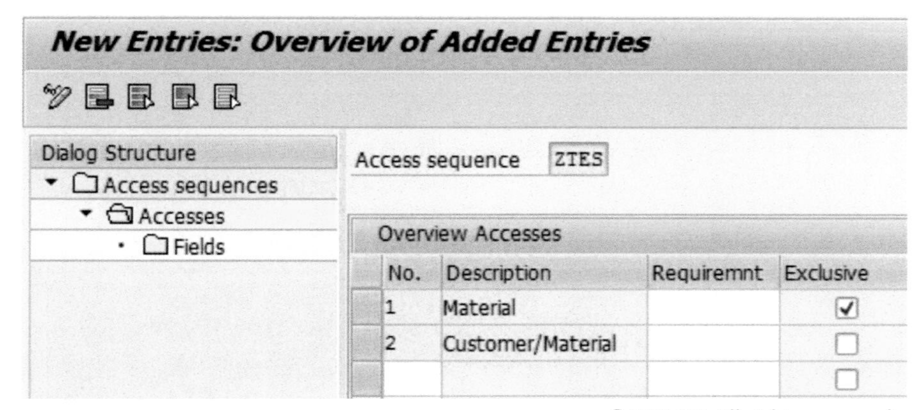

Tip: To navigate, select access sequence and click on the folder to go into access, and also table entries require additional enters to bypass soft error for table into a table.

Condition Type:

Condition type represents price, discount, taxes, freight, and surcharge on sales order. Each line able to feature multiple pricing conditions assigned to it. Pricing conditions able to manage further divided into different types of condition types: group condition, header pricing condition, and item pricing condition. The following are some of the pricing condition types:

- Price
- Discount
- Taxes
- Surcharge
- Freight

Business Use:

Each line able to have the multiple price condition. For example, using one pricing condition expected to be for MSRP and the other expected to be utilized for current price based on a percentage of MSRP. There are also a couple of discount condition types; one is discount and second one is off the first discount condition. Condition types able to fix price or percentage base. Pricing condition able to utilize for the header level or item level. The difference between the header and the item condition is that the header condition applied to the whole document and the item condition applied to each line level. The header condition divides the header amount into all the lines.

Condition Supplement:

Condition supplement is utilized for group conditions to be determined together. Based on one condition type, relevant supplement conditions will be determined together. The condition types should have the same pricing procedures in condition type setup. The condition supplement is created with Transaction Code VK11

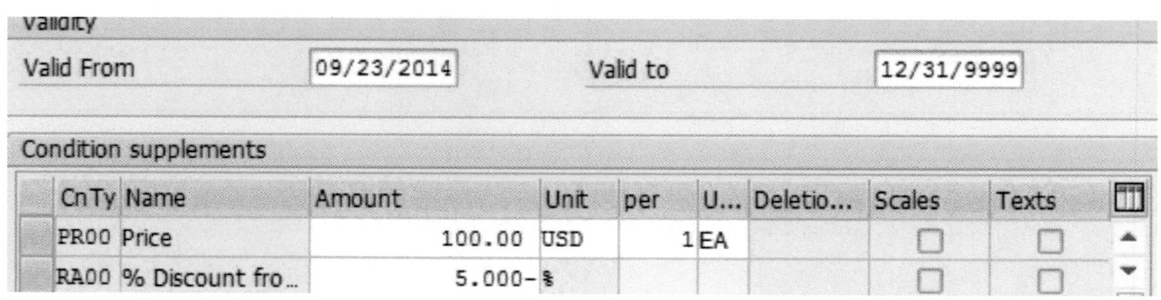

In the above screenshot, the condition record able to create for multiple condition type at once. From the configuration standpoint, the key element for condition supplement is to have condition pull together the pricing procedure assign to the condition type. The following is the screenshot of the Master data section of condition type customization; the default value is "PR0000".

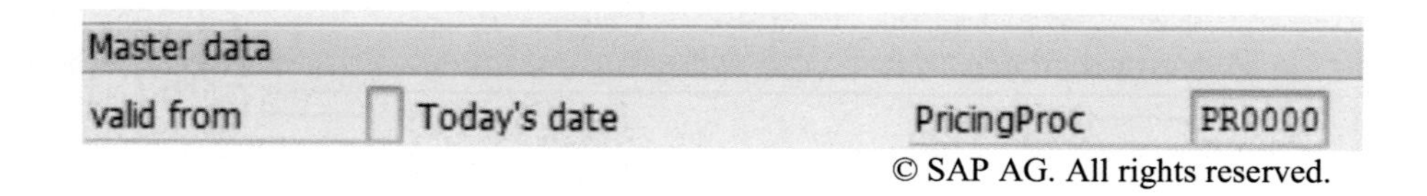

Customization:

Customization able to utilize for
IMG → Sales and Distribution → Basic Functions → Pricing → Pricing Control → Define Condition Type
The standard price condition is PR00

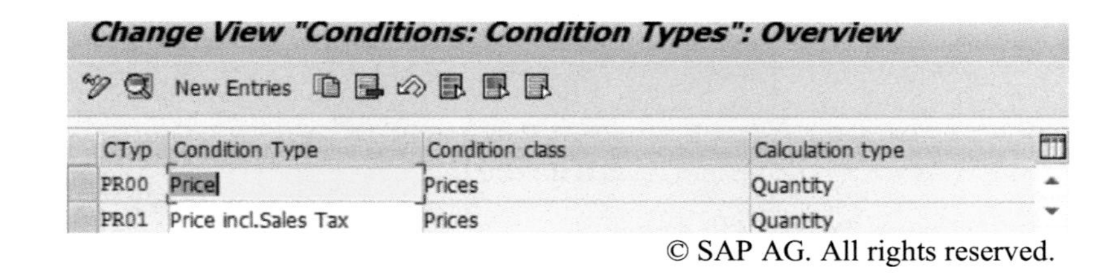

Change View "Conditions: Condition Types": Overview

New Entries

CTyp	Condition Type	Condition class	Calculation type
PR00	Price	Prices	Quantity
PR01	Price incl.Sales Tax	Prices	Quantity

Condition Type: PR00

Condit. type PR00 Price Access seq. PR00 Price

Records for access

Control data 1

Cond. class	B Prices	Plus/minus	positive a
Calculat.type	C Quantity		
Cond.category			
Rounding rule	Commercial		
StrucCond.			

Access sequence:

Access sequence, as we studied earlier, is utilized in pricing condition type. The access sequence determines the table.

Condition Class:

Conditional class classifies condition type, for example surcharge, discount, tax, etc.

Plus/minus: This identifies if the condition values are positive, negative or both.

Condition Category:

Condition category clarifies the condition type category. For example, tax condition category able to be selected.

Rounding rule:

The rounding rule rounds the value to closest decimal point (third place). It able to also round down or keep it commercial. If value selected rounds down the system, it will not consider any value from decimal point and keep it as is. When rounding up any value higher than five from third decimal point it will increase one value to the two-decimal point value.

Structure Condition:

This configuration is utilized for variant condition if condition type needs to be duplicated or accumulated.

Additional Condition Type Controls:

Group Condition:

Group condition is utilized when materials belong to the same group or price is set on the item in the group. It is for the item level of group material utilized for pricing.

Example: If material A and B belong to the same group and the price is set to the scale of ten for the group of materials together, then both material quantities able to mixed and matched and the sale price will be effective for the group of the materials.

Group Condition Routine:

Routine is utilized for group condition or it able to select for a non-group condition type.

Round Different Comparison:

This customization activates rounding calculations. It will start with header level, then condition level, and then add the condition with high value condition type.

Additional Condition Type Controls:

Changes which can be made
Manual entries C Manual entry has priority
☐ Header condit. ☑ Amount/percent ☐ Qty relation
☑ Item condition ☐ Delete ☐ Value ☐ Calculat.type

Manual Entries: This customization allows manual entry for the condition type. This customization allows several options for manual entries. "C" manual entry feature priority if this option, customized manual entry is allowed for the condition type and based on this if manual price is entered then it will overwrite the condition record. If option is left empty, then it features no limitation means it able to overwrite without limitation. If "B" is selected, then condition record feature priority over the manual. "D" option doesn't allow any manual entry for the condition type. The value is distributed based on net value.

Header Condition: If this customization is selected it will make it header condition. Header condition manually entered at header level. Header condition distributes its values into all items.

Amount / Percentage: This customization defines amount or percentage to be changed during processing. If this is not selected the amount and percentage cannot be changed.

Quantitative relation: It customization allows units of measure to be change in pricing.

Item Condition: Item condition identifies if condition type is at item level. It will only be unique to the item it has been entered for.

Delete: This customization will allow the item's condition to be deleted from the document.

Value: This customization allows value able to change during processing.

Calculation Type: This customization controls the calculation type, it changes during the processing.

Additional Pricing Controls with Limits:

Master data

valid from		Today's date	PricingProc	PR0000
Valid to		31.12.9999	delete fr. DB	Do not delete (set the delet...
RefConType			Condition index	
RefApplicatio			Condit.update	

Scales

Scale basis	C	Quantity scale	Scale formula	
Check value	A	Descending	Unit of meas.	
Scale type		can be maintained in con		

Valid from:

Valid from date is for the condition type to be valid from.

Valid to:

Valid to date is the validity of condition type.

Scale Basis:

The scale customization able to set for the condition type if it is required to be based on quantity or in weight or in volume.

Check Value:

This customization is utilized for the descending or ascending price scales.

Condition Limit:

Condition limit customization limits the value. The value does not surpass percentage or quantity or weight. Example for discount condition type able to limit to the limit so over or under discount is not given when user is using manual ever written on condition type.

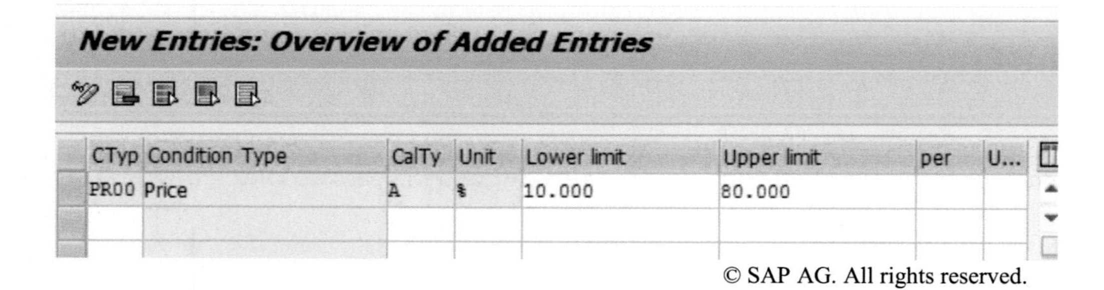

In the above screenshot the pricing limit able to set with calculation type unit percentage or quantity or weight, lower and upper limit, as per unit and unit of measure.

Pricing Procedure:

Pricing procedure customization based on the condition type calculation and functions. Pricing procedure feature 16 steps of control for each line. It is always recommended to copy existing SAP pricing procedure with “Z” or “Y” so it will stay with system upgrade.

Procedure RVAAUS Standard - USA /w/out Jur.Code

Control data

Reference Step Overview

Step	Counter	CTyp	Description	Fro	To	Manual	Required	Statistics	P	SuTot	Reqt	CalType	BasType	AccKey	Accruals
11	0	PR00	Price			☐	☑	☐			2			ERL	
13	0	PB00	Price (Gross)			☑	☐	☐			2			ERL	
100	0		Gross Value			☐	☐	☐	X	1					
101	0	KA00	Sales deal			☐	☐	☐	X		2			ERS	

16 Pricing Procedure field for customization:

1. **Step**
2. **Counter**
3. **Condition Type**
4. **Description**
5. **From**
6. **To**
7. **Manual**
8. **Required**
9. **Statistics**
10. **Print**
11. **Subtotal**
12. **Requirement**
13. **Calculation Type**
14. **Base Type**
15. **Account Key**
16. **Accruals**

Step:

Step is the sequence system start processing, pricing procedure. The first step starts with 10 and the second one 20 the reason for the steps to be numbered this way user able to add nine steps before them and nine steps after 10 if customization is required in between condition type steps. It is always recommended to use steps in gaps so if required additional steps able to add.

Counter:

The center is one of additional places where steps able to repeat and with different counter and the same step with combination able to set each new step.

Condition Type:

Condition type where we use condition type. This field is not required field and it able to left empty for other use in pricing procedure.

Description:

Description comes from condition type description. When condition type is not utilized, then the description field becomes free form to use and it is utilized for totals in group of condition types to be calculated and display in document processing at the header and item condition tabs.

"From" and "To":

"From" and "To" field are utilized to calculate in a selected range of steps to be calculated in that step.

Manual:

Manual option on pricing condition type to allow manual entry for the condition type. Similarly, for the condition type, this is another control to allow manual over write for the condition type. If this is option is marked, then the condition type allowed for manually overwrites.

Required:

Based on this option condition type become required for the document processing and if condition record is not found system will issue an error for the required condition type.

Statistics:

Statistics selection marks, a condition type for statistical use for the pricing in document processing. Some condition types are utilized only for statistical mean not effecting pricing of the document.

Print:

Print customization controls if a line needs to be printed in outputs.

Subtotal:

The subtotal field is utilized to subtotal condition types.

Requirement:

The requirement is a calculation program that provided by SAP form many formulas. New requirement able to set added as per requirements. In-depth; detailed summary of the subject is out of the scope of the book.

Calculation Type:

It is similar to the requirement field. Calculation type also utilized in condition type customization, but it is not same as the pricing procedure calculation type. Calculation type also feature many systems predefine selections, but a new one able to set introduced into a system with enhancements. Examples of Calculation type are: net value, cash minus tax, and initial price. The calculation type from condition type customization is similar to the customization but the pricing procedure feature many additional calculation type options available.

Base Type:

The base type is similar to the calculation type and requirement field, it feature many options to select from and additional option able to enhance into the system if needed.

Account Key:

Account key is utilized for account determination for the condition type. This customization is utilized for financial revenue recognition as per condition type.

Accruals:

Accrual field customization utilized for tracking accruals against the condition type. In this field account key for the accruals able to customize.

Pricing Procedure Determination:

Path for customization is
IMG → Sales and Distribution → Basic Functions → Pricing Controls → Define and Assign Pricing Procedure

After the above selection it will give a selection for the each of the component to select from for customization.

Short Definition:

Pricing procedure determines the formula = sales area + Customer Pricing Procedure indicator + Document Type Pricing Procedure.

Figure how pricing procedure gets to determine:

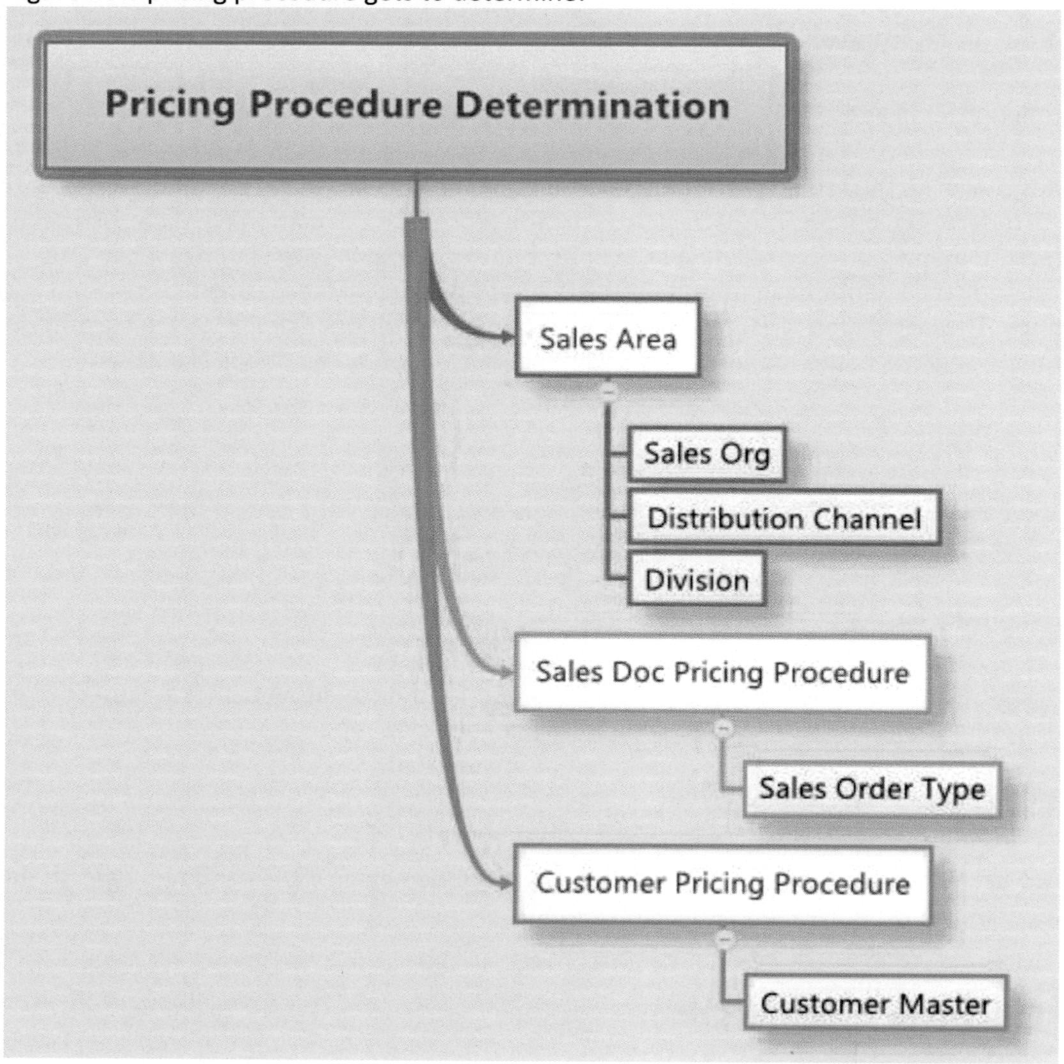

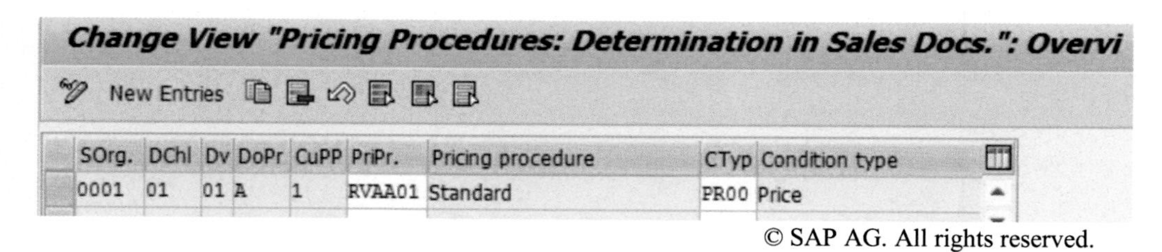
Change View "Pricing Procedures: Determination in Sales Docs.": Overvi

New Entries

SOrg.	DChl	Dv	DoPr	CuPP	PriPr.	Pricing procedure	CTyp	Condition type
0001	01	01	A	1	RVAA01	Standard	PR00	Price

The determination components:

Sales area is = Sales organization + Distribution channel + Division + Division

Document Procedure Indicator:

IMG → Sales and Distribution → Basic Functions → Pricing Controls → Define and Assign Pricing Procedure → Define document pricing Procedure

Procedure document is a single alphanumeric character is assigned to the document type.

Step1: Create the document procedure or use standard pre-define ("A" is standard)

Step2: Use T-code VOV8 for order type customization and add the document procedure to the document type.

Customers Procedure Indicator:

IMG → Sales and Distribution → Basic Functions → Pricing Controls → Define and Assign Pricing Procedure → Define customer pricing Procedure

The customer pricing procedure is a single alphanumeric character assigned to the customer master.

Step 1: Create the Customer pricing procedure or use standard pre-define ("1" is standard).

Step 2: Use T-code XD02 and in sales are data and in sales Tab add pricing procedure indicator in it.

Pricing with System Performance consideration:

Pricing affects system performance when many tables are utilized in access sequence and system keep searching. The access sequence able to stop searching with **exclusion** option and check box selection.

Condition Type limit able to affect the system performance as well too. It able to avoid if the process is monitored and only selected condition types are utilized for this function. Access sequence optimization also one of the functions is provided by system to improve the search result and system performance.

Condition Record:

Condition record is based on the field utilized in condition table and based on it, we create master data of condition record with t-code of VK11 or VK31. The condition record could have a validity period. Condition record considered master data.

T-code for condition record **VK11**
T-code to change condition record **VK12**
T-code to display condition record **VK13**

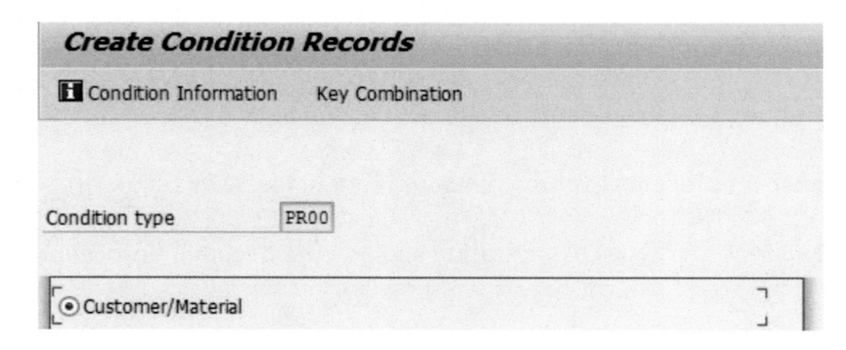

Condition Record:

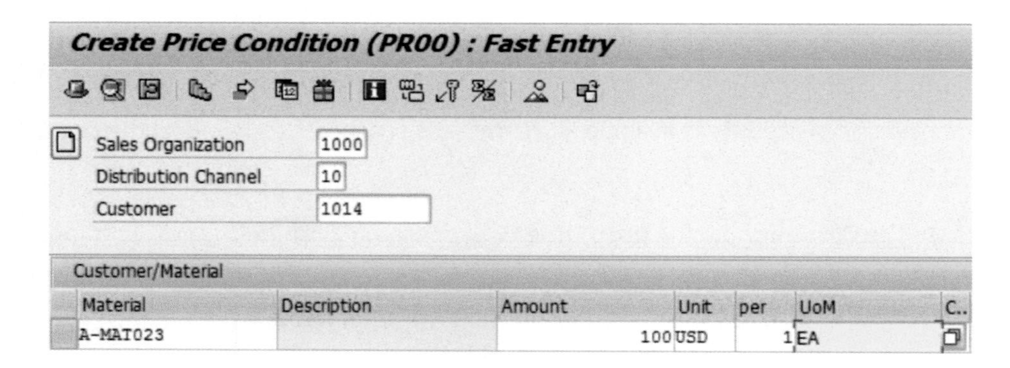

In the above screenshot condition record is created.

Condition record is pricing record saved using condition type. Base on the pricing setup and configuration, the condition record, master data able to create. Condition record feature many controls for the condition type. Condition record able to create with T-code VK11.

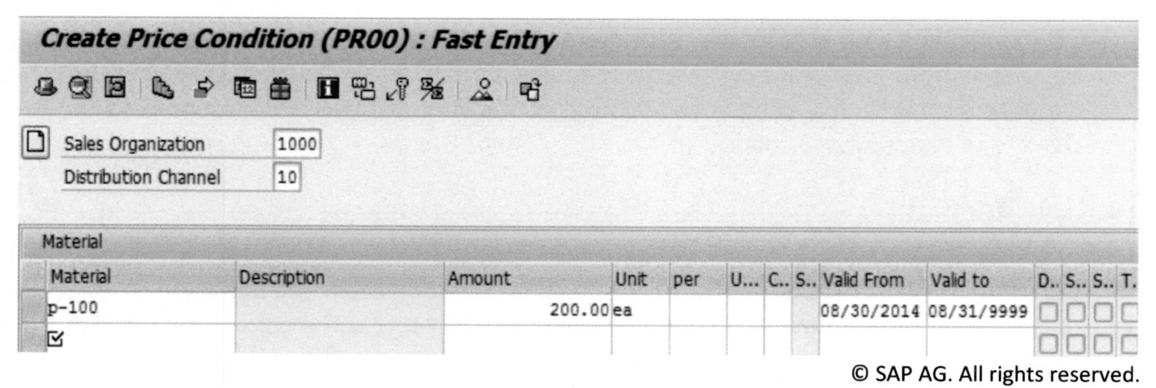

Condition record based on sales org and distribution channel and based on access sequence the condition will be based on it. It features price for unit and valid from and valid to date. If condition record is deleted the "D" check box will be selected. The first "S" represent condition supplement. The second "S" represent scale Pricing. The forth check box "T" represent Text. These options will come from if the additional option is allowed in customization and added in condition record creation.

Tables for Condition record are following:

KONV for Document
KONP for Item Condition

Field Catalog

When new field needed to be added into the field catalog, then it needed to be added into the structure of the following table. After table entry into the field catalog and then the new field is available for table creation in the pricing table.

Advance level tables for customization structures:

1. KOMG
2. KOMK
3. KOMP

SAP Pricing Routines:

What is SAP pricing Routine?

Introduction:
Routines are small enchantment programs. Routines are written for pricing procedures, condition type and many more objects in customization. Pricing Procedure contains routine customization. Pricing procedure feature SAP standard formula and calculation type. In sixteen steps in pricing procedure, few fields feature formulas and calculation type able to categories as routines. New routines able to write and utilized for the pricing and other customizations.

Routines:

Enhanced routines are written in ABAP Advance business application programing language. Pricing routine able to view and written by using T-code VOFM. The routine could be related to calculation type, requirement and base type field of pricing procedure.

Use of Routine

Pricing routines able to utilize in the calculation type field in the pricing procedure set or subtotal or requirement type and condition formula for basis. We able to use existing available routines, but if the requirements cannot meet with standard routines, then we create the new enhancement of routine.

Pricing in Order to cash:

Sales and Presales:

Pricing able to customize and utilized in presales process. Some business utilized inquiry document pricing copy to quotations pricing and that copy over to the sales order. So, pricing setup able to customize before sales order and the configuration is similar to sales order customization. Price able to change from inquiry to quotation and there would be price change. The sales pricing customization is flexible.

Delivery:

Delivery feature freight and handing related pricing condition setup and this pricing condition copy over to invoice. Pricing in delivery is optional.

Invoice:

Pricing in invoice is copied over from sales order, but Pricing able to recalculate in invoice.

Pricing is very flexible it able to set customized in Most of order to cash cycle process. Pricing copy over from document to document and each document able to update the pricing based on business requirement.

Summary for Chapter 6

In this chapter we covered pricing, customization with standard setup with detail to the field level definitions.

- Pricing table customization
- Access Sequence customization
- Condition Type customization
- Pricing Procedure Customization
- Condition record
- Pricing determination

Notes

CHAPTER 7

BILLING & CREDIT MANAGEMENT

Chapter 7 Topics

- Introduction to Billing
- Customization in Billing Document
- Copy control
- Billing Reports
- Resource Related Billing
- Credit and Debits
- Charge back
- Pricing in Billing
- Billing Plan
- Credit Management
- Revenue recognition

Objectives:

- Learn Billing Order type customization
- Lean how to customize copy control for billing
- Learn how to customize billing plan
- Learn how to customize periodic billing
- Learn How to Customize credit management
- Learn how to customize revenue determination
- Learn end user transection to unblock credit from worklist
- Learn how to customize Accrued and Deferred
- Learn how to customize revenue recognition

Introduction to Billing:

Billing is one of the last steps in order to cash cycle, followed by order or delivery. Billing able to set based on orders when we look into service industry billing is based on order or contract. From a customization standpoint, billing expected to be based on delivery. Billing is an integration point between FICO and SD Sales and Distribution.

Billing Customization:

Billing type customized from the billing order type. Additional customization able to set done with item category customization. Sales order type feature billing type define into it and based on the order type billing type determines in order to cash cycle. Pricing able to also be reprocessed in billing.

T-code for billing Customization is **VOFA**
SPRO
IMG → Sales and Distribution → Billing → Billing Document → Billing Document Types

The standard billing document type is "**F2**"
Customization of billing document is the same framework for all the billing type but with different values. If all the fields are understood all other billing types able to set understood easily.
The customization of F2 document is the following.

Billing Type F2 Invoice Created by SAP

Number systems

No.range int.assgt.	19		Item no.increment	

General control

SD document categ.	M	Invoice	☐ Posting Block
Transaction group	7	Billing documents	☑ Statistics
Billing category			
Document Type			
Negative posting		No negative posting	
Branch/Head office		Customer=Payer/Branch=sold-to party	
Credit memo w/ValDat	☐	No	
Invoice list type	LR	Invoice List	
Rebate settlement			☐ Rel.for rebate
Standard text			

General Controls

Number Range: The number range field controls the number that will be utilized for the billing document.

IMG → Sales and Distribution → Billing → Billing Document → Define number range for billing document.
T-code for number range is VN01

N..	From No.	To Number	NR Status	Ext
Z2	900000	000999999		☐

Ext: In the number range, Ext represents an external number range defined in billing that able to set created with manually entered numbers. If the Ext is not selected, then the system picks the next available billing number. Billing document numbers are increments that able to define so the next number able to automatically create according to the controls.

SD Document Category:

The Sales and Distribution document category is the document type that is the representation type of document. "M" represents an invoice which is a standard document type of any invoice.

Posting Block:

Posting block able to set so that when the billing document is created it will have a billing block in it. This control blocks any posting for the billing document.

Transaction Group:

Transaction group is also similar to the Document category field. It categorizes the document type by its group and processing functions with the group.

Statistics:

This checkbox controls the billing document that is required for reporting and statistical use.

Negative Posting:

This field controls if negative posting is allowed. If negative posting is allowed or if not allowed, it able to control from this field.

Invoice list:

An invoice able to process in groups or batches. The invoice list, type in F2 billing is "LR". The invoice list allows group to processing of invoices.

Rebate Settlement and Related for Rebate:

These two fields are relevant for the rebate process. What type of rebate settlement is utilized for the billing document type, and if the billing document is relevant for the rebate related accruals.

Controls for Cancelation of billing document:

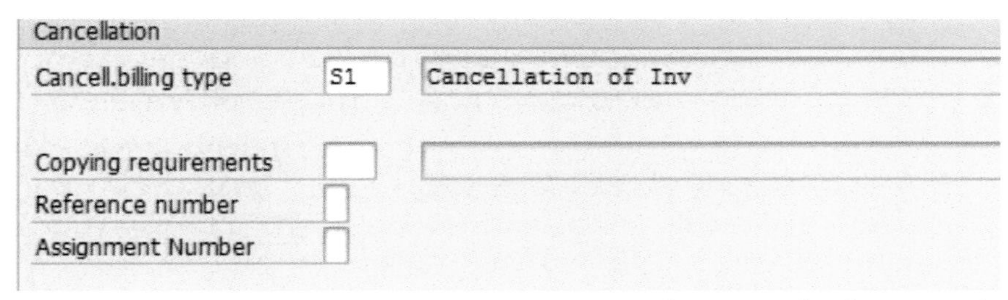

Cancellation		
Cancell.billing type	S1	Cancellation of Inv
Copying requirements		
Reference number		
Assignment Number		

If "F2" billing type needs to be cancelled based on the billing type system, it will check in the billing document type controls and use the cancel billing type. Relevant controls are in the screenshot and the standard cancel billing type is "F2" is "S1".

Controls for Account Assignment / Pricing

The first field of these controls is an Account determination for the billing type. The field value is a standard account determination procedure utilized in the screenshot, "KOFI00" and document procedure is utilized for pricing, "A". Document procedures are utilized if pricing is required to be recalculated in billing.

Account assignment/pricing		
AcctDetermProc.	KOFI00	Account Determination
Doc. pric. procedure	A	Standard
Acc. det. rec. acc.		
Acc. det. cash. set.		
Acc. det. pay. cards		

Output / Partner and Texts Controls:

The first filed for customizations is "output determination procedure". It is utilized for output customization from billing type. The standard output condition type is "RD00" which is utilized for "Output type" field.

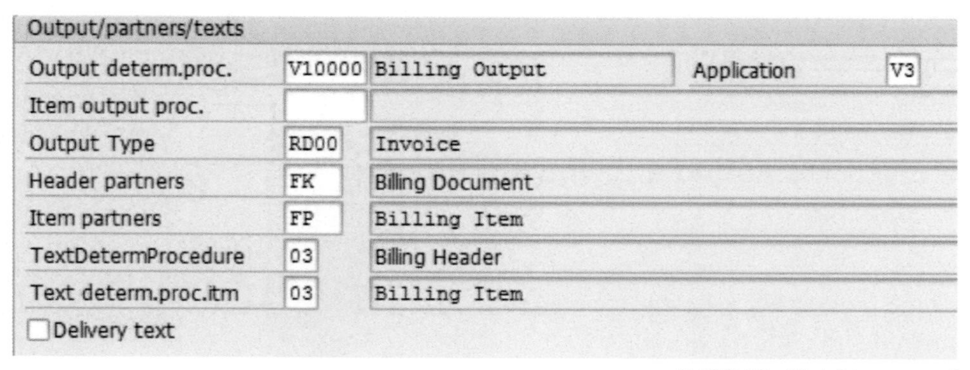

For partner and text determination these are the standard fields that are utilized for partner determination. "Delivery text field" copy text from a delivery document to the billing document text.

Invoice List

Invoice List is the process where billing documents able to process together in a list, group, or batches. The invoice list is also utilized in billing document control and further additional customization able to utilize.

Assign Invoice list to the Billing Type:

IMG → Sales and Distribution → Billing → Billing Document → Invoice List → Assign Invoice List to Billing Type.

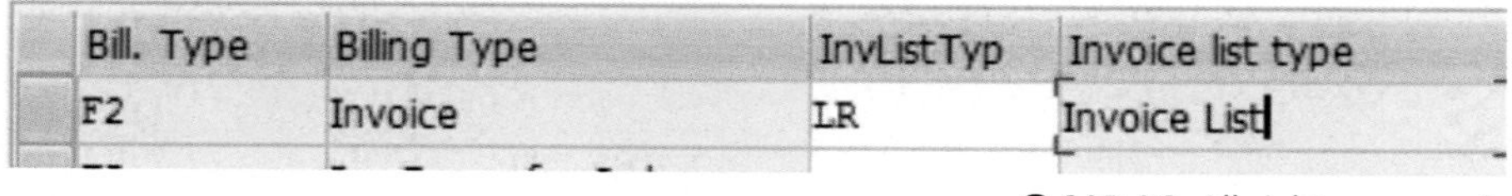

Bill. Type	Billing Type	InvListTyp	Invoice list type
F2	Invoice	LR	Invoice List

In this customization, the invoice list is assigned to the invoice list type. The based on this customization it will determine the invoice list by billing type.

Copy Control for Billing Document:

Copy control copies appropriate values to proceeding document. The customization menu path able to follow by following the menu path from T-code SPRO:

IMG → Sales and Distribution → Billing → Billing Document → Maintain Copy Controls for billing Document

T-code: **VTFA**

Copy control is based on header level and item levels is based on the header level. It is based on the invoice order type to sales order type level header level and also on item level it is based on item category level.

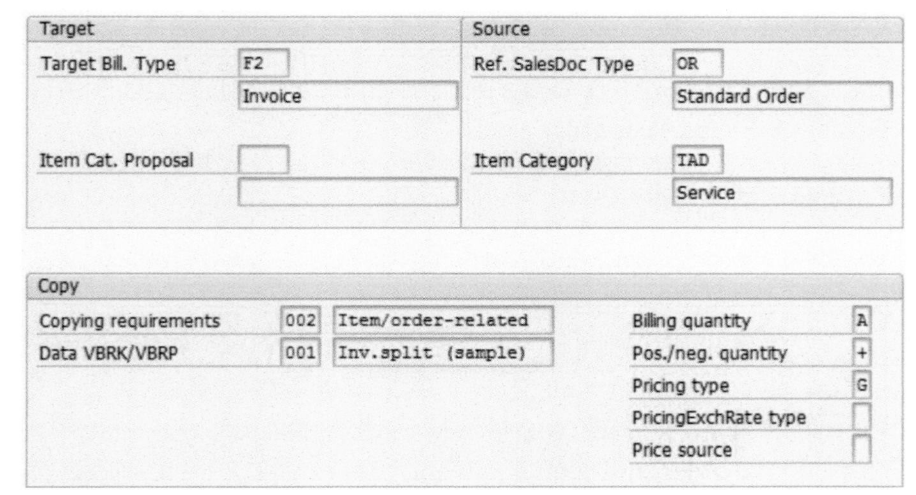

The source to target controls the header level and also the item category level.

Copy:

Copy controls field description is the following.

Copying Requirements:

The first field in customization is the “Copying Requirements”. The requirement is predefining program to choose from. The standard “copying requirements” value is “002” which represents the order related so billing is based on order.

Data BBRK / VBRP:

The data is also a similar filed as "Copy requirements" but the requirement is made for billing table "VBRP." The billing item data and billing header data table "VBRK" is the standard requirement utilized on "001" with controls for the invoice split.

Billing Quantity:

Billing quantity controls which quantity supposed to copy into the billing document.

Positive and Negative quantity:

This customization allows positive or negative quantity to be copied over to the billing document.

Price type:

This customization determines if price needs to be recalculated in the billing or copy price element from the sales order.

Pricing Exchange rate Type:

This field controls what pricing exchange rate date is valid for billing. Pricing exchange rate expected to be based on order date.

Price Source:

Price source filed indicates where the price is copied from the source of the price. Price source is based on the order, and if left empty this able to also be based on purchase order, delivery or external.

Billing Plans

Two different types of billing plans are available in SAP

- Milestone Billing
- Periodic Billing

Milestone Billing:

Milestone billing is utilized where billing is issued for services in increments of services or billing where the issued based on milestone completion of services. For example, when building a house, the payment able to set for completion of each room or percentage and at that point the billing will be issued by milestone by milestone.

IMG → Sales and Distribution → Billing → Billing Plan → Define Billing Plan Type

T-code: **OVBI**

Billing plan type is 01 for the milestone billing.

BillingPlanType 01 Milestone Billing

Origin of general data

Start date 01 Today's Date

RefBillPlanNo.

Billing data: date proposal

Date category 01

Control data: create dates

Online order X

General control data

FCode-OvervScrn 0003

Start date: Selecting the start from calculating date, using value "01" to represent todays date. When this plan is utilized in the document, it will consider the start date of the document date for the milestone billing needs.

Date category: This defines the processing date, also considering what type of date. 01 represents milestone relevant date, 03 represents down payment relevant date.

Online Order:

If "X" is marked, the system will purpose the dates, but when it is not marked the dates able to be manually.

Periodic Billing:

Periodic billing is billing of service or product which is divided into periods of time. Periodic billing is like a rent payment on a house or product which is charged periodically.

IMG → Sales and Distribution → Billing → Billing Plan → Define Billing Plan Type

T-code: OVBI

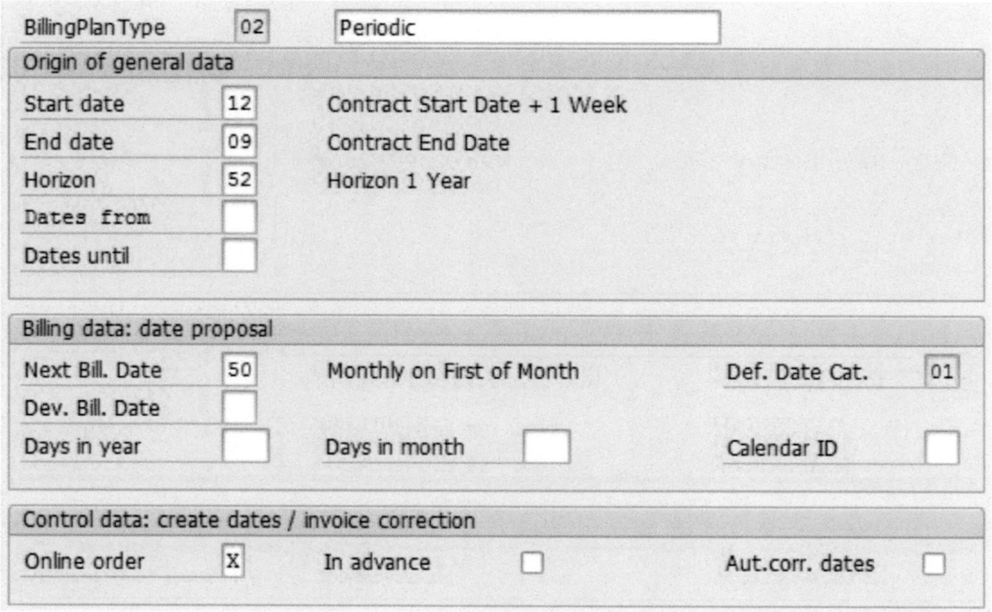

BillingPlanType	02	Periodic		
Origin of general data				
Start date	12	Contract Start Date + 1 Week		
End date	09	Contract End Date		
Horizon	52	Horizon 1 Year		
Dates from				
Dates until				
Billing data: date proposal				
Next Bill. Date	50	Monthly on First of Month	Def. Date Cat.	01
Dev. Bill. Date				
Days in year		Days in month	Calendar ID	
Control data: create dates / invoice correction				
Online order	X	In advance ☐	Aut.corr. dates	☐

Periodic billing feature start and end dates that able to customize in the billing plan. The start date is based on: yearly, contract period, Billing date, contract validity + contract validity period, etc. The contract end date expected to be based on similar factors such as contract start date. Horizon define is not the contract end date, but it defines the length of the billing plan.

Dates "from" and "dates until" are the rule base dates determination. The next billing date controls when the next billing date is determined for the billing plan. The "Dev Billing Date" represents deviating billing date so that the original billing date able to change. For accounting the days in the year and days in a month able to set in these fields. Online order dates automatic allows for manual entry. Advance field allows for advance billing. The auto correction date field automatically corrects the invoice for the processing.

Credit Management:

When the customer creation credit master issues a credit limit for sales process, the customer can do this with a credit limit. The credit limit automatically blocks transactions when the credit limit is reached. Credit functionality able to utilize to block sales order, delivery, and billing documents. Customer credit is calculated against the customer's open document and credit exposure.

Credit master data controls the credit related transactions.

Credit Master:

Credit master is created with the combination of customer and credit control area. Credit is based on credit limit and credit risk assigned to the customer. Credit is calculated based on the horizon and credit exposure. Credit exposure means it's an open order, open delivery and open invoice.
T-code for credit management is FD32

T-code to display Credit Master FD33

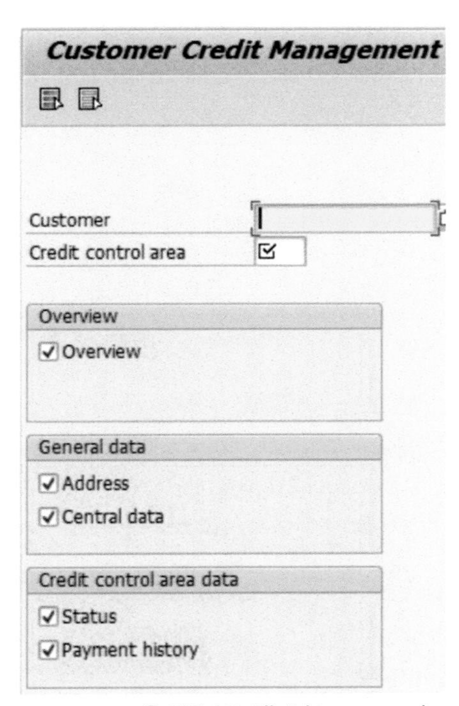

The following are 5 different views of credit master:

- Overview
- Address
- Central data
- Status
- Payment history

Credit Exposure:

Credit management is the combination of risk category and credit control area of credit master. Credit exposure is considered a customer's open sales orders, liabilities, delivery, billing, and posting open document's value, which then adds them all together. The credit exposure is utilized for credit controls for the transactions to be blocked.

Credit Check:

There are credit checks.

Credit reports and functionalities

Customer Credit Block:

Customer credit block controls and stops the sales and delivery of document for further processing. The sales order requires processing of approval to release it from the credit block. The credit block able to remove with the work list report and by following T-codes:

- VKM4 Release credit for sales order and Delivery document
- VKM3 Release credit for sales document
- VKM5 Release credit for Delivery Document

To release credit use T-code VKM4

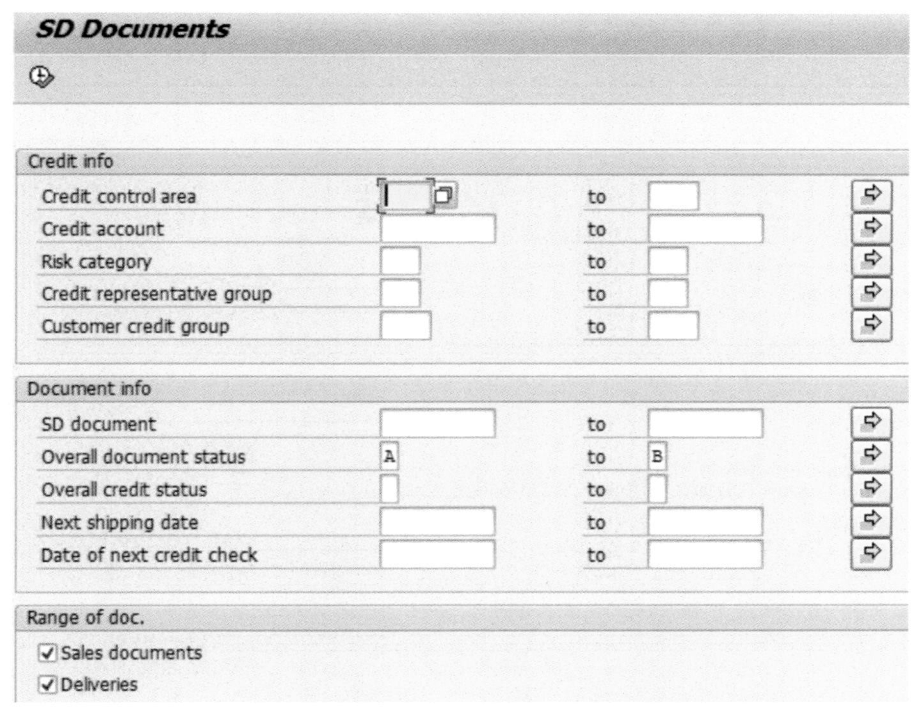

Credit able to release by the report VKM4.

Revenue Account Determination:

Account determination is based on condition technique. Revenue recognition is an accounting related functionality. The two types of revenue recognition in the systems are:

1. Accrued revenue
2. Deferred revenue

Accrued Revenue:

Accrued accounting revenue is based on recognizing revenue before cash is received. For example, the customer pays for the invoice later, but the review soon realizes that the invoice is issued.

Deferred revenue:

Deferred revenue is realized later at a point of time until the amount is received.

Example: when an invoice is created, but the payment is not received, and when the payment is received, then the revenue is recognized. In other words, the transaction is created, but the realization of revenue is not recognized until the payment is cleared then the revenue able to recognize.

Revenue Recognition Configuration:

Revenue recognition is basic and major customization object is part of the item category. In Item the category, we able to define what kind of revenue recognition supposed to apply in the system.

Customization Path from SPRO t-code is the following

IMG →Sales and Distribution → Basic Functions → Account Assignment / Costing → Revenue Recognition → Set Revenue Recognition for Item Categories

Screenshot:

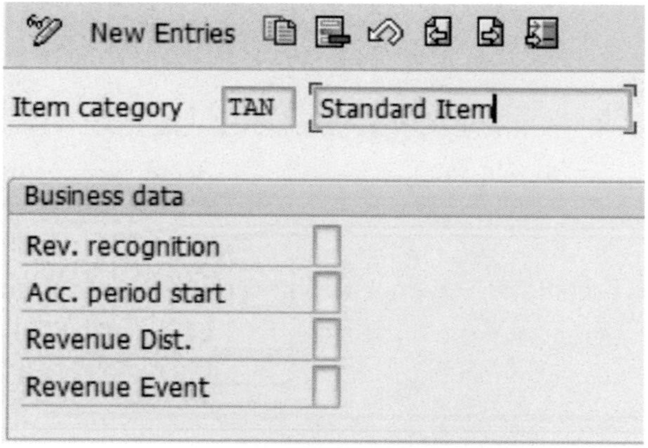

New Entries

Item category TAN Standard Item

Business data

Rev. recognition

Acc. period start

Revenue Dist.

Revenue Event

The revenue recognition field controls any of the following: the standard review of recognition, time related or service related revenue, or billing related time of service.

If the accounting period field is left empty it means that it is not relevant to the accounting period start date. This field is utilized for contract and billing related data.

Revenue Distribution: This field defines a billing plan related or value with distribution or non-distributions.

Revenue Event: In this field revenue is recognized based on the events that are defined in the field. Any of the following apply, the event is invoiced, date is acceptance, or based on customer types.

Account Determination Configuration:

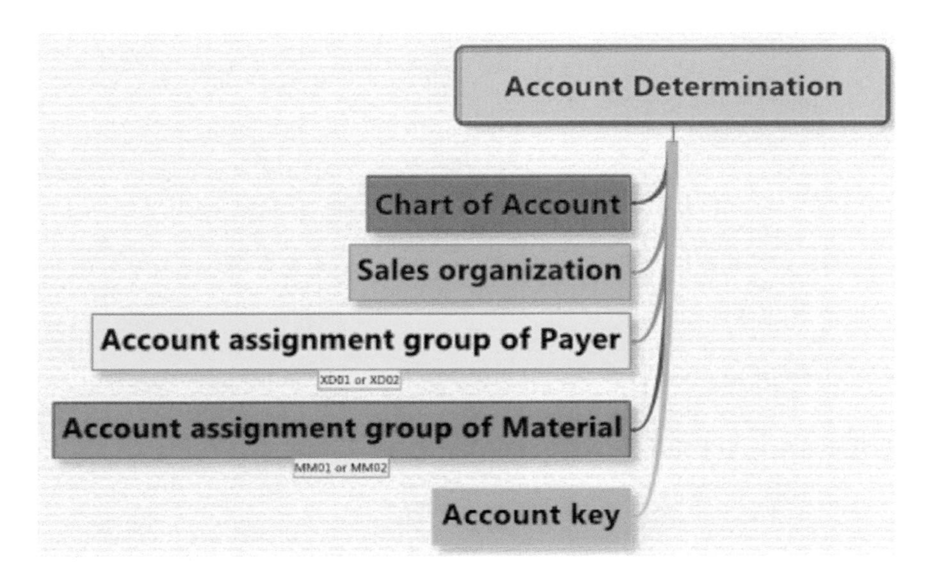

Master Data Account Group:

Revenue account determination is based on customer and material master.

Customization Path from SPRO T-code is the following:

IMG →Sales and Distribution → Basic Functions → Account Assignment / Costing → Revenue Account Determination → Check Master data relevant for account assignment

In this customization the account group gets assigned to customer and material master.

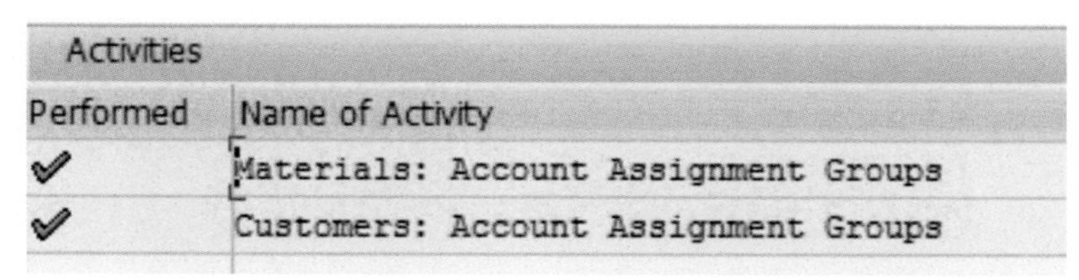

Performed	Name of Activity
✔	Materials: Account Assignment Groups
✔	Customers: Account Assignment Groups

Dependency for Account Determination:

Dependency for account determination is based on defining the table. The table will be utilized in the condition technique for account determination. The following standard tables are utilized in account determination.

Customization Path from SPRO t-code is the following

IMG →Sales and Distribution → Basic Functions → Account Assignment / Costing → Revenue Account Determination → Define Dependencies of Revenue Account Determination

Tab	Short Description
001	Cust.Grp/MaterialGrp/AcctKey
002	Cust.Grp/Account Key
003	Material Grp/Acct Key
004	General
005	Acct Key

An additional table able to utilize for maintaining the account determination tables.

Define Access Sequence and Account Determinations Type:

In access the sequence customization is assigned to the condition type. The access sequence, then assigns it to the account determination type.

Customization Path from SPRO t-code is the following

IMG →Sales and Distribution → Basic Functions → Account Assignment / Costing → Revenue Account Determination → Define Dependencies of Revenue Account Determination

Screenshot:

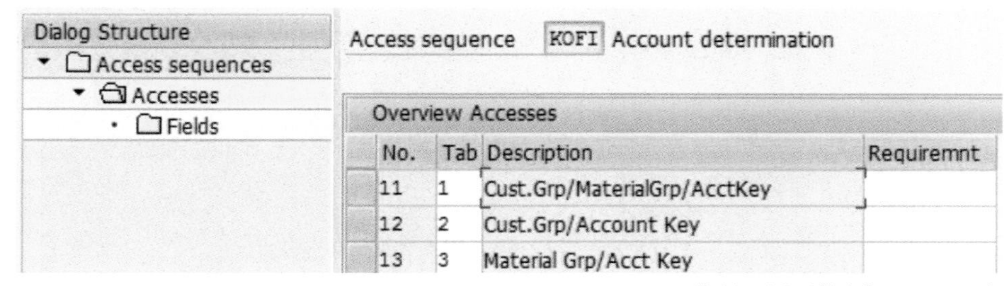

The requirement able to utilize for system defined options.

Define Condition Type and Assign assess sequence to it

Overview of Condition Types

CTyp	Name	AS	Description
KOFI	Accnt Determination	KOFI	Account determination

In the screenshot above, the standard condition type is assigned to the standard access sequence, KOFI. In the configuration we will focus on KOFI condition type. In any standard system two condition types are utilized for account determination

- KOFI
- KOFK

KOFI is utilized for sales, for example from stock where controlling related functionality is not utilized. The KOFK is utilized to make an order scenario and controlling involves variant configuration made to order and WBS related project system projects.

Define and assign account determination procedure:

In this step we define Account determination procedure controls and assign it to the billing document type.

Customization Path from SPRO t-code is the following:

IMG →Sales and Distribution → Basic Functions → Account Assignment / Costing → Revenue Account Determination → Define and assign Account Determination procedure

Screenshot:

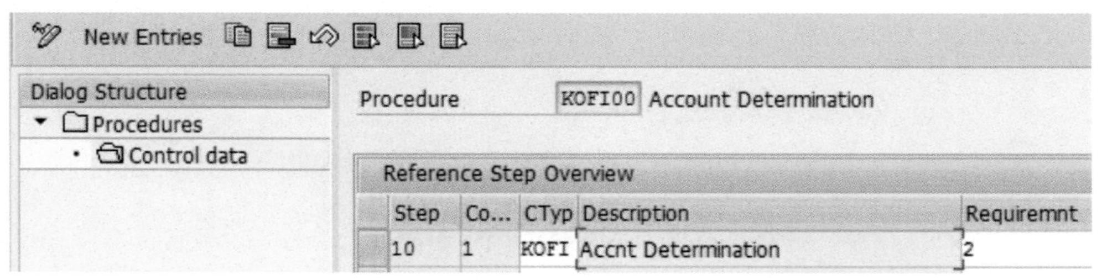

The first field is the procedure and second field are the customization that contains the condition type. The requirement type defines the condition type relevant to the controlling assignment without the controlling assignment.

Define and Assign Account Keys

Customization Path from SPRO t-code is the following

IMG →Sales and Distribution → Basic Functions → Account Assignment / Costing → Revenue Account Determination → Define and assign Account Keys

T-CODE: OK11

Screenshot:

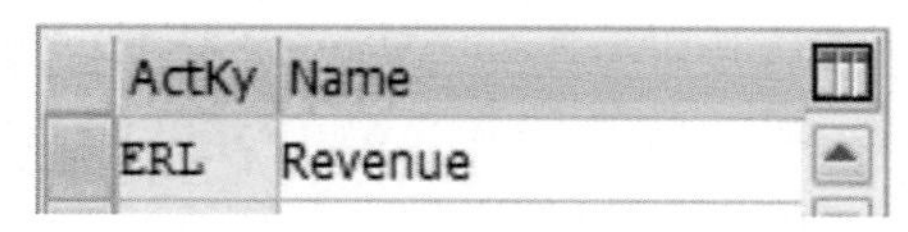

In the above screenshot we define an account key.

PR0000	10	0	PR00	Price	ERL	Revenue
	20	0	KA00	Sales deal		
	40	1	RA00	% Discount from Net		
	40	2	RB00	Discount (Value)		

In the above screenshot we assign the account keys to the pricing procedure so that each condition type of pricing able to have different account determination according to the revenue.

Assign G/L Accounts:

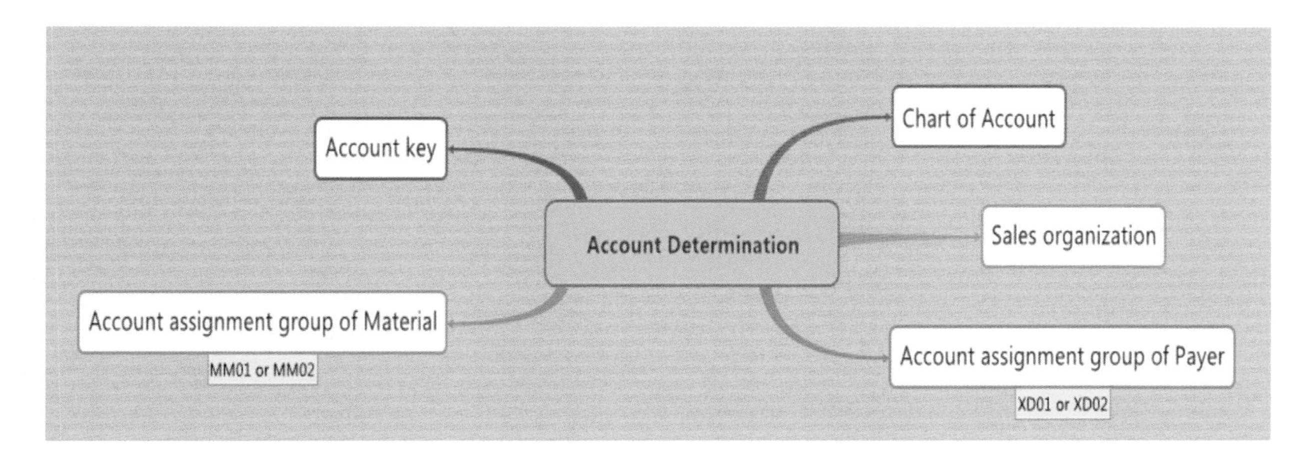

In the last step of account determination G/L account gets assigned to the table conditions that are selected in the table.

Customization Path from SPRO t-code is the following:

IMG →Sales and Distribution → Basic Functions → Account Assignment / Costing → Revenue Account Determination → Assign G/L Accounts

T-code: **OK15**

Screenshot:

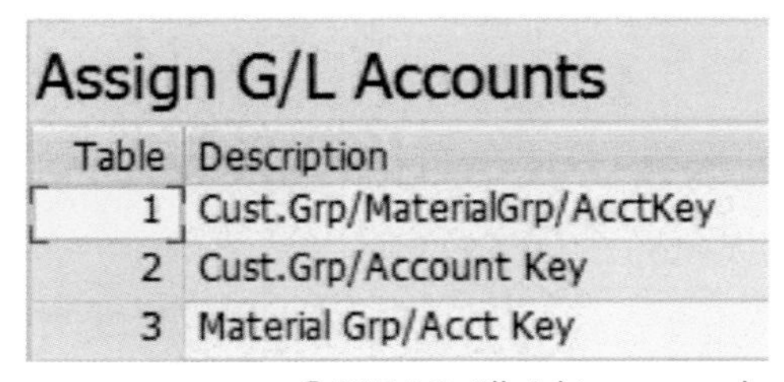

Assign G/L Accounts

Table	Description
1	Cust.Grp/MaterialGrp/AcctKey
2	Cust.Grp/Account Key
3	Material Grp/Acct Key

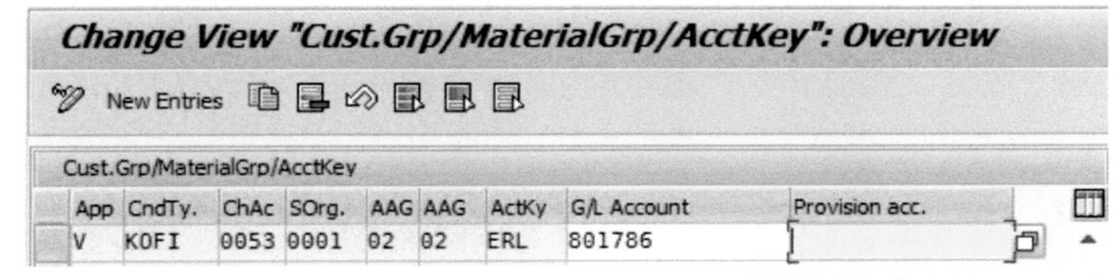

Change View "Cust.Grp/MaterialGrp/AcctKey": Overview

New Entries

Cust.Grp/MaterialGrp/AcctKey

App	CndTy.	ChAc	SOrg.	AAG	AAG	ActKy	G/L Account	Provision acc.
V	KOFI	0053	0001	02	02	ERL	801786	

This is the general account determination, but it defers based on combinations of Account Key, chart of account, sales organization, account assignment group of customer master, and account assignment group from material master.

App field defines the "V" for sales and distribution related account determination. "CondTy" is utilized for condition Type. "ChAc" field is utilized for chart of account. Field "SOrg" is utilized in Sales Organization. G/L Account is utilized for General Ledger Account and Provision Acc. The field is utilized for accruals for the rebate.

Posting Period:

Posting period is an accounting function from monthly statement. It is a monthly period to be opened for transactions or closed at the end of the month. A posting period in SAP goes with a month plus years and the status of being open and closed for the period.

Chapter 7 Summary

Billing and Credit Management

In Billing the following topics are covered in the chapter

- Introduction to Billing
- Billing Order Type Customization
- Billing document type Copy Control
- Invoice List Customization

For Credit management the following topics are covered in the 6th chapter

- Credit Control area customization
- Credit Management
- Credit reports and functionalities

Revenue Recognition

- Accrued Revenue
- Deferred Revenue
- Revenue Determination

Notes

CHAPTER 8

AVAILABLE TO PROMISE

Chapter Summary

- Available to Promise (ATP)
- Availability check
- ATP Scope of check
- ATP and Master Data
- Requirement Type
- Transfer of Requirements
- Allocation

Objectives:

- Learn How Available to Promise work
- Learn how to configure ATP and AC
- Learn Master data and availability check
- Learn how to configure Requirement type
- Learn allocation configuration

Production Order MRP and ATP

Over period of time ERP systems designed out of MRP system development. At first companies develop a system to calculate available to promise and scheduling.

Business Introduction

ATP is a process where business plan when the product can be deliver to customer with calculation of time. ATP process include times for buying, selling, producing and shipment. Available to promise is based on stocks availability. There are two types of basic processes for allocation:

- Stock to order
- Make to order

In the stock to order system look at the stock. Looking at the stock it expected to be from purchasing of raw material to production to lead time calculations included in it. If there is stock already in the plant, then the ATP able to calculate the shipping time and schedule it accordingly and issue the correct ATP date so that the customer able to have the exact date. There are two variations in it:

- Backward scheduling
- Forward scheduling

Both backward and forward scheduling able to utilize with the scope of the check.

Make to Order:

Make to order is a good example of custom order. When the customer needs a special produced that is more customized.

SAP ATP

ATP stands for available to promise. When the sales orders are created, it runs a MRP based on an ATP setup. What is MRP? MRP stands for Material Requirement Planning. It is one of the compound parts of the ERP system to process materials planning according to the requirements.

To confirm the customer's order against the scope availability is known as the "Availably to Promise"

Available to Promise and Availability Check:

Available to promise is a function of sales, calculating stock at hand and feature the availability to be shipped to the customer. The system able to consider the following elements in ATP check. The screenshots are very descriptive to how the system able to configure with these elements are utilized for ATP.

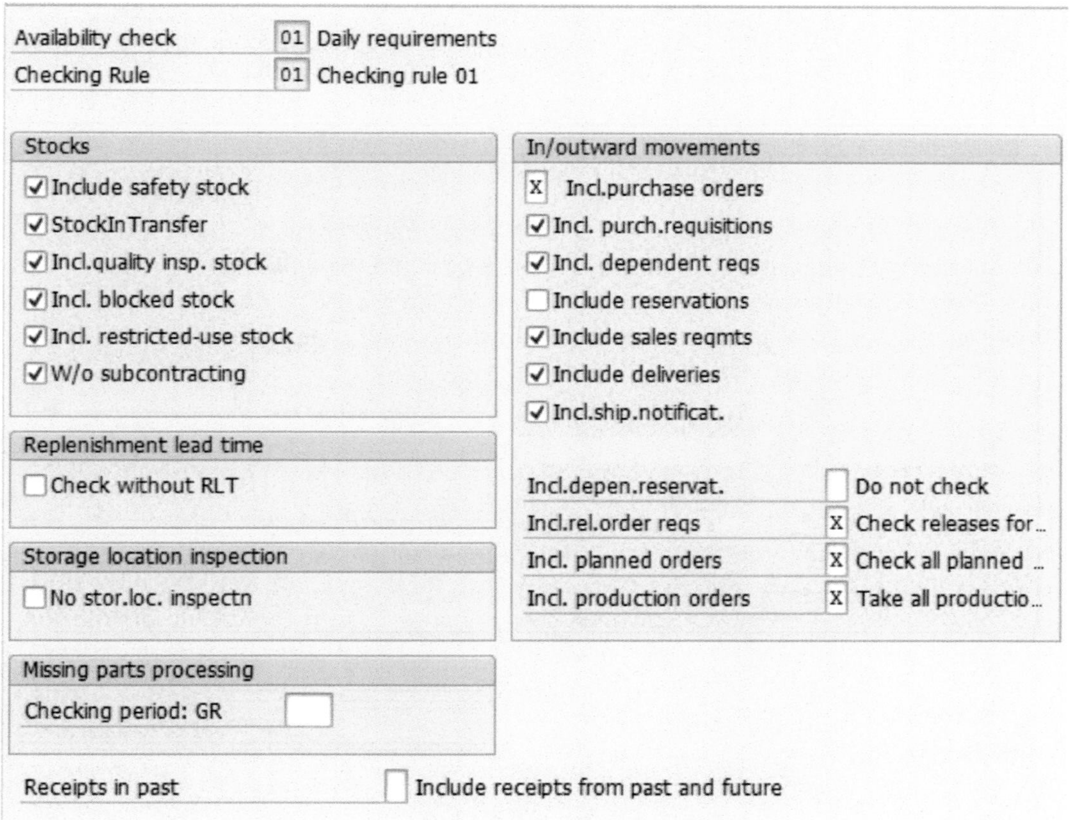

Availability check 01 Daily requirements
Checking Rule 01 Checking rule 01

Stocks
- [x] Include safety stock
- [x] StockInTransfer
- [x] Incl.quality insp. stock
- [x] Incl. blocked stock
- [x] Incl. restricted-use stock
- [x] W/o subcontracting

Replenishment lead time
- [ ] Check without RLT

Storage location inspection
- [ ] No stor.loc. inspectn

Missing parts processing
Checking period: GR

In/outward movements
- X Incl.purchase orders
- [x] Incl. purch.requisitions
- [x] Incl. dependent reqs
- [ ] Include reservations
- [x] Include sales reqmts
- [x] Include deliveries
- [x] Incl.ship.notificat.

Incl.depen.reservat. Do not check
Incl.rel.order reqs X Check releases for...
Incl. planned orders X Check all planned ...
Incl. production orders X Take all productio...

Receipts in past Include receipts from past and future

The above screenshot explains the systematic consideration to calculate and process how ATP should work.

There are five major areas considered:

- Stocks
- Replenishment Lead Time
- Storage Location Inspection
- Missing Parts Processing

- In / outward Movements

For example, if we wanted to consider stock in the transfer or block stock. These are all situations and business processes that need to be streamlined then the configuration part able to be done in the system. ATP stands for Available to Promise and it is based on the master data and transactional data.

How does the master data affect MRP?

Material Master Data feature four different views for MRP and they all integrate with all different modules. To view the MRP views, the user able to look into MD04 requirement screen.

What is Requirement Type?

The requirement type function is utilized in the form material requirement planning views. In MRP the view of material master requirement types able to be defined. The transfer of requirement functionality is a prerequisite for carrying out the availability check. Transfer of requirement able to be configured without the availability check, but the availability check will not work without the transfer of requirement.

Transfer of requirement

Material requirement is created with the customer's requested delivery date and quantity.
Transfer of requirement takes the requirement and transfer into Material requirement.
The following are two types of requirement:

1. **Individual**
2. **Collective**

Availability check:

Available to promise a date is confirmed by the availability check. For the transfer of requirements, the availability check is a prerequisite. It is on a schedule line confirmation, and date confirmation for the delivery date. The scope able to be configured to check the following:

Plant Stock/warehouse (Delivering Plant)
(Procurement/Production) Lead times
Plant / warehouse processing time (Pick/ pack, load/Unload, transportation planning time/ Good issue/ receipt time)
Schedule line also determines if the AC needs to be activated. When a sales order is created, the schedule line determines a new delivery data based on stock level and processing time of the

product out of the plant.

ATP:

Available to promise functionality based on current stock in hand and also ATP check future purchase order and stock transfer coming in and adding them into ATP logic and also calculate material going out. The options and flexibility of the system allow adopting according to the business needs and turn one and off options in ATP function.

Allocation:

Allocation is the name of a process where stock is allocated to the sales order. When the user allocates this stock, it is exclusively assigned to the sales order and there are many variations that able to be configured. Allocation controls the system with options of available quantity, future available quantity, how much per period able to be allocated, allocation based on sales history, allocation based on geographical location, allocation based on limited quantity, and many various options available for customization. Material quantity able to be limit for the allocation. Allocation quantity able to be based on the customer / region.

The three types of allocations are:

- ATP Quantity base
- Product Allocation
- Planning

AC based on Planning:

It is based on demand planning generated from SAP APO-DP. These are based on the markets not based on the customers.

Customization of ATP and AC

- Availability Check and Transfer of Requirements
  - Transfer of Requirements
    - Define Requirements Classes
    - Define Requirements Types
    - Determination Of Requirement Types Using Transaction
    - Define Procedure For Each Schedule Line Category
    - Block Quantity Confirmation In Delivery Blocks
    - Maintain Requirements For Transfer Of Requirements
    - Maintain Requirements For Purchase And Assembly Orders
  - Availability Check
    - Availability Check with ATP Logic or Against Planning
    - Availability Check Against Product Allocation
    - Rule-based Availability Check

- Availability Check and Transfer of Requirements
  - Transfer of Requirements
    - Define Requirements Classes
    - Define Requirements Types
    - Determination Of Requirement Types Using Transaction
    - Define Procedure For Each Schedule Line Category
    - Block Quantity Confirmation In Delivery Blocks
    - Maintain Requirements For Transfer Of Requirements
    - Maintain Requirements For Purchase And Assembly Orders
  - Availability Check
    - Availability Check with ATP Logic or Against Planning
      - Define Checking Groups
      - Define Material Block For Other Users
      - Define Checking Groups Default Value
      - Carry Out Control For Availability Check
      - Define Procedure By Requirements Class
      - Define Procedure For Each Schedule Line Category
      - Determine Procedure For Each Delivery Item Category
      - Checking Rule For Updating Backorders
      - Define Default Settings
    - Availability Check Against Product Allocation
      - Maintain Procedure
      - Define Object
      - Specify Hierarchy
      - Define Consumption Periods
      - Control Product Allocation
      - Define Flow According To Requirement Category
      - Process Flow For Each Schedule Line Category
      - Permit Collective Product Allocation In Info Structures
      - Check Settings In Product Allocation
    - Rule-based Availability Check
      - Define business transaction
      - Assign business transaction to sales order type

Requirement Class Controls:

1. MRP
2. Requirement consumption strategy

3. Requirement planning strategy

Once ATP and (A.C) availability checks are activated, then it is activated globally, but it able to be controlled by scheduling the line to activate or not activated both the functions.

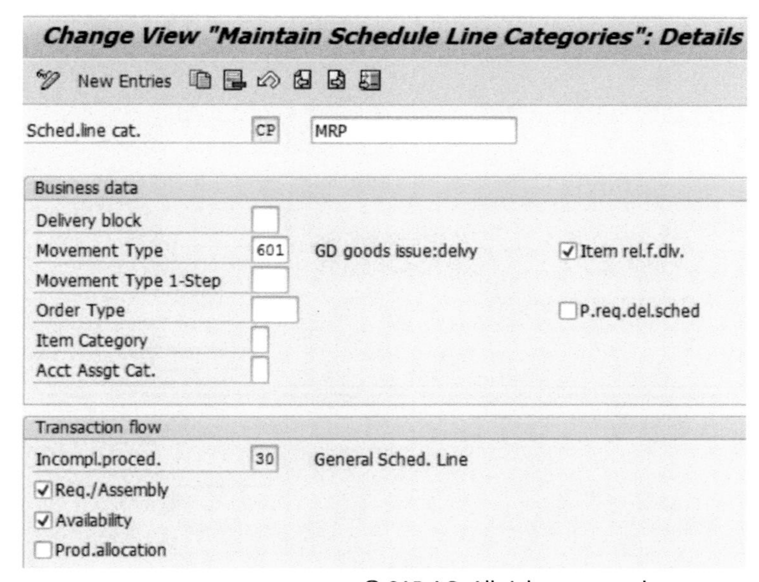

Customization of Requirement Class

from the SD prospective the focus on requirement class controls for ATP and AC only; additional customization is out of scope for this book.

In following screenshot, the requirement class feature the availability to check and transfer requirements marked, so these functions are active.

In requirement class the following elements are controlled:

- Requirments
- Configuration
- Assembly
- Costing
- Account Assignment

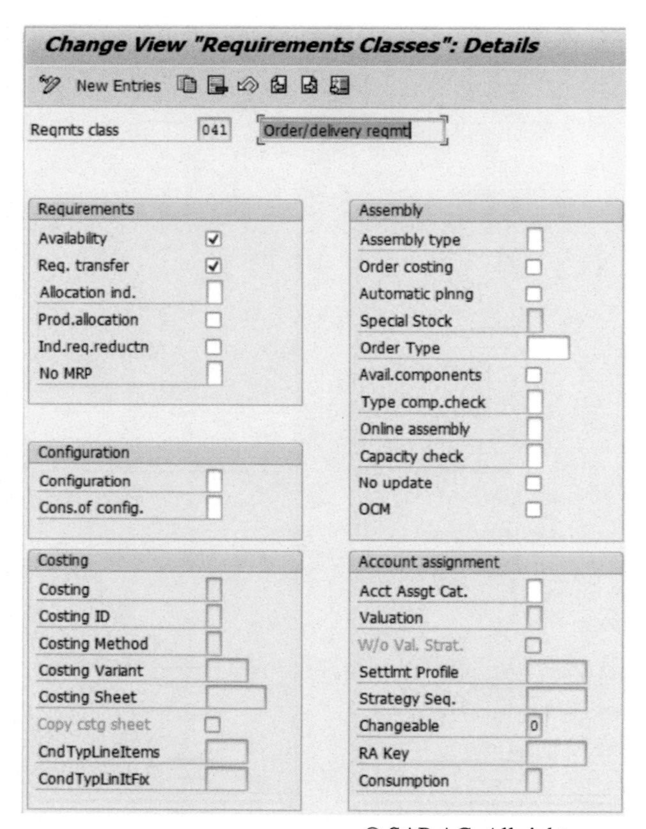

With each customization section it features detail controls for ATP.

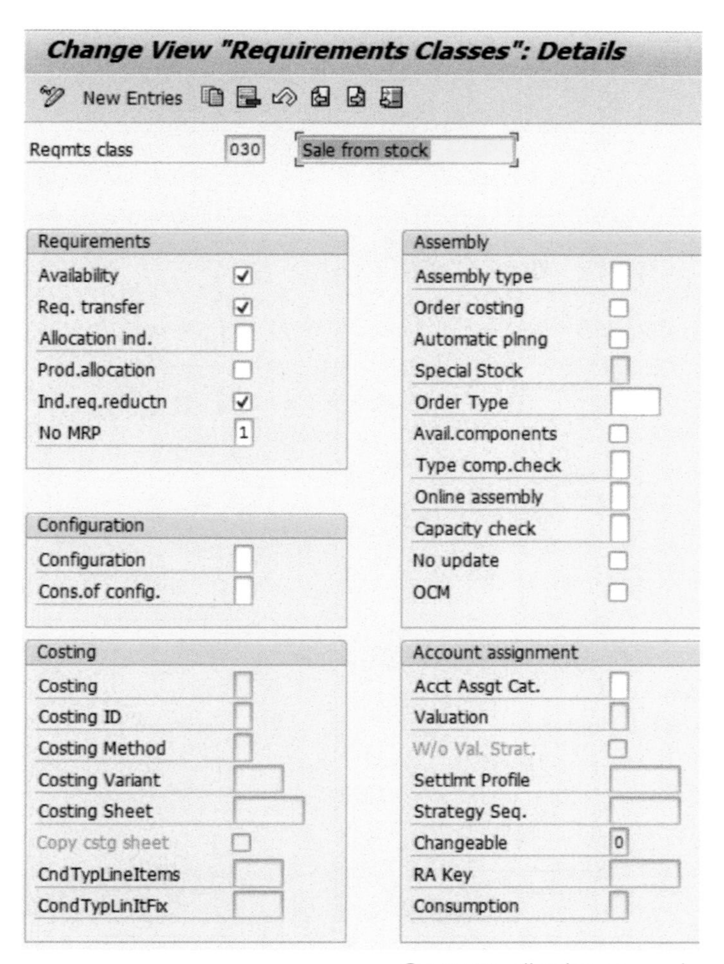

Transfer of requirement and availability checked able to be controlled from class.

Requirement Type:

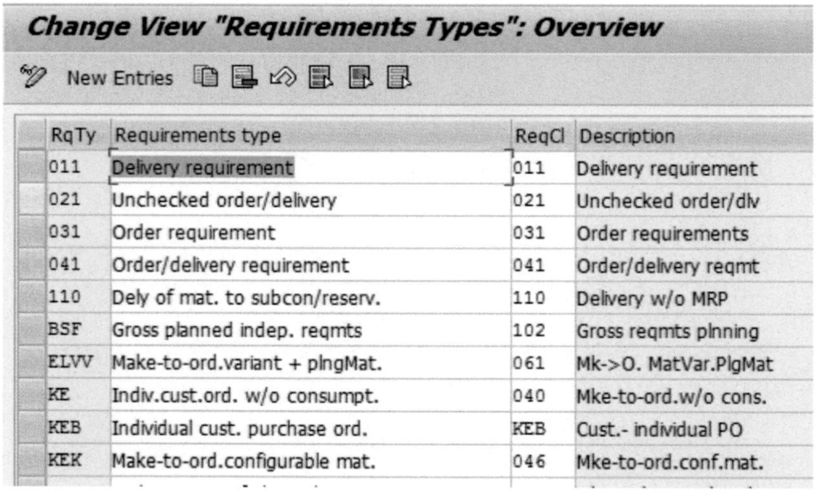

Change View "Requirements Types": Overview

New Entries

RqTy	Requirements type	ReqCl	Description
011	Delivery requirement	011	Delivery requirement
021	Unchecked order/delivery	021	Unchecked order/dlv
031	Order requirement	031	Order requirements
041	Order/delivery requirement	041	Order/delivery reqmt
110	Dely of mat. to subcon/reserv.	110	Delivery w/o MRP
BSF	Gross planned indep. reqmts	102	Gross reqmts plnning
ELVV	Make-to-ord.variant + plngMat.	061	Mk->O. MatVar.PlgMat
KE	Indiv.cust.ord. w/o consumpt.	040	Mke-to-ord.w/o cons.
KEB	Individual cust. purchase ord.	KEB	Cust.- individual PO
KEK	Make-to-ord.configurable mat.	046	Mke-to-ord.conf.mat.

Requirement Type determination

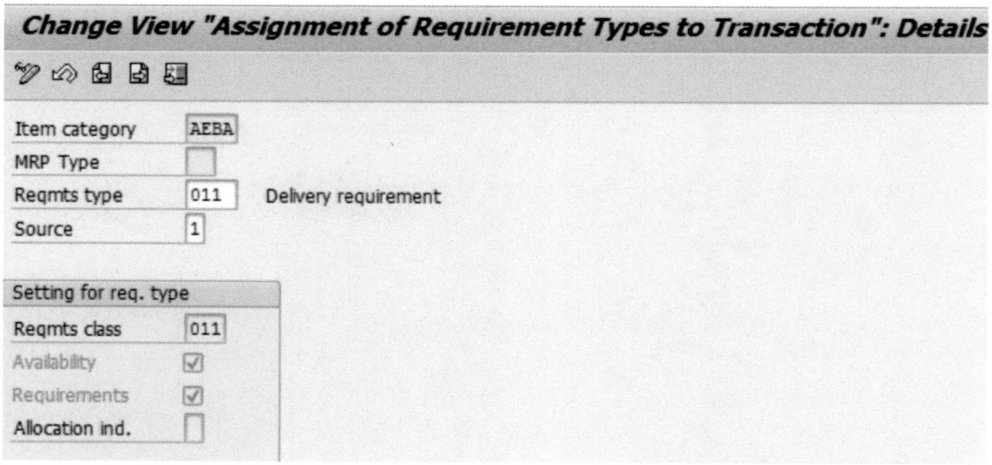

Change View "Assignment of Requirement Types to Transaction": Details

Item category	AEBA	
MRP Type		
Reqmts type	011	Delivery requirement
Source	1	

Setting for req. type

Reqmts class	011
Availability	☑
Requirements	☑
Allocation ind.	☐

Activate ATP and AC at schedule line category or USE VOV6 same controls

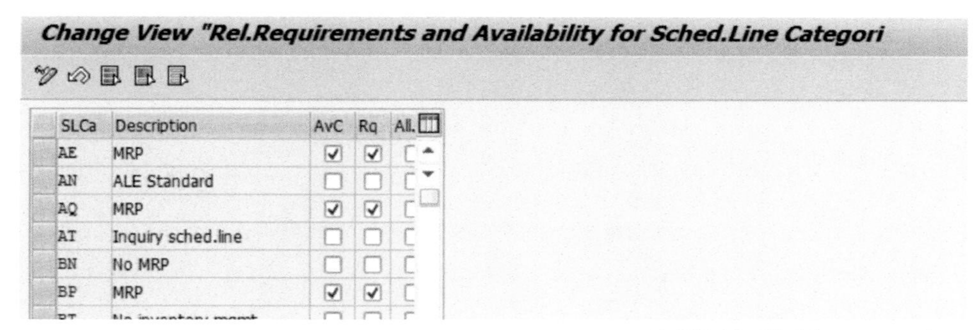

Checking Group:

Checking group controls the AC and ATP further controls.

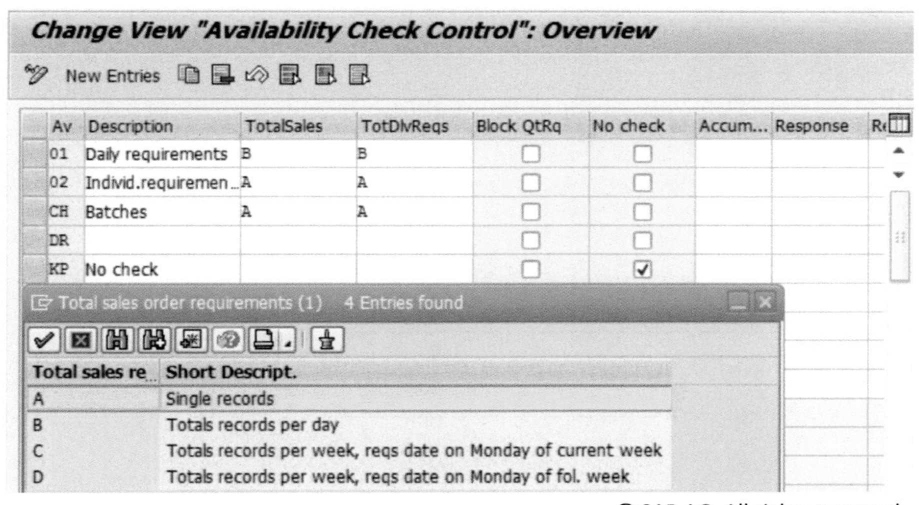

Total Sales requirements:

This configuration is based on sales order requirements along with how the system controls and should behave for material requirement planning process.
The requirement selections feature four options for customizations. These requirements will be generated during sales order creation.

The two different requirements are:

1. Individual requirement
2. Collective requirements

(A) Individual requirement is a single record requirement that is a generated requirement for a single item for MRP. The individual requirement processed at a sales level is to run MRP and confirm the order and the allocation.

(B) Total records per day is a Collective requirement generated based on this option.

(C) It is also a collective requirements option. Based on this selection it runs the total requirement based on the week starting from Monday to current week.

(D) It is also similar as option "C", but the exception of it generates requirement for the week, but it generate the requirements on following Monday of the current week.

Total Delivery Requirements:

In this configuration, it controls the delivery requirement and how the system should calculate it in material requirement planning.
Requirements selections have four options for customization. These requirements will be generated during sales order creation.
Two different requirements are available for selection:

1. Individual requirement
2. Collective requirements

(A) It is in the category of individual requirement that single record requirements generate a requirement for a single item for MRP.

(B) Total records per day is a collective requirement generated based on this option.

(C) It is a collective requirements option. Based on this selection it runs the total requirement based on the week starting from Monday to current week.

(D) It is similar to option "C" but the exception is that it generates requirement for the week, but it generate requirements on following Monday of the current week.

Block Quantity:

As specified in the settings for quantity block, the material will be blocked during the availability check. The quantity is reserved for this transaction that is recorded in the blocking table. Any other user processing the material at that time receives this information. This complements the information gained from the availability check and gives a more accurate picture of the current availability situation. If the block is set, then the purchase order, sales order, and master data will be blocked from processing.

No Check:

This customization is configured when the availability check is not required for the checking group related controls. If the material planning is controlled by a third-party application or it is maintained out of system, then this functionality is utilized to turn off the MRP in SAP.

Accumulation:

It's customized to avoid inconsistence in confirming quantity of the sales order. Four options are available for the configuration of the accumulation calculation. These settings will affect the conformation of sales order conform quantity.

1. No Accumulation:

If this is selected in customization, then there will be no accumulation for the sales order. To avoid inconsistency, the alternative option supposed to utilize: backorder processing, planning, and rescheduling.

2. Accumulation of confirmed quantity when created and changed:
Based on this customization, the total quantity will be added together on sales order creations. The "accumulation" checked is the ATP quantity and then sales order checked against the available quantity. Confirmation of sales order sum the previous quantity and additional quantity. It basically accumulates the quantity based on customization.

3. Required quantity when created, no accumulation when changed:
It only accumulates quantity only for sales order creation and is based on the sales order change. It will not consider ATP quantity.

4. Required quantity when created, conf. Quantity when changed:
It creates a required quantity requirement on sales order creation and based on change. It also confirms the quantity by checking the ATP.

Response:
This function is customized for shortage of material then the system generates an output for the shortage.

RelChkPlan:
This stands for "Relevant check against Planning" and controls for which material supposed to checked against the planning or plan independent planning.

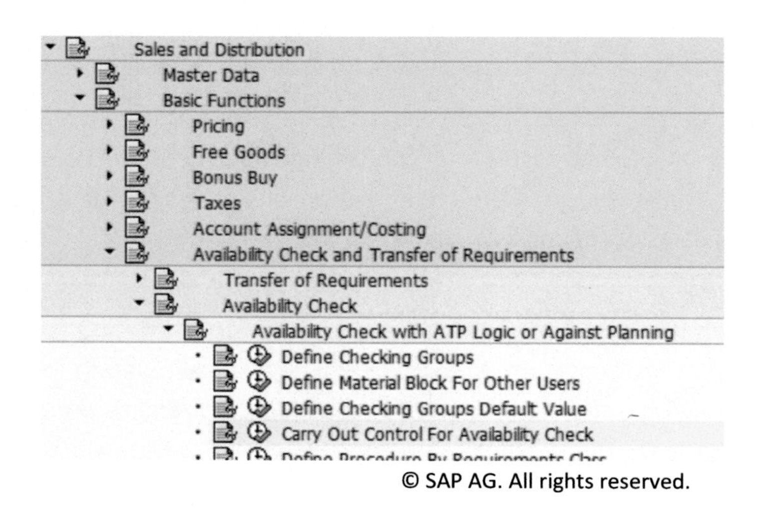

Availability Check Controls:

Availability check able to be configured on the following levels of controls:

- Stocks
- Replenishment Lead Time
- Storage location Inspection
- Missing Parts processing
- In/outward Orders Moment

Availability check scope able to be customized with many elements to be considered as per the screenshot. The screenshot represents the following controls:

Change View "Availability Check Control": Details

New Entries

Availability check | 01 Daily requirements
Checking Rule | A SD order

Stocks
- [ ] Include safety stock
- [ ] StockInTransfer
- [ ] Incl.quality insp. stock
- [ ] Incl. blocked stock
- [ ] Incl. restricted-use stock
- [ ] W/o subcontracting

Replenishment lead time
- [ ] Check without RLT

Storage location inspection
- [ ] No stor.loc. inspectn

Missing parts processing
Checking period: GR

In/outward movements
- [X] Incl.Purchase Orders
- [ ] Incl. purch.requisitions
- [ ] Incl. dependent reqs
- [x] Include reservations
- [x] Include sales reqmts
- [x] Include deliveries
- [ ] Incl.ship.notificat.

Incl.depen.reservat. | Do not check
Incl.rel.order reqs | Do not check
Incl. planned orders | Do not check
Incl. production orders | Do not take into ...

Receipts in past | Include receipts from past and future

Stocks:

Based on the selection, safety stock able to include or exclude the availability check. If stock is transferred between the plants, the system will calculate the time for pick/pack, shipping and loading time. The stock is in quality that able to include or ignore in availability check.

Replenishment Lead Time:

Replenishment Lead Time is based on the master data, shipping, loading time and the calculation able to activate the availability check. The default value able to be maintained in the material master.

Extra: Same controls also are utilized for Total Delivery requirements.

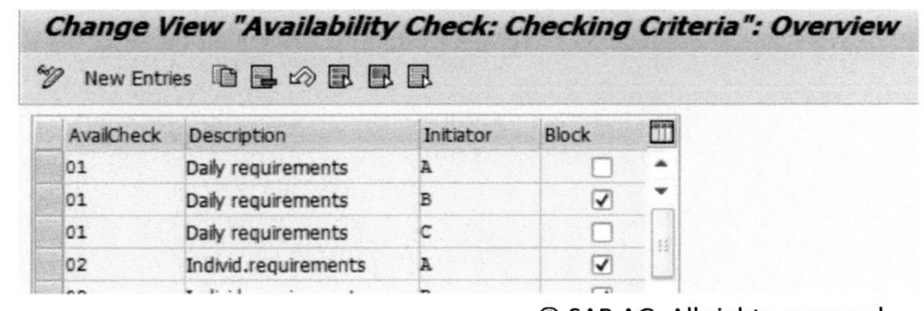

Change View "Availability Check: Checking Criteria": Overview

New Entries

AvailCheck	Description	Initiator	Block
01	Daily requirements	A	☐
01	Daily requirements	B	☑
01	Daily requirements	C	☐
02	Individ.requirements	A	☑

Chapter 8 Summary

In chapter 7 we cover the following topics:

- Material requiring planning
- Available to promise
- Transfer of requirements
- Availability Check
- Allocation
- Availability check based on Planning

Notes

CHAPTER 9

LISTING / EXCLUSION & OUTPUT DETERMINATION

Chapter Summary:

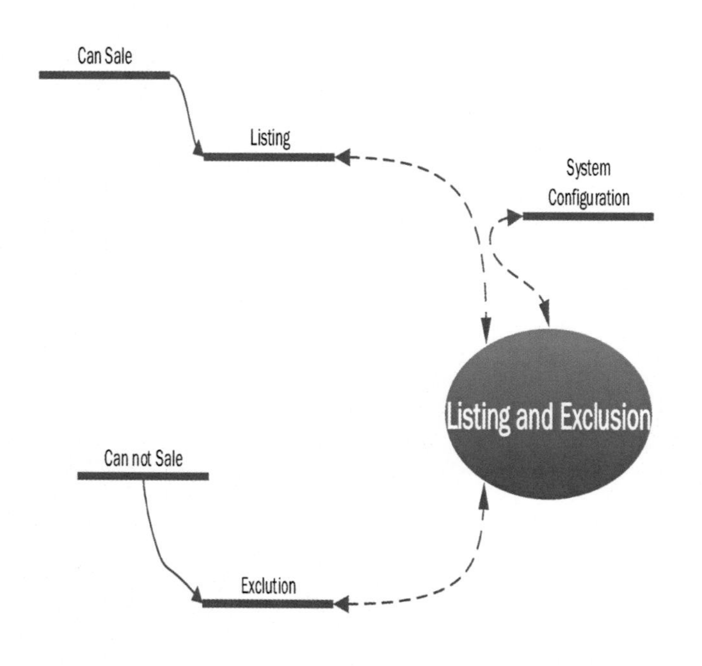

- Output Determination
- Text determination
- Listing and Exclusion

Objectives:

- Learn how to configure output Determination
- Learn how to configure text Determination
- Learn how to configure Listing and Exclusion

Output Determination:

In SAP Output means any type of print form or report that able to be printed. In SAP any type of "form" that is created from the transaction able to be configured. Output configuration is based on the condition technique. Output type able to be utilized for Email, EDI, Fax and other type of interfaces. The following are few document types where output able to be utilized:

- Inquiry
- Quotation
- Contracts
- Sales related documents
- Delivery
- Billing

The output is not limited to the above transactions; it able to be utilized with other transactions.

The output configuration in Sales and Distribution

In Sales and Distribution output configuration customized on following transactions areas:

- Sales activity
- Sales Document
- Billing Document

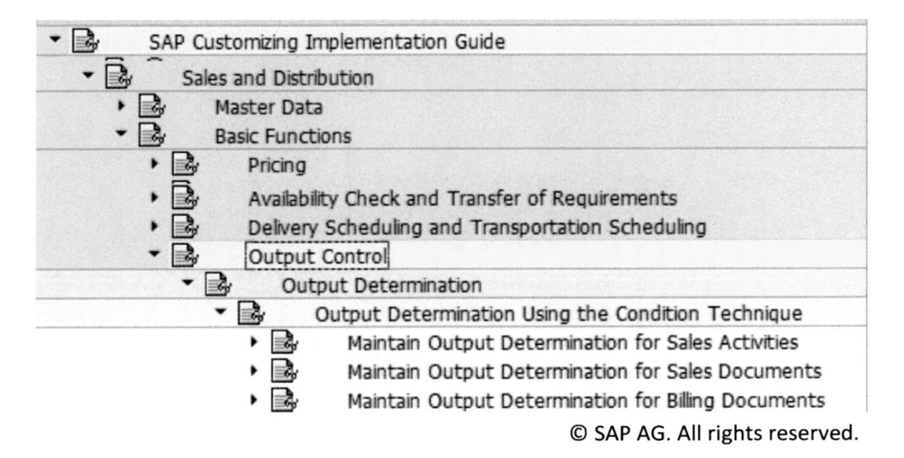

SAP Output used for print, email, EDI (more) processed from transections

Output Configuration:

Output determination customization is based on condition technique. The following are customization steps:

- Condition Table
- Access sequence
- Condition Type
- Output procedure
- Condition Record

Output Type Table:

Table customization is based on the fields. The fields are the basis of triggering the output type. Also, the standard table's entries able to be utilized with access sequence.

Customization Path from SPRO t-code is the following:

IM Customization Path from SPRO t-code is the following:

IMG →Sales and Distribution → Basic Functions → Output Determination → Maintain Output Determination for Sales Document → Maintain Condition Table

T-code for customization: **NACE**

Screenshot:

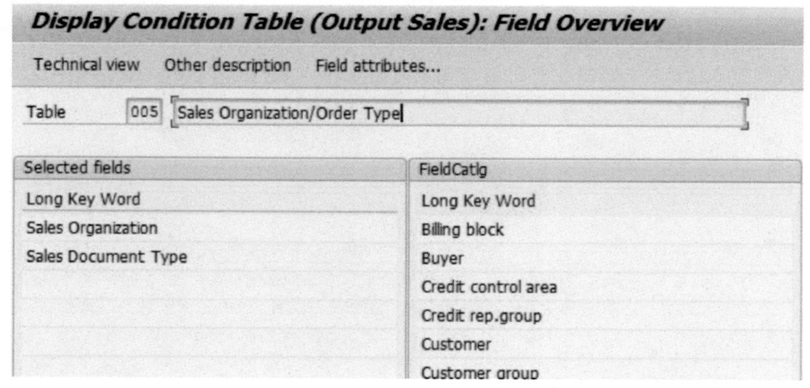

In the screenshot above, the left side displays the table field and the right side feature the field catalog. The field catalog allows for the field to be utilized for the condition

table. If the field is not maintained in the field catalog, then it's considered an enhancement to adding fields in field catalog.

Output Type Access Sequence:

Access sequence is some search criteria, where table entries are maintained. The table eatery able to be excluded by customization so that the search will stop if the table entry is marked exclusive.

Customization Path from SPRO t-code is the following

IMG →Sales and Distribution → Basic Functions → Output Determination → Maintain Output Determination for Sales Document → Maintain Access Sequence

T-code for customization: **NACE**

In a first step the folder access the sequence that is selected, and a new access sequence is created. In the second step the access folder is selected with the selection of access sequence and table entry able to be maintained with requirement and exclusive check box.

Output Condition Type:

Output condition Type is utilized for the transactional output issue. The output condition type able to be manual or able to be auto populated with condition record.

Customization Path from SPRO t-code is the following

IMG →Sales and Distribution → Basic Functions → Output Determination → Maintain Output Determination for Sales Document → Maintain Condition Type

Screenshot:

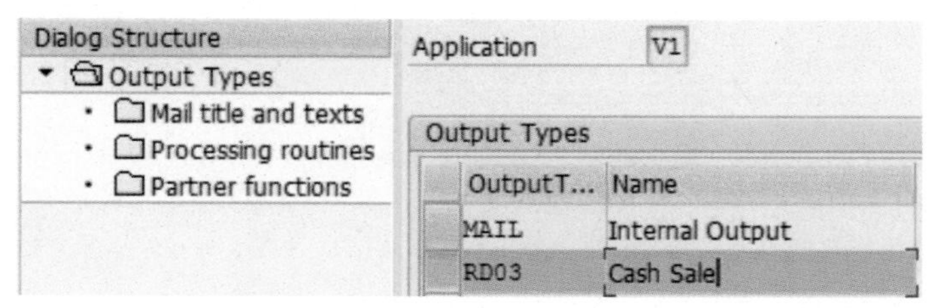

Above is the example of standard output type "RD03" cash sale. The condition type controls are on left side of screenshot. "Mail title and text," "Processing routine," and "Partner function" have further output condition type controls for customization.

Mail title and text:

Mail title and text are utilized to control the language and document title.

Processing routine:

The layout module controls the type of output program being utilized. There expected to be multiple processing routines that able to be utilized for the single output condition type as per medium. The processing routine is utilized to define the program in the form and routine is utilized for the condition type. The customized form is attached to the folder. The PDF/smartform Form is defined in this control and form type.

Partner Function:

Partner function control is utilized to allow the partner type.

Output type Partner Function Assignment:

Partner functions are maintained with output type for the transaction processing.

Customization Path from SPRO t-code is the following

IMG →Sales and Distribution → Basic Functions → Output Determination → Maintain Output Determination for Sales Document → Assign Output Type to Partner Function

T-code for customization: NACE

Screenshot:

Out.	Med	Funct	Name	Name
RD03	1	SP	Cash Sale	Sold-to Party
RD03	1	BP	Cash Sale	Bill-to Party

Above screen shot defines the kind of medium is utilized for the partner function.

Output Determination Procedure:

Output determination procedure contains all the condition types for the output process. With the output procedure, it is identified with application and usage.

Customization Path from SPRO t-code is the following:

IMG →Sales and Distribution → Basic Functions → Output Determination → Maintain Output Determination for Sales Document → Assign Output Type to Partner Function

T-code for customization: NACE

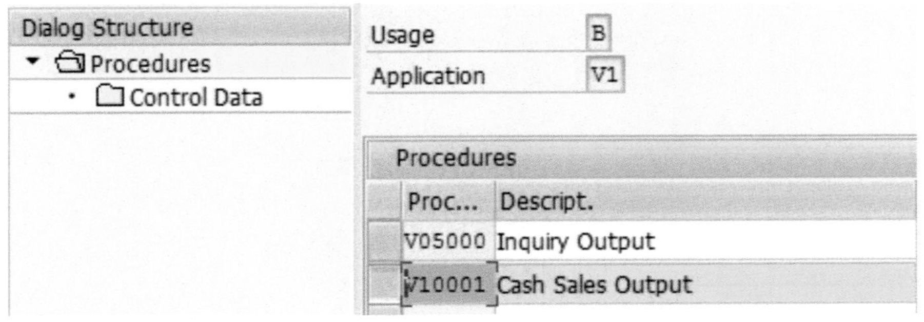

The above screenshot feature output procedure type “V10001” for cash ales output type.

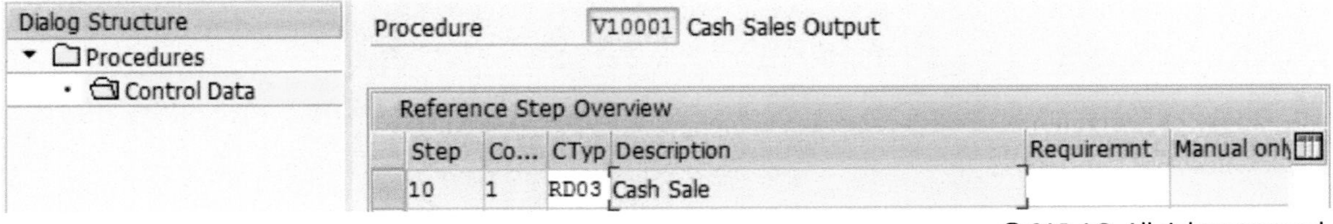

This screen represents the controls and condition types in the output procedure.

The step field represents the sequential procedure. **Setup** is the starting point for processing and **counter** is utilized for same control, which sequences the procedure process the condition type with the same step. The "requirement" is based on what kind of transaction this condition type supposed to utilize. Manual only controls the condition type is manual only in transection.

Output Determination Procedure Assignment:

Output procedure able to be assigned on order header and item level.

IMG →Sales and Distribution → Basic Functions → Output Determination → Maintain Output Determination for Sales Document → Assign Output Determination Procedure

T-code for customization: **NACE**

Screenshot:

SaTy	Description	Out.pr	Description	OutputT...	Name
BV	Cash Sale	V10001	Cash Sales Output	RD03	Cash Sale

Output type and procedure get assigned to the order type.

Item Level Output determination, assignment:

Item category	Description	Item output proc.	Description
TAN	Standard Item	V10001	Cash Sales Output

In the above screenshot the output determination procedure is assigned to the item category at the item level.

Text Determination

Text is utilized in the master data for the transactions and also customized at the transactional level. The text types are utilized in text determination to be determined for different order type and customer master account group. Document text determination is utilized in the header and item level. In text determination, we do not create a condition record.

The following steps are utilized for configuration:

- Define Text Type
- Define Access Sequence
- Define Text Determine Procedure

Define Text Type:

Text type is utilized in document type and master data. It defines what kind of text it is and assigned to the text procedure.

Customization Path from SPRO t-code is the following:

IMG →Sales and Distribution → Basic Functions → Text Control →Define Text Type

T-code for customization: VOTXN

Screenshot:

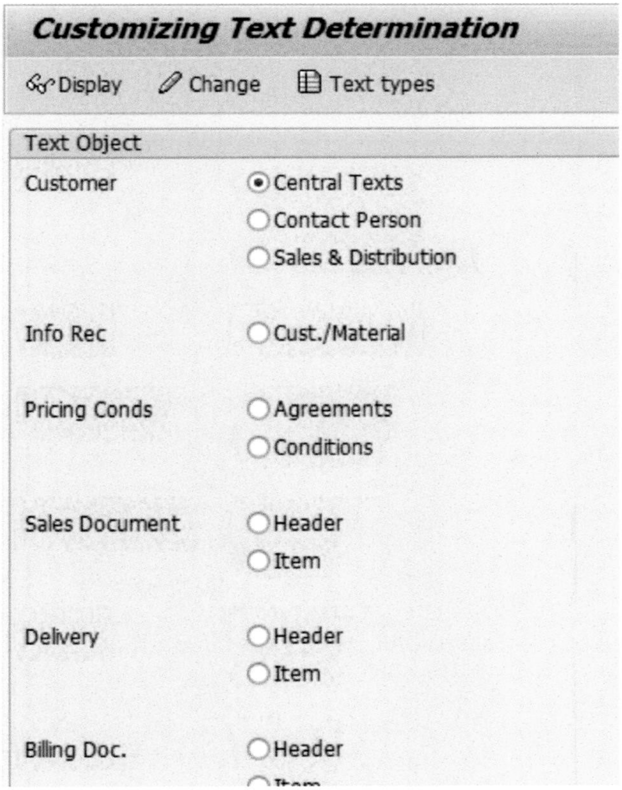

Customizing Text Determination

Display Change Text types

Text Object

Customer Central Texts
Contact Person
Sales & Distribution

Info Rec Cust./Material

Pricing Conds Agreements
Conditions

Sales Document Header
Item

Delivery Header
Item

Billing Doc. Header

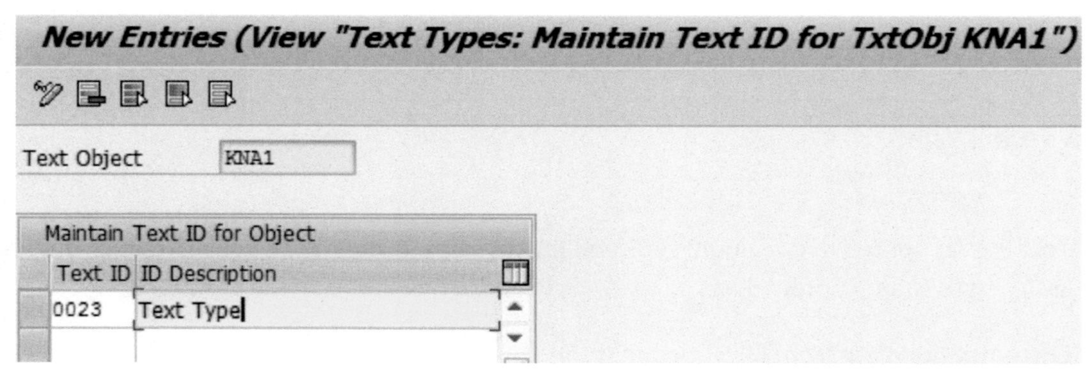

In the above screenshot customization defines the text ID type and it its description according to the text object.

Define Access Sequence

The access sequence contains the entries for an item and header level text types.

IMG →Sales and Distribution → Basic Functions → Text Control →Define Text Access Sequence

T-code for customization:

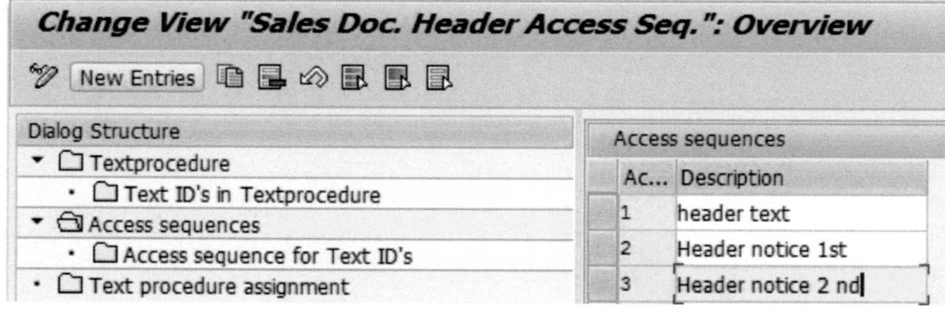

The text access sequence gets assigned to the Text ID type, with additional controls.

Text ID Controls are the following:

- Text object
- Text ID
- Partner Function
- Take a language from Sales Org
- Language

- Requirement Type
- Data Transfer Routine

Text is utilized in transections and master data. SAP Text object expected to be a master data relevant or a transactional relevant. Text ID is a text type. Partner function defines the partner function of ship to or sold to. The sales organization language took preference for the text. Language able to be selected to what language is relevant for the text type. Requirement Type is the program that calculates how the text should behave. Requirements are enhancement that the program able to developer by. Data transfer is the development object if the text needs to be utilized for selected a group of customer or objects.

Define Text Determine Procedure

Text Procedure contains the Text ID types and access sequence controls.

IMG →Sales and Distribution → Basic Functions → Text Control →Define and Assign text determination Procedure

T-code for customization:

Screenshot: **VOTXN**

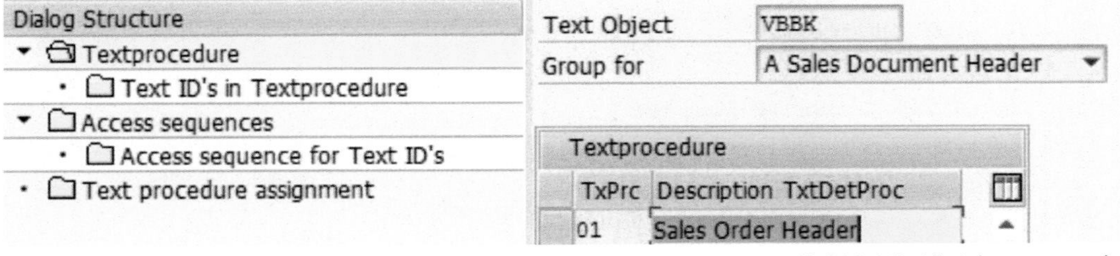

In the above screenshot first, we define a procedure with Text object type.

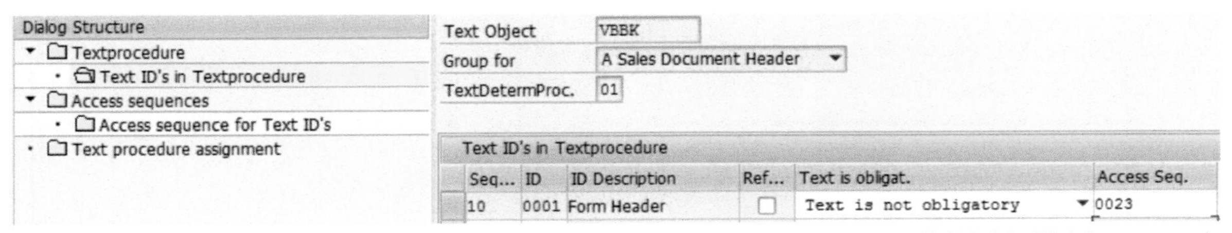

In the above screenshot we define procedure controls with Text ID in Text procedure. The reference field controls if text ID type need to be referenced. The Field "Text is Obligate"

controls text to be obligated or not obligate and if it require being display during copying. The access sequence is assigned to the procedure.

Listing / Exclusion

Listing and exclusion functionality define which customer able to buy selected product and which product they are not allowed to buy. It is a simple listing concept where material and customer are included. For this we need to group customers and materials and use listing and exclusion.

Listing and Exclusion Customization:

Listing and exclusion is based on the condition technique. The customization is maintained under a single place where defining table, access sequence, condition type, procedure, assigning listing and exclusion type to the document type are maintained.

Customization Path from SPRO t-code is the following:

IMG →Sales and Distribution → Basic Functions → Listing and Exclusion → Marinating
Condition Table:

The standard table fulfills most of the requirements.

Listing and Exclusion Access Sequence:

The table is utilized in access sequence, for the customization.

Customization Path from SPRO t-code is the following:

IMG →Sales and Distribution → Basic Functions → Listing and Exclusion → Marinating Access Sequence

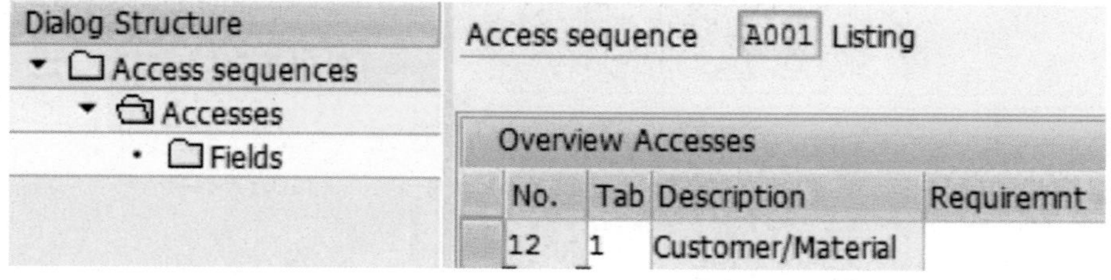

Listing and Exclusion Condition Type:

The condition type feature access sequence assigned to it and validity period.

IMG →Sales and Distribution → Basic Functions → Listing and Exclusion → Marinating Condition Table

CTyp	Name	AS	Description	Valid from	Valid to
A001	Listing CndTyp	A001	Listing		

Listing and Exclusion Procedure:

Procedure contains condition types with requirement types for additional requirements in the procedure.

Customization Path from SPRO is the following:

IMG →Sales and Distribution → Basic Functions → Listing and Exclusion → Marinating Procedure

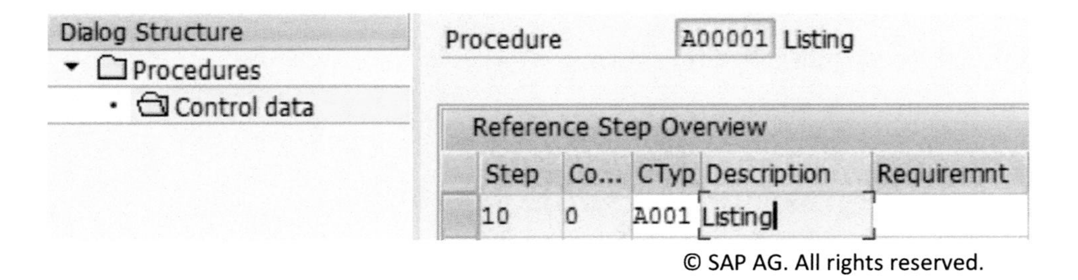

Step	Co...	CTyp	Description	Requiremnt
10	0	A001	Listing	

Listing and Exclusion Activate sales Document Type:

The listing and exclusion type is assigned to the sales document type. The order type assigned with the listing and exclusion procedure is to be determined for the order type.

Customization Path from SPRO t-code is the following:

IMG → Sales and Distribution → Basic Functions → Listing and Exclusion → Activate Listing/Exclusion by sales document Type

SaTy	Sales Doc. Type	Pro	Listing	Listing	Exclusion	Exclusion
IN	Inquiry		A00001	Listing	B00001	Exclusion
QT	Quotation					

Listing and Exclusion utilized for "list" and "exclude" products from sales

Chapter 9 Summary

In chapter 9 we cover the following topics:

- Output Determination
- Output determination condition technique
- Output Table customization
- Output Access Sequence customization
- Output condition Type customization
- Output partner function customization
- Output determination
- Output condition Record
- Text Determination
- Listing and Exclusion Customization

Notes

CHAPTER 10

ADVANCED SAP TIPS & TRICKS with Variant Configuration

Chapter Summary:

- SAP SD Determination
- SAP EDI
- User Exit
- BADI
- Rebate Process
- LSMW
- Sales cross matching
- BAPI
- Condition Technique
- Third party drop ship
- Variant Configuration
- SQVI reports
- ABAP Debugging
- Variant Configuration
- Table view Old and New
- Mass updates

Objectives:

- Learn Variant Configuration Material setup
- Learn SAP SD Determinations cheat sheet
- Learn about SAP EDI.
- Learn how to Mass updates in SAP SD
- Learn about SAP user exit
- Learn about SAP BADI
- Learn SAP SD Rebate process
- Learn about SAP LSMW
- Learn about BAPI
- Learn about Third-party drop ship process
- Learn about SAP Report variants
- Learn how to ABAP debug
- Learn how to create SQVI Report
- Learn how to use SAP parameters for auto population in transection
- Learn SAP Enhancement point for routines VOFM
- Learn how to setup Auto startup transection for GUI

SAP Sales and Distribution Determinations:

The following are major determinations of sales and distribution module determinations.

#	Type	Determination	Comment
1	**Plant Determination**	Customer Material Info Record if exist then Customer Master Record if exist then Material Master Record	System look for first available record
2	**Item Category Determination**	Sales Order Type + Item Category Group + Higher Level Item Category + Usage	item category group come from material master
3	**Schedule line Category Determination**	Item Category + MRP (Materials requirements planning type on the material master record of the item)	
4	**Route Determination**	Departure Zone of Delivering Plant + Shipping Condition of the Sold - to party + Transportation Group + Transportation Zone of the Ship - to party	
5	**Shipping Point Determination**	Shipping Condition of the Sold - to party + Loading Group + Delivering Plant	Loading group come from material Master
6	**Pricing Procedure Determination**	Sales Area + Sales Document Pricing Procedure + Customer Master Record	
7	**Partner Determination**	Sales Document Header/item Customer Master + Delivery Billing Header/ Item	
8	**G/L Account Determination**	Charts of Accounts + Sales Organization + Account assignment group of Payer + Account assignment group for Material + Account Key.	
9	**Warehouse**	Plant + Storage location	
10	**Billing Plan Types Determination**	Sales Document Type + Item Category	
11	**Material Determination**	Sales Document type + Procedure + (condition types + access sequence + condition tables + fields)	
12	**Text Determination Procedure**	Sales Area + Sales Document + Customer Master Record	
13	**Batch Determination**	Material master record	

14	**Staging Area**	Warehouse Number	
15	**Business Area**	Plant + Item Division / Sales Area / Sales Org. + Distribution Channel + Item Division	
16	**Tax Determination**	Taxes according to the Country of the Delivering plant + The Country of the Customer receiving goods + Tax indicator of the Customer master record + Tax indicator of the Material master record	

SAP EDI

SAP EDI stands for electronic data interface. EDI is utilized between two systems to transfer the electronic document for business and information exchange. EDI is standardized by the National Institute of Standards and Technology for organizations. EDI is one of the means for SAP system to another system via EDI because both SAP and non-SAP able to speak EDI language so that the data able to be transmitted. When the SAP system talks to the non-SAP system, middleware severs will enable the SAP system and the non-SAP system will communicate regarding the documents.

IDOC

IDOC stands for intermediate document. IDOC is a SAP framework for interface and transmits data from the EDI interface. IDOC contains data through EDI and the middle ware use of data packet between systems.

To monitor IDOCS T-code: **WE02**
Test IDOC: **WE19**

How to Monitor IDOCS?

To Monitor IDOC for errors and success, the following is a screen shot from WE02. IDOCs able to be monitored ranged from "Create at" time range. Additional filters able to be utilized to pinpoint the IDOC or periodic monitoring.

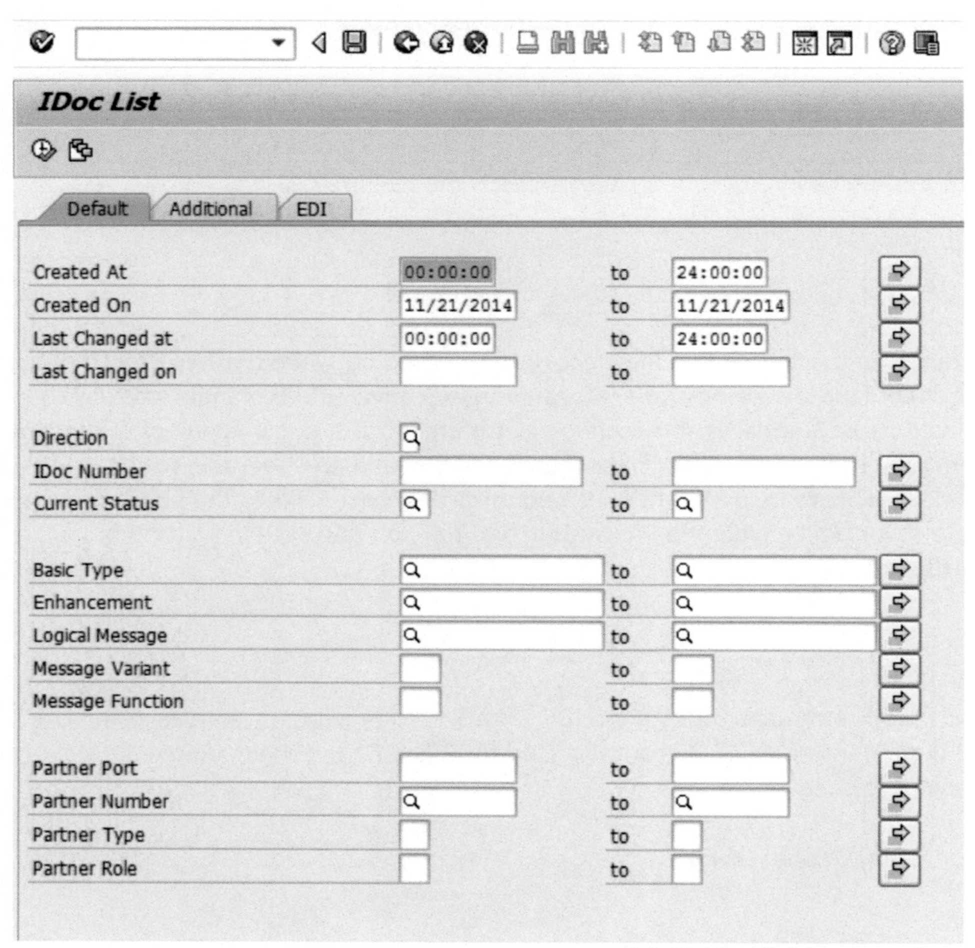
IDoc List
Default
Additional
EDI
Created At
00:00:00
to
24:00:00
Created On
11/21/2014
to
11/21/2014
Last Changed at
00:00:00
to
24:00:00
Last Changed on
to
Direction
IDoc Number
to
Current Status
to
Basic Type
to
Enhancement
to
Logical Message
to
Message Variant
to
Message Function
to
Partner Port
to
Partner Number
to
Partner Type
to
Partner Role
to

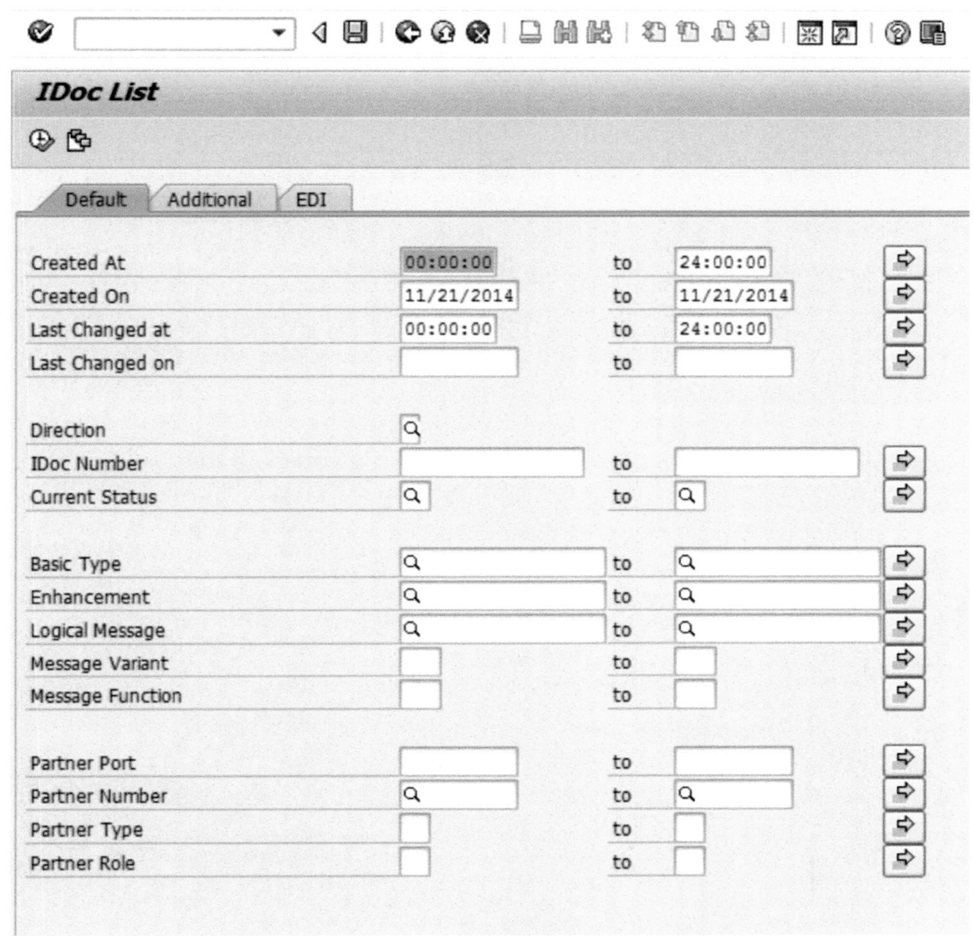

User Exit:

SAP is built by ABAP programs, which designed and allowed for change called user exit. The user exit is a safe place to be enhanced because it affect original functions. These areas are made from modifiable codes. The complexity of each business requires their own way of modifying this area this may be different from SAP standard and editions.

User exit is a SAP enhancement area where programs able to be edited and SAP able to be molded by the requirement. Each module feature their user exits.

BADI:

BADI is a SAP related enhancement that functions at the application layer. BADI is a SAP original object that able to be enhanced without touching the original object.

For example, the user able to find a BADI and use it to enhance it, while the original transaction will not be enhanced, only the BADI will be enhanced. BADI stands for Business add in. BADI is able to change similar object oriented in the programing concept. BADI is utilized with in the bundle of business add-ins, business add-in class and screen enhancements. BADI able to use multiple times without touching original object.

BADI is only utilized for the application layer changes. On the creation on BADI the two classes get auto created, while one is for interfacing and the other is for the trigger of BADI.

To create BADI use t-code SE18

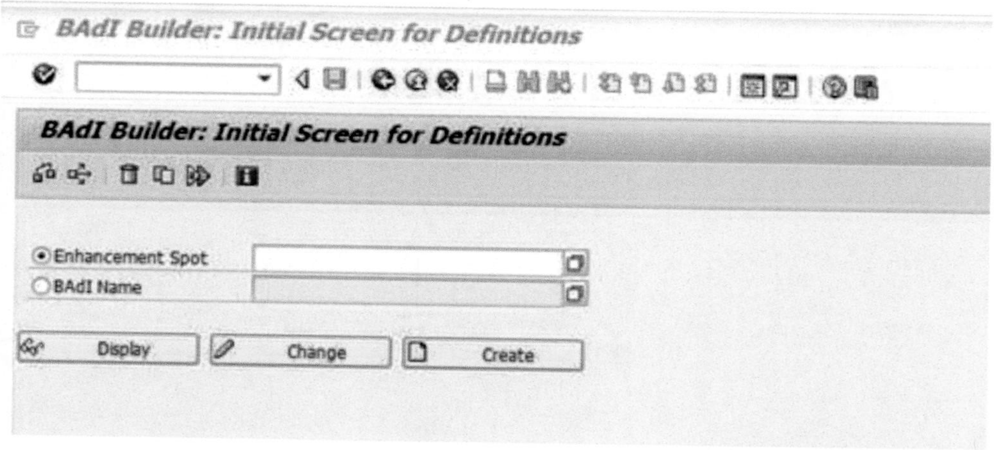

BAdI Builder: Initial Screen for Definitions

BAdI Builder: Initial Screen for Definitions

Enhancement Spot

BAdI Name

Display Change Create

To enhance BADI the user must have the developer access it.

SE19 is utilized for the enhancement implementation.

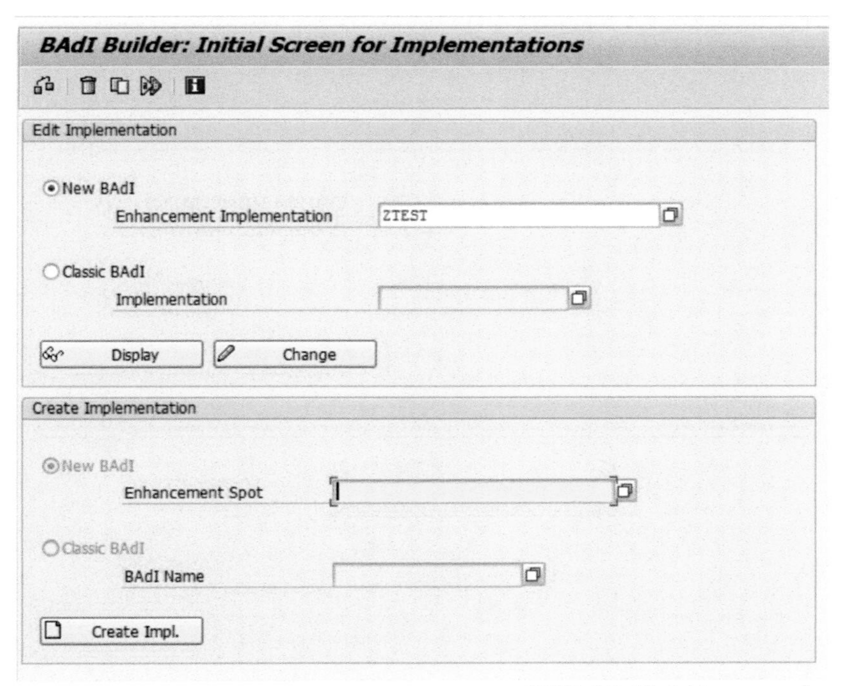

The four sections in this function

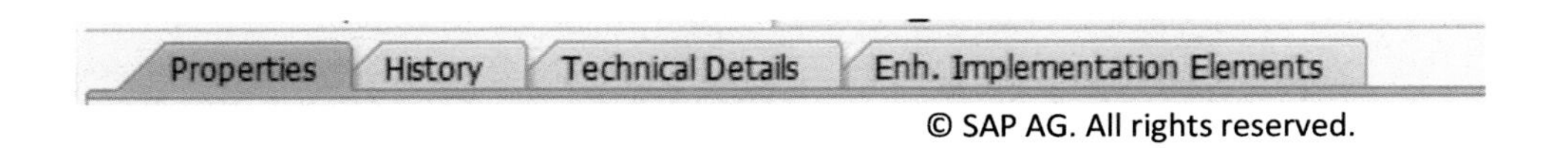

Properties
History
Technical
Enchantment Implementation Element

It is more technical in nature, it is technical ABAPER Responsibility.

How to Get BADI?

To search BADI in the transaction, the user needs to set a debugging in class and the transaction program will stop at BADI.

The steps are:

SE24 and enter Object Type:

Double click on Get Instance

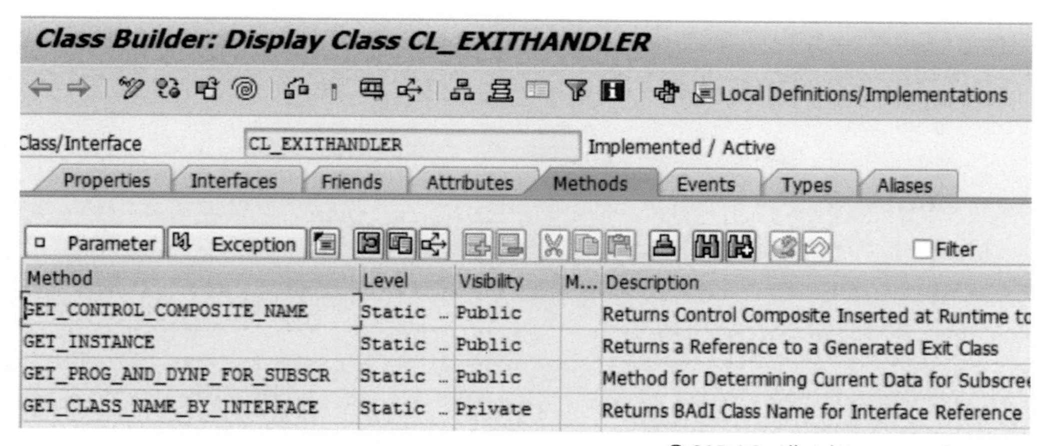

Online no 14 or go to the line which feature this value
“CALL METHOD cl_exithandler=>get_class_name_by_interface”

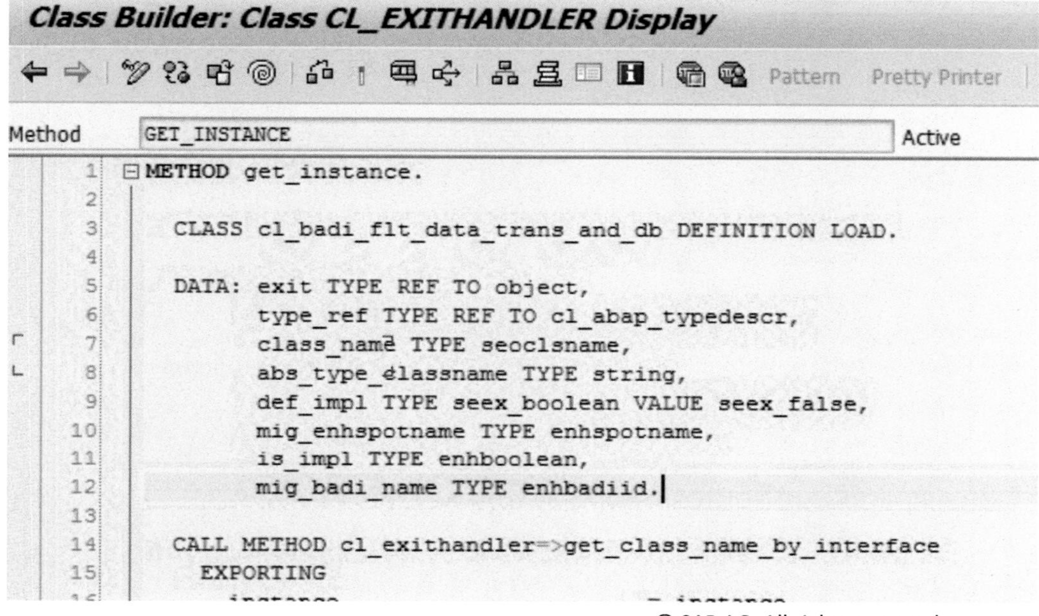

Then select this line and click on Set/delete session break point or press (Ctrl + Shift + F12)

it should look like this after the breakpoint is set.

```
12         mig_badi_name TYPE enhbadiid.
13
14   CALL METHOD cl_exithandler=>get_class_name_by_interface
15     EXPORTING
```


After this, set in the same session or the new session then run your transaction to capture BADI

For this example, sales order transaction is utilized: VA01

The ABAP debugger will pop up and in the standard tab and under the local tab on it the EXI name is BADI_SD_SALES is the name of the BADI.

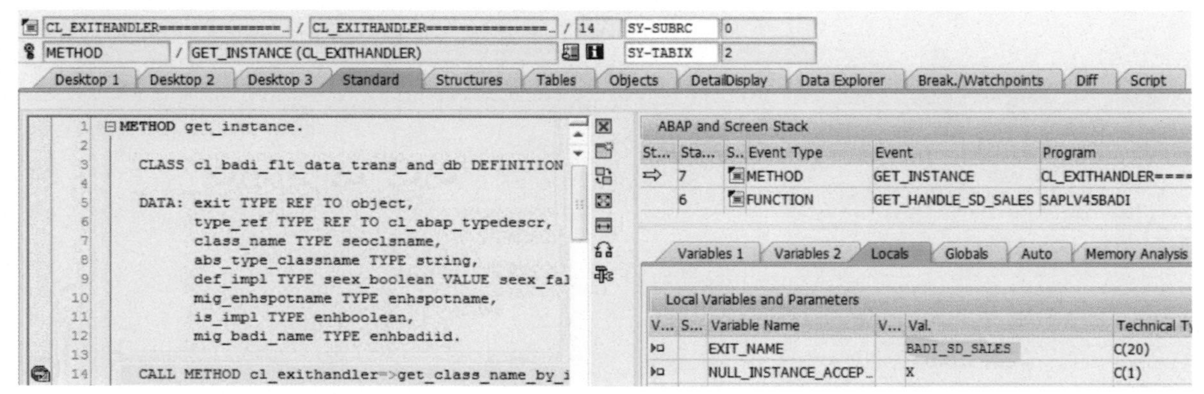

SAP SD Rebate Process and configuration

The rebate process is similar to a discount. In the rebate when a customer buys the product they are offering a discount on a quantity and volume based on date range. The rebate discount is not given to the customer immediately, but the discount is given to customer after a period of time based on the accumulation or periodic basis. The rebate process involves additional conditions and controls that able to be utilized in a rebate customization. SAP sales and distribution rebate process is based on the rebate agreement. The rebate agreement becomes the basis of accruals on the conditions on the sales process. After the accruals are calculated, credit able to be issued to the customer. The rebate able to be based on customer, material, customer hierarchy, sales volume, and groups. The rebate basis able to be changed.

The repeat process able to set for customers of products with a time frame. When the condition of term is met then the payment will be issued to the customer. In SAP the first rebate agreement is setup based on different criteria and condition master is creating with the time period. Here is a screenshot of how the rebate agreement looks.
T-code VB01 to create rebate agreement

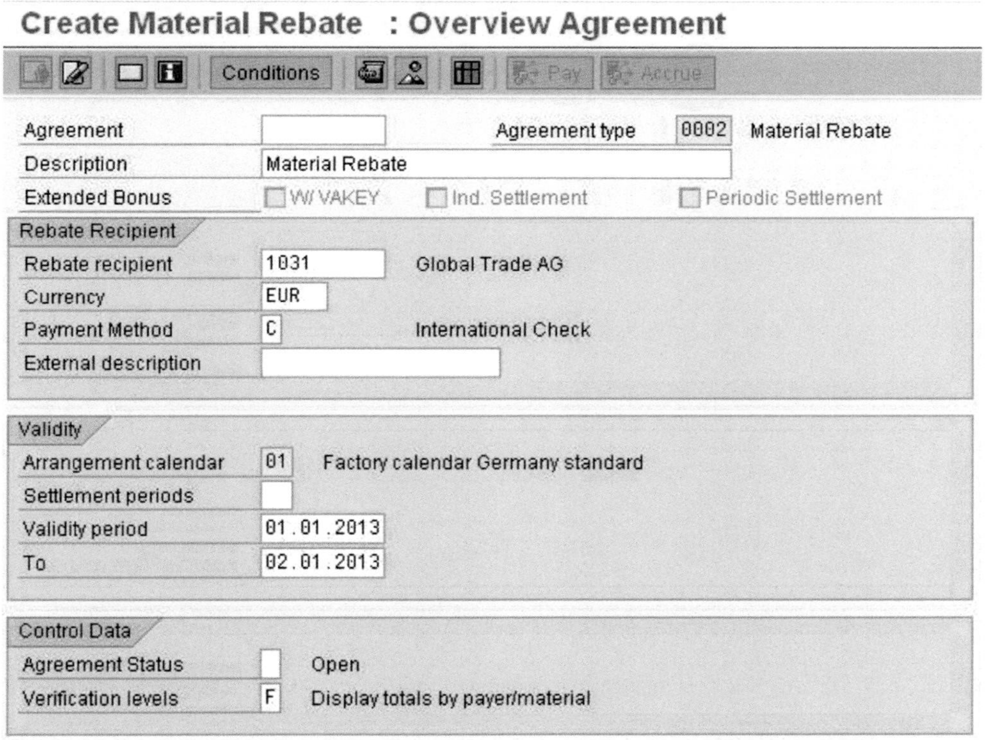

Create Material Rebate : Overview Agreement

Conditions | Pay | Accrue

Agreement		Agreement type	0002 Material Rebate
Description	Material Rebate		
Extended Bonus	W/ VAKEY	Ind. Settlement	Periodic Settlement

Rebate Recipient

Rebate recipient	1031	Global Trade AG
Currency	EUR	
Payment Method	C	International Check
External description		

Validity

Arrangement calendar	01	Factory calendar Germany standard
Settlement periods		
Validity period	01.01.2013	
To	02.01.2013	

Control Data

Agreement Status		Open
Verification levels	F	Display totals by payer/material

T-Code	Description
VB(1	Rebate number ranges
VB(2	Rebate Agreement Type Maintenance
VB(3	Condition Type Groups Overview
VB(4	Condition Types in Condition Type Groups
VB(5	Assignment Condition -> Condition Type Group
VB(6	Rebate Group Maintenance
VB(7	Rebate Agreement Settlement
VB(8	List Rebate Agreements
VB(9	Maintain Sales Deal Types
VB(A	Promotion Type Maintenance
VB(B	Copying Control Maintenance
VB(C	Maintain Copying Control
VB(D	Rebate Agreement Settlement

LSMW:

LSMW stands for Legacy System Migration Workbench; it is a data migration tool that comes with SAP 5.0 and 6.0. LSMW transfer data is from Legacy system to SAP. It actually takes data from a file and then migrates it into SAP. It is utilized for transferring to Master Data and Transnational data before cutover activities. We able to use this tool for each object with the required fields and additional fields. The most common effective ways is to transfer the data into flat files and load into LSMW. In LSMW data able to be transferred using existing BAPI, BDC and recording. Flat files are mapped to the BDC (Recording), Program, IDOC, and BAPI and loaded into the SAP.

T-code: LSMW

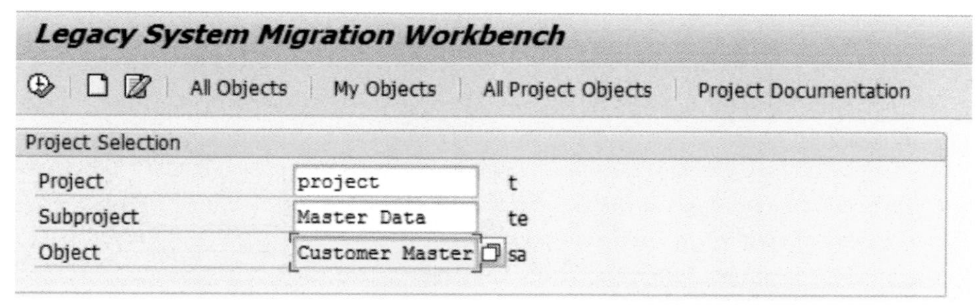

Master and Transactional Data Migration to SAP (add in data migration)

In the SAP project implementation, data migration is a critical part of the project. Master Data is the basis of transactional data. After the data extraction from the legacy system the data supposed to be ready for the next steps. The diagram below is an example of the data migration process.

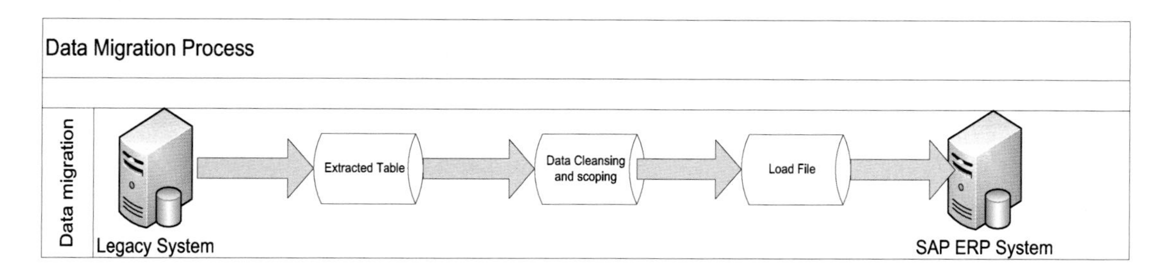

The above diagram shows the data migration that uses many tools and process of the steps for data migration. After processing the steps of data extraction, data transformation, and load file preparation, mapping the load file is utilized for final data population. The extracted data expected to be based many tables. If the data is spread across many tables and feature multiple records, then it require very careful mapping for comprehensive mapping of valid master data.

Cross matching for Duplicates

Cross matching report identifies the duplicate sales order. The duplication of order expected to be based on many reasons but with this the duplicated order able to be caught and fixed.

Benefits:

The crosshatch transaction able to help avoid error and data duplication. If the sales order is created due to many reasons the order able to be identified in this report. The transaction able to be ran by the end user, which is the customer service representative or the manager. They able to monitor it if any duplicated sales orders are generated and they able to avoid duplication.

Transaction code is: **VC15**

Screenshot of **VC15**

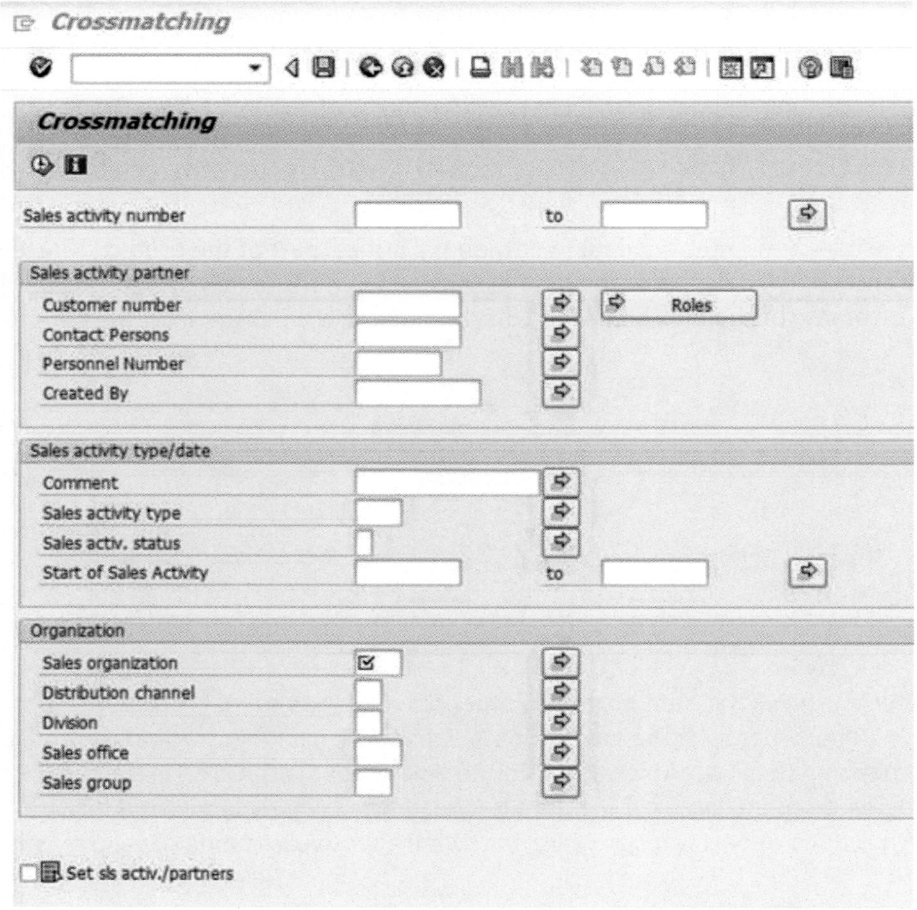

Crossmatching

Crossmatching

Sales activity number to

Sales activity partner

Customer number Roles

Contact Persons

Personnel Number

Created By

Sales activity type/date

Comment

Sales activity type

Sales activ. status

Start of Sales Activity to

Organization

Sales organization

Distribution channel

Division

Sales office

Sales group

Set sls activ./partners

Sales organization filed is a required field for the Crosshatching report.

Multiple options are available to search the cross match to monitor. The search able to be based on the customer number, sales activity or searched by "Created By" user if user wants to validation.

Matrix Copy:

In SAP copy control requires an additional shortcut to copy, paste. This copy paste function is in SAP, it is called Matrix Copy.

CTRL + Y Select
CTRL + C
CTRL + V

Reports:

Reports in all modules able to be viewed by T-code **SAP1**
Tip: it should be utilized from the easy Access Menu

T-codes for Reports:

Description	T-code
Sales Order Report	VA05
Inquiry Report	VA15
Quotation Report	VA25
Scheduling Agreement Report	VA45
Contract Report	VA45
Customer Sales Summary	VC/2
Price Report	V/LD
Incomplete Order	V.02
Billing Report	VF05
Rebate Report	VB(B

All the T-code in Tables:
To view all the t-codes table use table **TSTCT**

Looking Up T-codes

To find t-codes use the table TSTCT.
The easy trick is to use language: EN
if you are looking for a sales related t-code, then use a text field to search for the description.

Controls	Description	Example
*	Use asterisk before the word and it will only search word starting from "*".	*sales
*	Use asterisk it in the beginning and end: then it will look in all the text and display at-code no matter where the sales values is utilized, beginning, middle or end.	*sales*

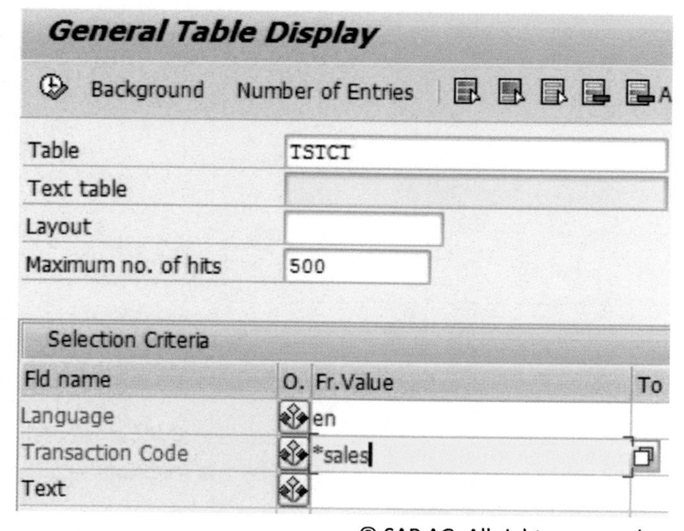

Mass Update:

The following are T-codes utilized for a mass update.

Description	T-code
Customer master mass update	XD99
Martial master Mass updates	MM17
Mass Update (many objects)	**MASS**

Mass update Example:

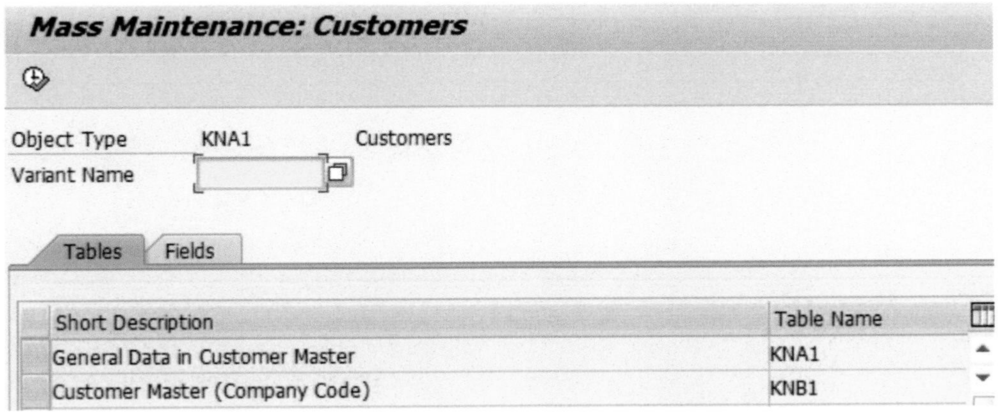

The customer master mass update is based on the tables and field level of the customer master. First the table is selected then the field is selected. The customer range is then being selected for the mass update and the field values able to be updated at once.

To view the table:

To view tables in SAP, the following t-codes are following:

Description	T-code
Table View (Old)	SE16
Table View New	SE16N
ABAP Dictionary	SE11
Run Query	SQVI

Maintaining Pricing:

Pricing tips and tricks for end user

Pricing able to be maintained with a single T-code: VK32

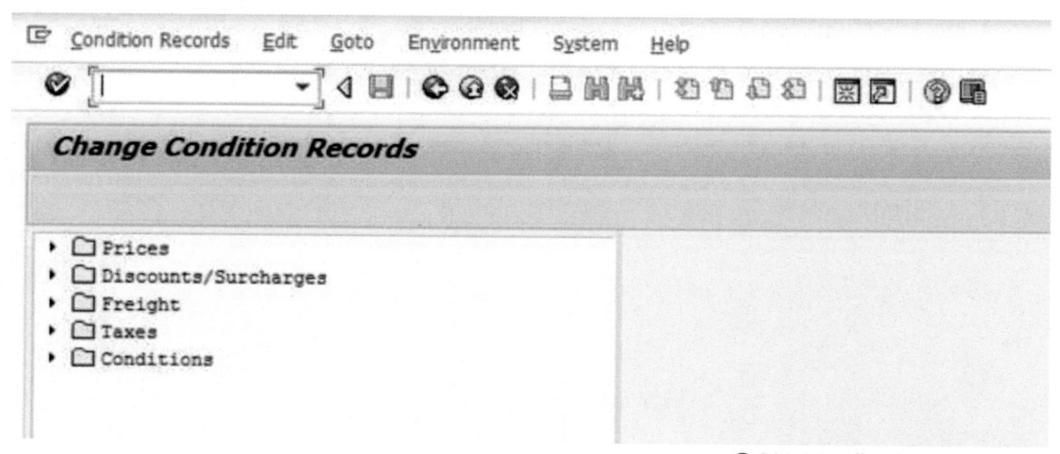

There are different types of condition types that will be grouped under the respective folder.

Click on the triangle (on the left side of folder icon) and it will drop down the list of condition types under the teach folder. The user able to double click on each one of them to add additional condition records.

Pricing also able to be maintained by the following T-code:

VK11
VK12
VK13

Create Pricing Record:

VK11 is utilized for pricing condition record from conditioning type. When the condition record is created the respective option on the condition type is setup and will prompt for the pricing record. The VK11 user able to define the scale pricing and condition supplement.

Change Pricing Record:

To change the pricing condition, record the t-code VK12 is utilized. It only able to be utilized if the pricing condition record exists. With pricing condition record change the record able to be marked for delete. .

To view pricing:

To view the pricing condition record, VK13 is utilized for displaying. With the selected combination multiple records able to be displayed in this transaction.

To view pricing report:

This able to be viewed from VK32 and also able to be displayed from the T-code "V/LD" pricing report.

SAP official training "Open SAP" and SAP training

Free SAP Training is provided by "Hasso Plattner Institute" with the collaboration of SAP. The training is provided to individuals and students who would like to gain knowledge of SAP.

To gain SAP official training the user must goes to https://open.sap.com/ and register for current free courses. The courses have opening times and have opening enrolling period. After the enrollment, the student will receive an ID and password to start the multimedia course. Their interactive forum for students is to contribute toward the class and ask questions on the topic. The courses are based on video lectures, presentations and it is modular base. At the end of each modular training section it will have a quiz. By the end of course there is a final quiz, this is similar to the training quizzes. The successful candidate will be granted a certificate online.

SAP also offers a promotional, training official website https://training.sap.com/de/en/. It is called a SAP Learning Hub edition. To registers for the course please use this code "HUB001". Users able to sign up for a free course under the code of HUB001. It is a combination of multiple courses for individuals to learn from. Log in and start learning SAP training today; it feature many areas that cover SAP for new students. It also helps those who are SAP end users or consultants who wish to gain more knowledge. Please go the website for more details. Generally, it feature basic courses for free, however advance level courses are not free. The course content is also limited to the SAP learning Hub edition.

How to register for the SAP Learning Hub edition?

If you are interested in this program, the user requires an S-ID.

What is S-ID?

S-ID is utilized for the training of a prospective student. It is utilized to keep track of the student's t activities. S-ID is a unique ID that is associated with user and need to be requested from SAP training website. First register and then request for SAP training ID. It has a limited time service that might change based on the offer of SAP training services. There is one more website that able to offer free courses, open.sap.com

BAPI:

BAPI is also called a functional module that is utilized for interfaces and programs. BAPI stands for Business Application Programing Interface. BAPI is also called functional module, the BAPI transactions able to be viewed with Transaction Code BAPI. BAPI able to be called remotely with interface; they able to be synchronous or as asynchronous. BAPI is utilized for interfacing between SAP components to communicate in-between. It able to also utilize with third party system to communicate with the SAP system to process the transaction. To view SAP available BAPI's, use the T-code able to be utilized BAPI.

The following are screenshot of transaction: BAPI

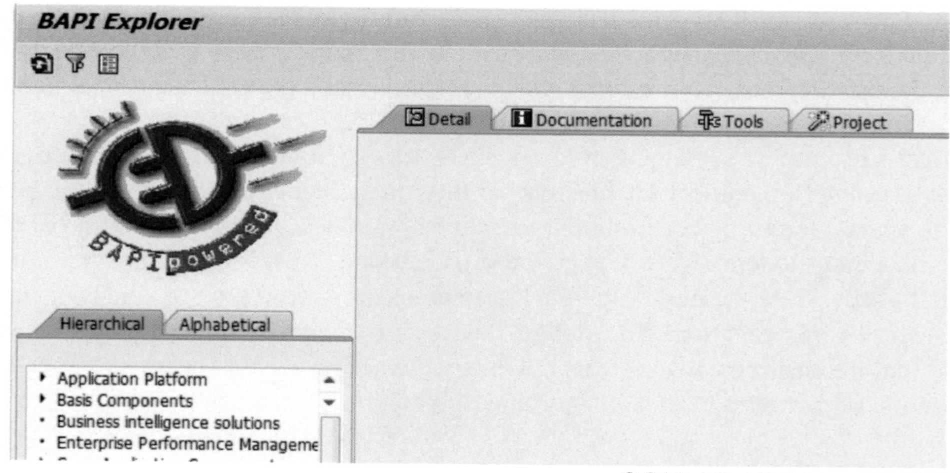

BAPI able to be tested with transaction Code: SE37

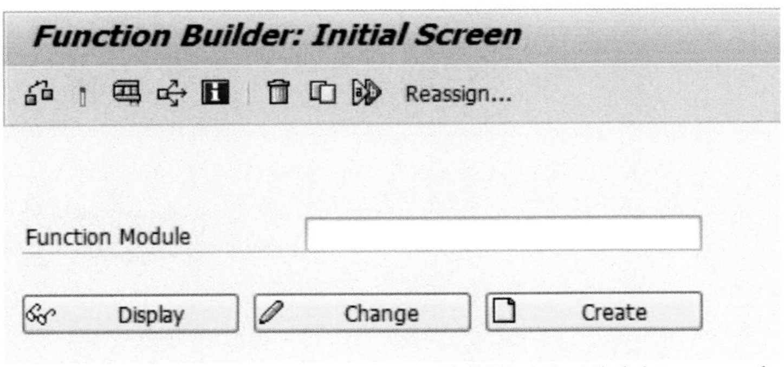

The above screenshot represent the functional module view.

Condition Technique utilized at following configuration:

- Material Determination
- Pricing (Sales Order, Invoice)
- Text Determination
- Output determination
- Partner determination
- Batch determination
- Free Good
- Rebates
- Revenue account determination
- Listing / exclusion

Third party drop ship

The third party drop ship is based on the standard SAP Sales and Distribution functionality.

Business Process:

When a business behave to keep a stock of items and feature their vendor directly ship their item to the customer, it considered drop ship. By drop ship the company's saves on logistics and make their vendor ship directly to their customer.

Process in Sales and Distribution:

In Sales and Distributions the drop ship requires a minimal customization. This process involves sales and procurement cycles. From the sales side, it involves sales order, billing and from procurement side. It involves purchasing requisition, purchase order, good receipt, and vendor invoice. This process involves order to cash cycle and procurement to pay cycle.

The following is how it works.

1. Sales order creations
2. Purchase requisition
3. Purchase order
4. Good receipt (Statistical)
5. Vendor Invoice
6. Customer Invoice

Sales Order for Third Party Order:

Sales order flow

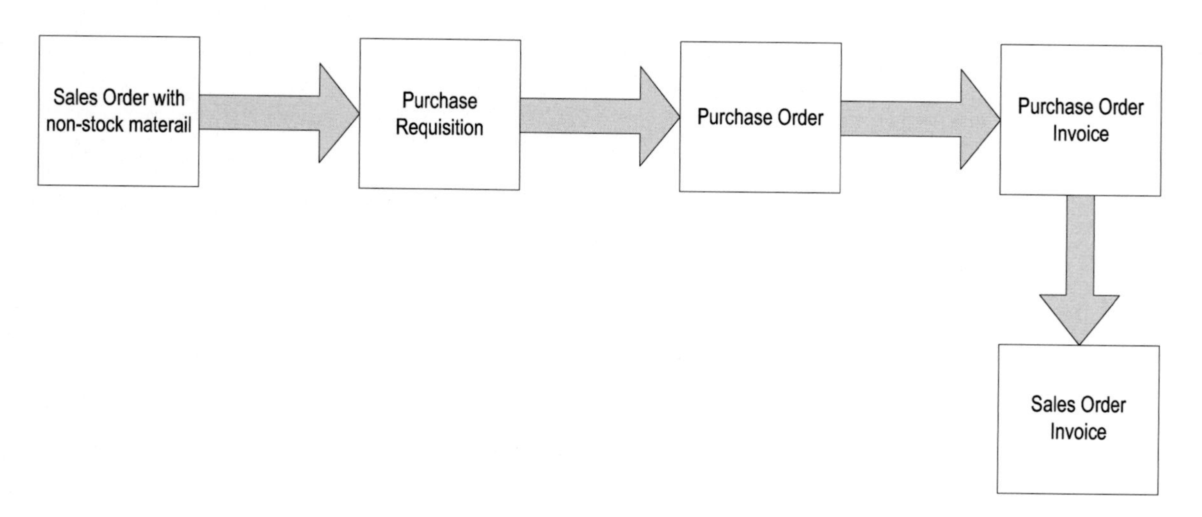

That is a simple third-party process where sales invoices are based on sales order related. The third-party sales order feature item category "TAS". The item category determine, based on item category group "BARN" from material master. The schedule line feature purchase requisition type assigned to it to create purchase requisition. The purchase requisition copies it into a purchase order and then based on the material management, procurement related controls. If statically it's a good receipt, then it is required before the vendor invoice or the vendor invoice cannot be created without good receipt. After vendor invoice the sales invoice able to be created.

Variant:

Variant is a shortcut values in SAP transactions. It is utilized if the value needs to be auto populated in transactions, reports and master data processing. The variant icon able to be identified with the folder.

Variant able to be global or local. The global variant able to be seen and utilized by all the users with the same client. The user variant only able to be viewed by the user who created it.

SQVI:

SQVI is a table joins view t-code. SQVI tool is utilized for the database table to connect and create a report. It able to create reports from two or more tables together. With this tool reports it able to be generated with detail customization. SQVI expected to utilize with caution because a bad setup of this T-code able to affect the entire system performance and hang the database. It is for supper users.

Screenshot:

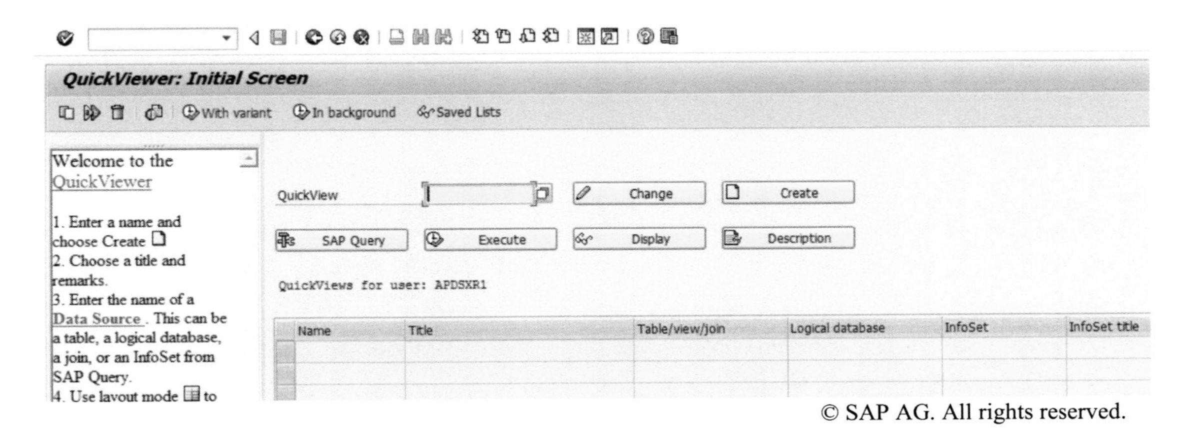

SQVI query expected to be based on a single table or expected to be based on the join of tables, logical database or SAP query infoset. The table and join table supposed to sufficient for most of the requirements. The layout of the tables able to be select "basic mode" or Layout mode. The layout able to be changed even after the tables are selected with filter and selection criteria.

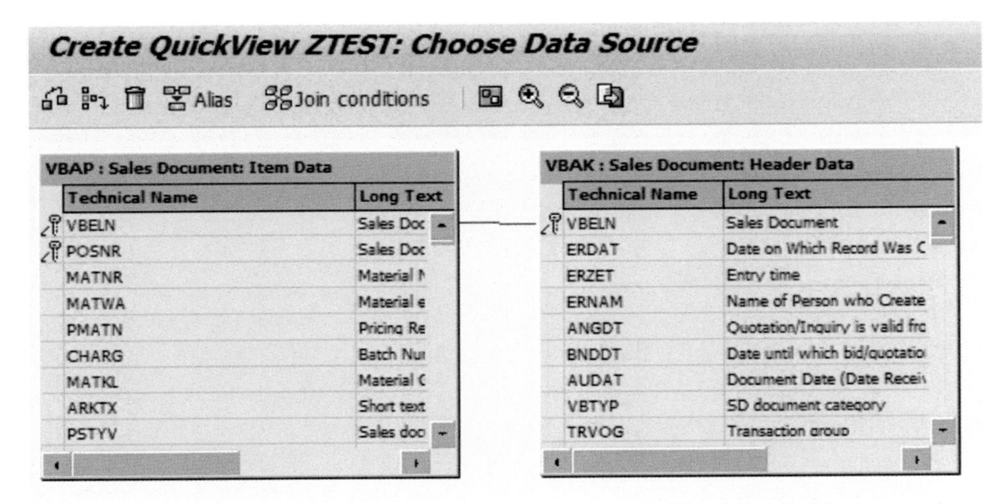

The above screenshot is an example of join tables. The join of tables should base on key fields or correct join fields; otherwise the table entry will not work.

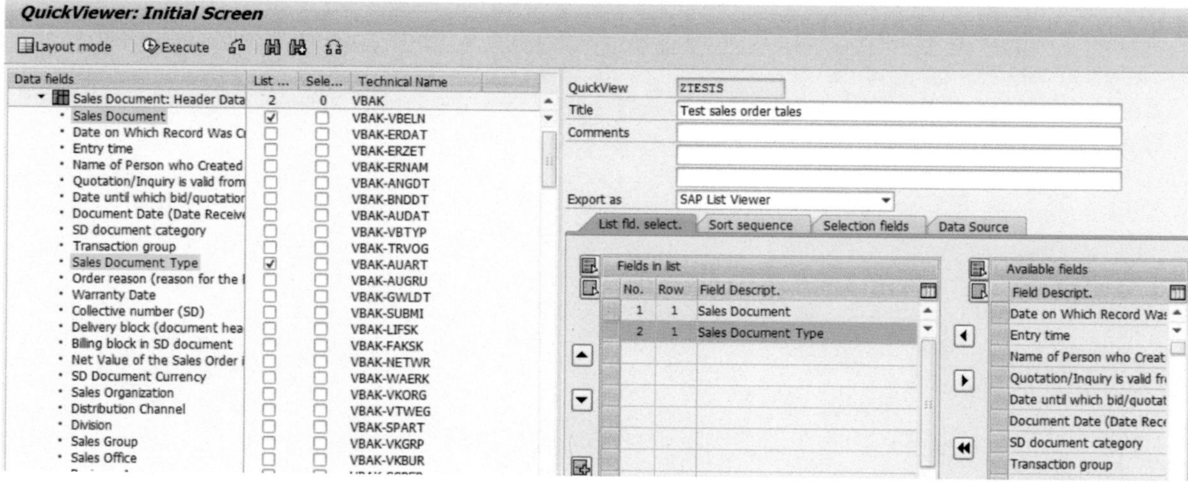

The above screen represents how the report able to be selected. The left side of the screen fields able to be selected and on the right side of screen fields able to be selected and in addition to that the report able to then be executed.

Edit Table Entry:

Table entry should not be updated because it is not recommended by SAP, unless the table is a custom table, and it able to also cause an error in the database.

The table able to be edited a few different ways:

- EDIT table from Table View (SE16n)
- Edit Table with ABAP
- Edit Table with SM30
- Maintain Table with SE11

Edit Table with Table View (SE16N):

The table view tool is utilized for the table display and table data. This transaction does not allow data to be edited in it, so it is only a display. Data able to be edited from this transaction, but it is not recommended.

Follow the following steps:

1. Go to Table view by entering T-code: SE16N
2. Enter another t-code in the Table view “sap_edit”

3. Execute the table.

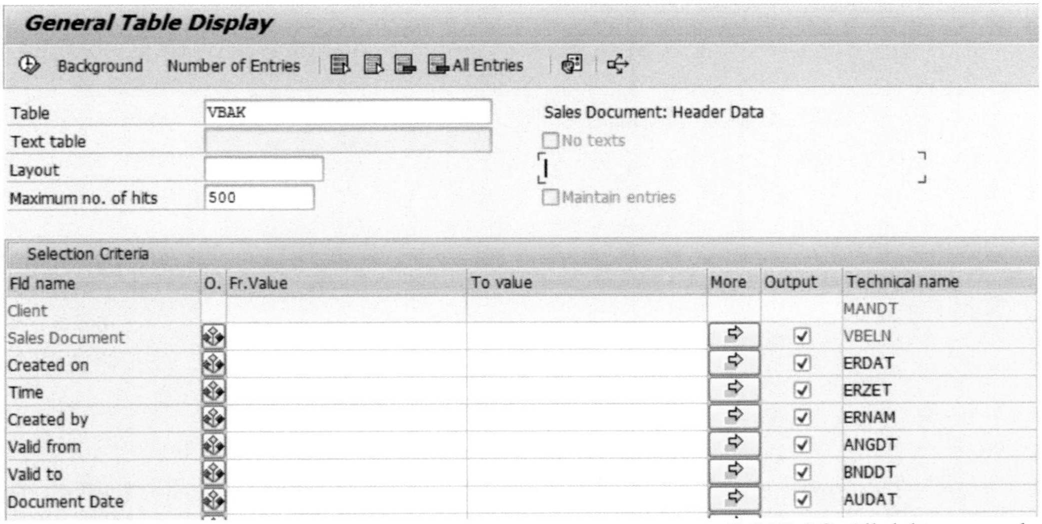

General Table Display

Background Number of Entries All Entries

Table	VBAK	Sales Document: Header Data
Text table		No texts
Layout		
Maximum no. of hits	500	Maintain entries

Selection Criteria

Fld name	O.	Fr.Value	To value	More	Output	Technical name
Client						MANDT
Sales Document					✓	VBELN
Created on					✓	ERDAT
Time					✓	ERZET
Created by					✓	ERNAM
Valid from					✓	ANGDT
Valid to					✓	BNDDT
Document Date					✓	AUDAT

With the “More” button additional values able to be searched at once.

SM30 Table Maintenance:

The transaction code is utilized for table maintenance. With this table customization table and standard tables, it able to be edited and entries able to be added into it.

ABAP and SE11:

ABAP programmer uses SE11. It also maintains the tables that are possible, and it is more technical compare to functional.

Debugging ABAP program:

Debugging the program is utilized for fixing issues and identifying problems. It able to identify what is getting processed by ABAP program. Debugging requires ABAP knowledge to understand ABAP programing.

Debugging:

To start debugging use the T-code“/h” it will turn on the debugger and as soon as the transaction or program is started, the system will open a new screen where the debugging able to be analyzed.

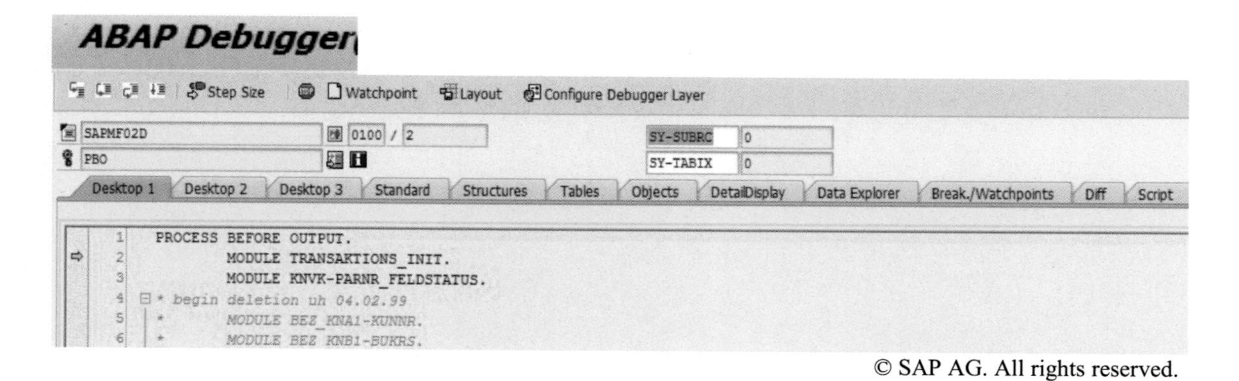

The program sustain lines with numeric values whereas the ABAP debugger able to be utilized for line by line code runs or also process all the line and able to stop on a certain line value that able to be viewed.

Tip: To understand the ABAP select on Syntax and click on F1. It will show description and maybe an example of the code.

Variant Configuration:

Variant Configuration is a SAP term, which refers to options in sales order processing with selections. This function is mostly utilized in the automotive industry. Variant configuration is a single material that is entered in the sales order and the new screen will pop up which is where the user able to configure or select options. It also is considered, as a made to order because the selections are unique with a combination of vagrants in the sales process. For example, if we use a car sell options, the customers able to request five CD players instead of a single CD player. There expected to be many other options available to choose from. The benefit of this option is that the material master data maintenances would be only one material with many options or variants. If the variant configuration is not utilized then there would be different materials for each different option, including the combinations which able to cause a data overload and confusions. A variant configuration also reflects its variants in bill of material and pricing. In this book variant configuration setup is based on the very basic. Variant configuration involves the following modules.

Variant Configuration Sales and Distribution:

Variant configurations are related function that would be pricing related configuration that setup for the material. Variant level pricing feature different option. This functionality is dependent and requires to be written, and pricing characteristic is also requiring to be attached to the main class.

Material Master:

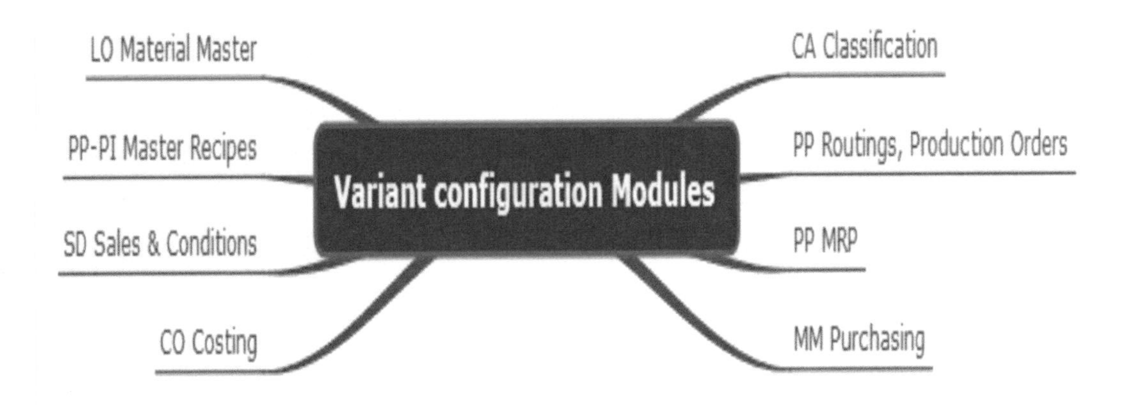

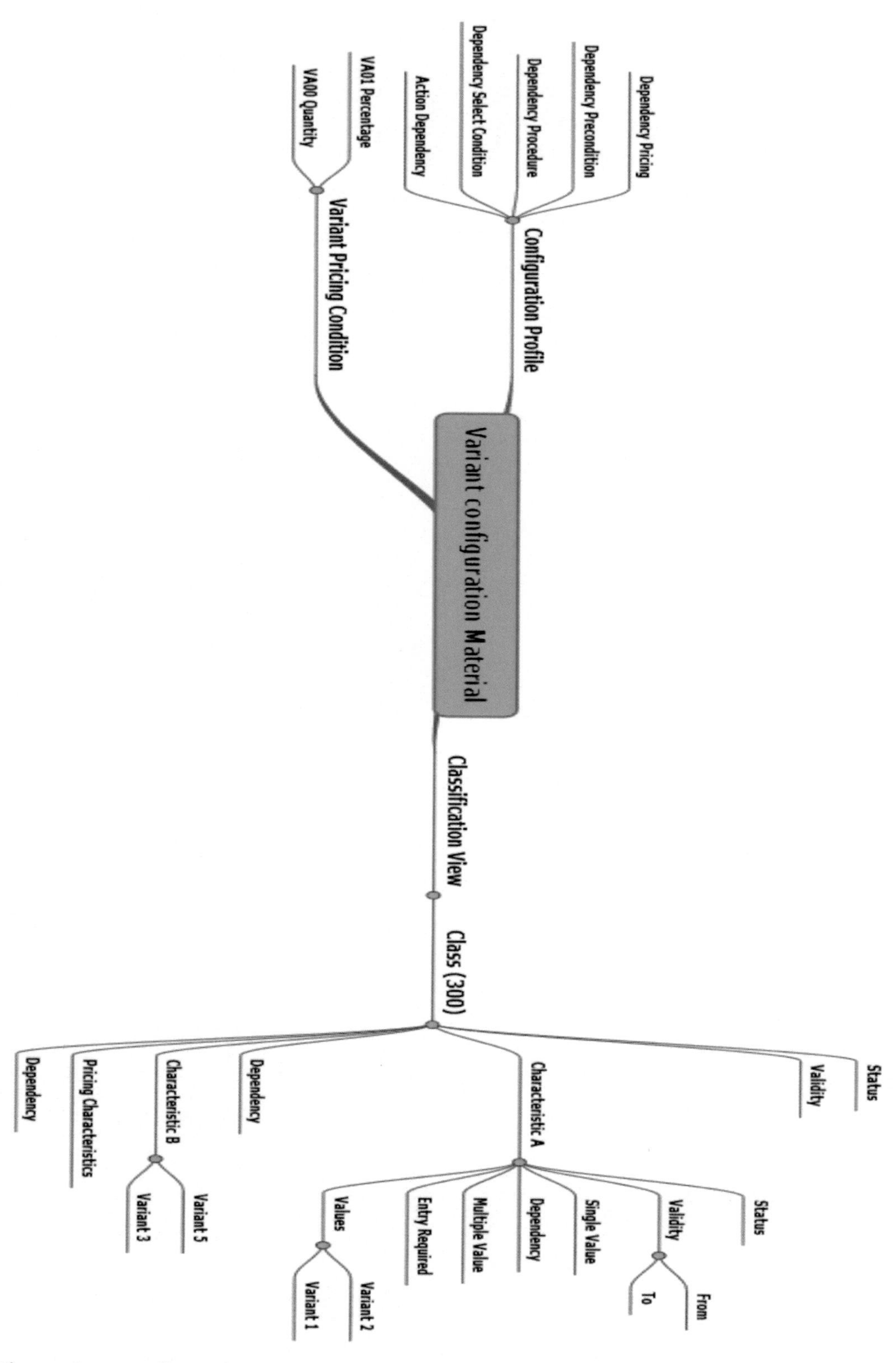

The variant configuration material is created with material master type "KMAT". KMAT stands for configurable material. With material type, KMAT it comes with configuration preset for

variant configurable views and controls for the material.
To create a variant configuration material use: MM01

Create Material (Initial Screen)

Select View(s) Org. Levels Data

Material Vehicle
Industry sector M Mechanical engin...
Material Type KMAT Configurable...

Change Number

Copy from...
Material

With Material Master Basic Data 2 the field "Material is Configurable" should be checked.

Also, for Classification view expected to select by Class type 300.

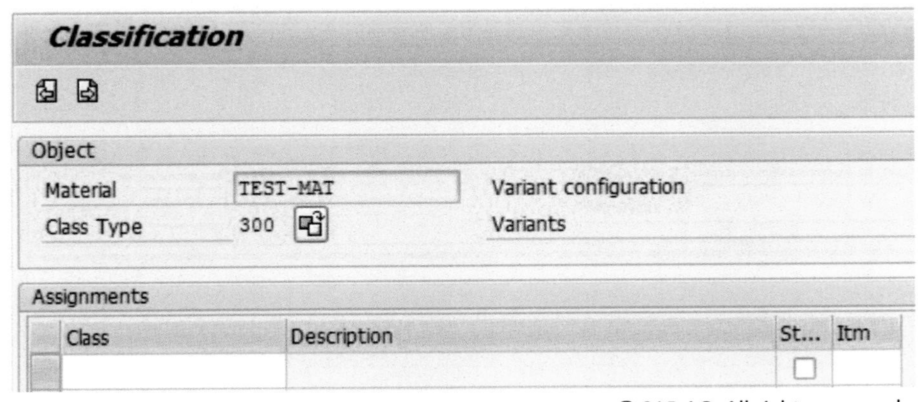

The class required to be created to enter in the material master.

Class:

The class contains many characteristics in it and characteristic feature variants in it. It also contains many other types of classes, but Class 300 represents the variant class. Variant class 300 allows the function of variant configuration for the material. The class feature a validity period. Class feature status, and class able to be created specific to organizational area.

To create a class T-code, use "CL01".

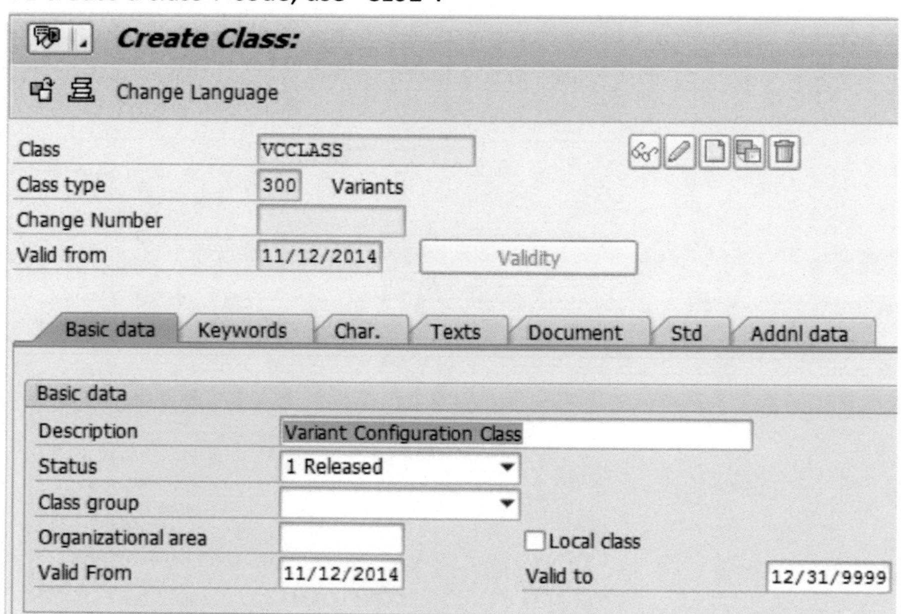

Characteristic are assigned in class which are in the following screenshot

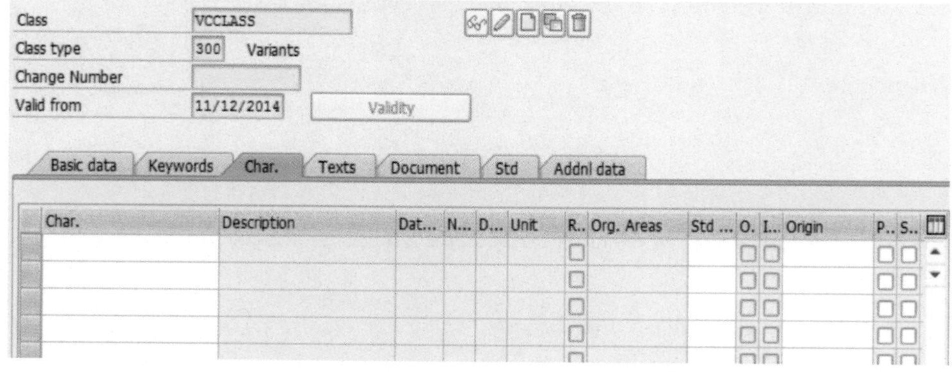

After the class creation characteristic, it required to be created to populate in class. Dependency able to be written if characteristic is needed to be selected based on a rule. That means based

on the condition or requirement, only a few characteristics able to be utilized at the same time as the sales order creation.

Characteristic

Characteristics contain the variants on it, which are selected as an option which at the same time make a sales order creation. Characteristics also have validity periods and status and each characteristic feature a group of variants grouped in it.

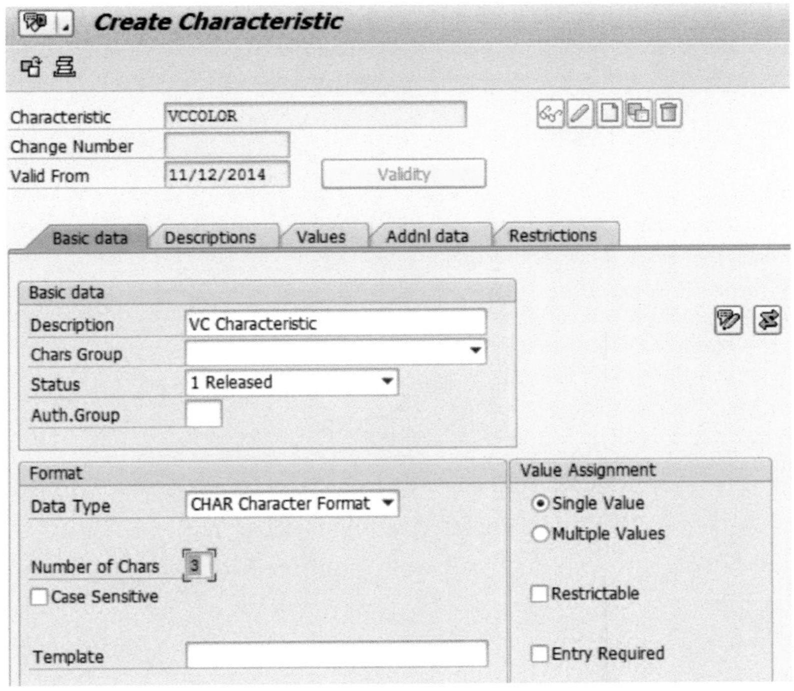

In the Basic View the data type contain a Character type and length of key, which represent the variant selected in basic data.

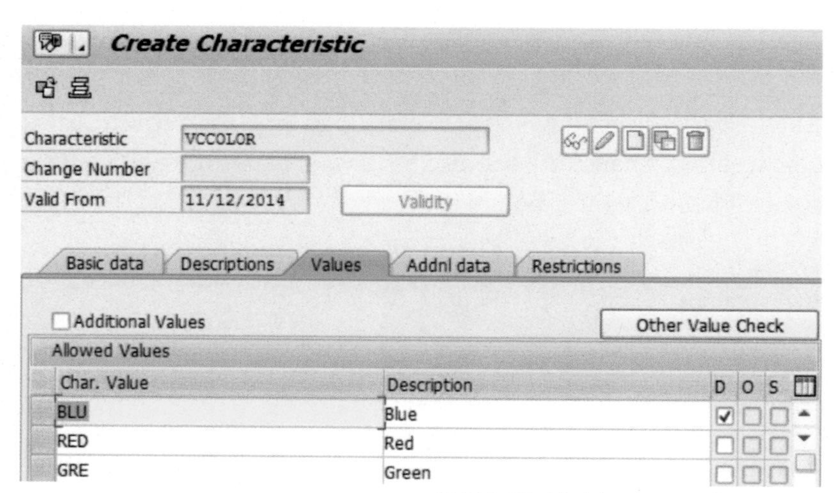

The keys or variants are defined in the Values tab.

Pricing Characteristic

Characteristic for pricing defined without the Values; the pricing Characteristic will be assigned in same class. Base on the pricing, the Characteristic will be utilized for the pricing dependency setup and condition records.

T-code for Characteristic is: **CT04**

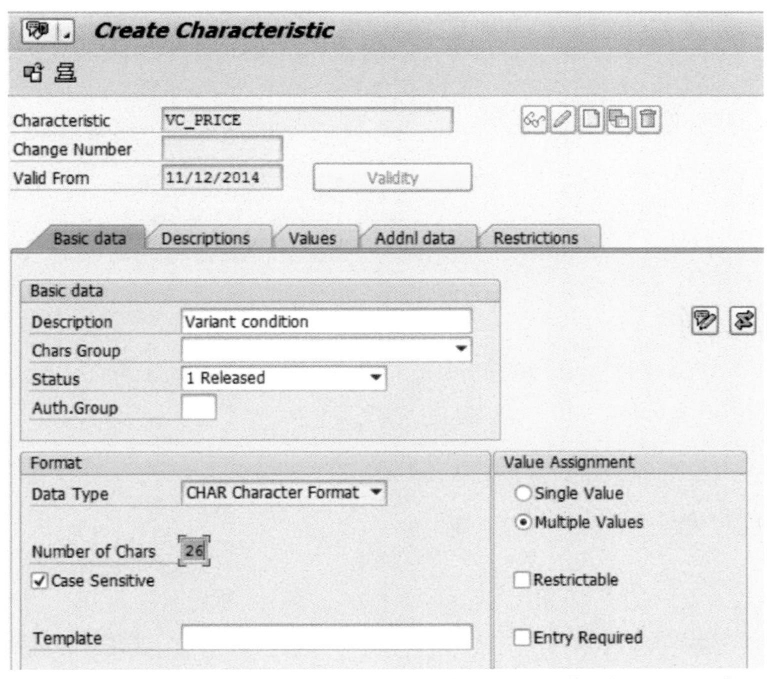

To get the pricing characteristic value assignment, it needs to be set in multiple Value option and number of char option expected to "26".

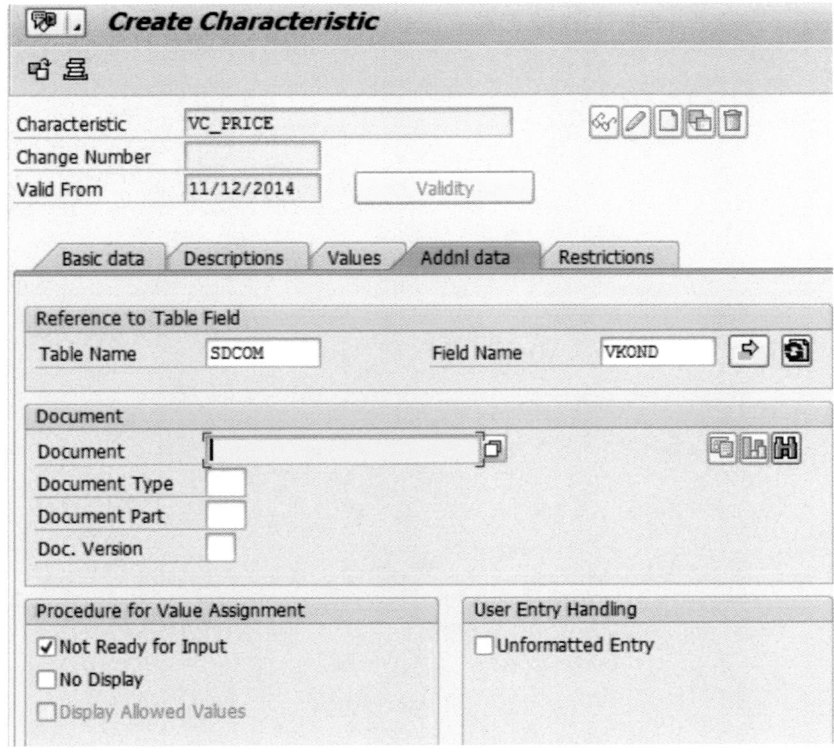

With Additional data the view table name needs to be populated as "SDCOM" and field name as "VKNOD". With the table reference, multiple variants able to be utilized for pricing. This characteristic does not take direct input so far "procedure for Value Assignment" tab option expected to select "not ready for input".

Variant Configuration Pricing:

Pricing in variant configuration part of Sales and Distribution module. The pricing condition type is for the variant condition, these are the following:

- VA00 Condition type utilized for the fix amount
- VA01 Condition Type utilized for the percentage

Pricing requires characteristic to be created with the table value. With the value of the tables in, additional data tab and maintains tables. A screenshot of characteristic attached. To create a Characteristic use transaction code: CT04

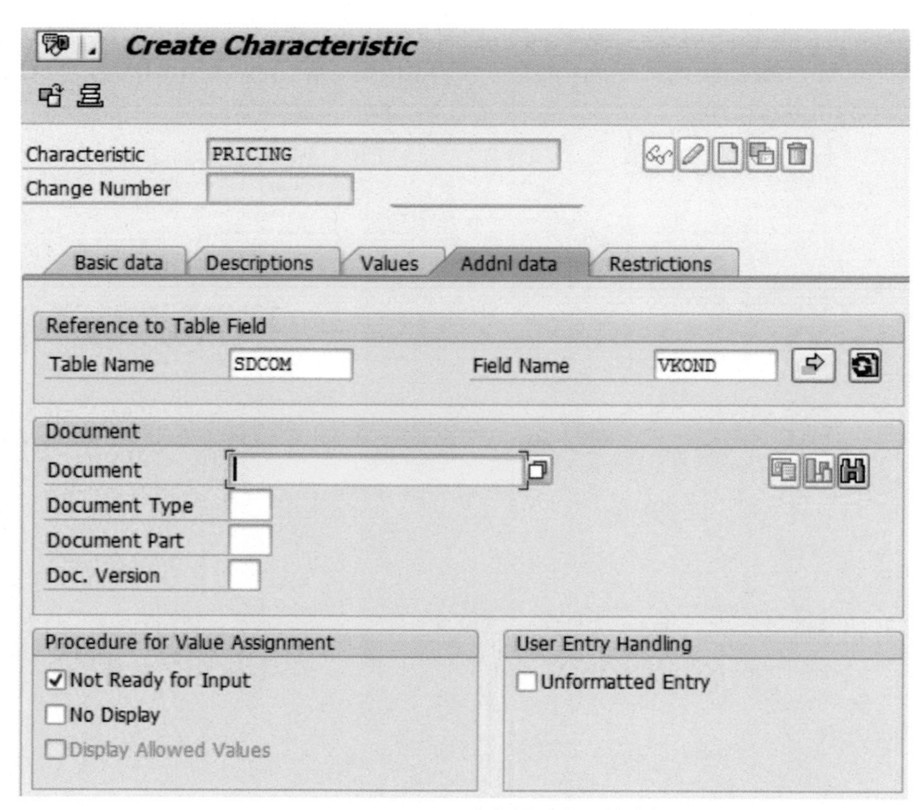

The characteristic attached to the class that contains variant characteristic. Pricing characteristic essentially required for pricing to work. Then after the pricing characteristic maintained, the dependency required to be written for the variant material.

The pricing characteristic gets assigned to the main class where all characteristics are maintained.

Following steps:

The class needs to be assigned into the material master, all the characteristics needs to be assigned to the class. After the assignment of classification and characteristics into material master, the configuration profile needs to be setup.

Configuration Profile:

Configuration Profile represent the setup for the martial so the decadency able to be assigned to the profile and make the bill of material and Sales and Distribution related function possible for the material.

T-code: CU41

Variant Configuration Simulation:

After the configuration profile setup, it needs to be tested. The test able to be done for sales configuration, bill of material and plant relevant. Another way to simulate the variant configuration martial also in the sales order.

T-code: CU50

Dependency:

Dependency make utilization of condition and calculation controls for the characteristic and class. Dependency able to be written in the configuration profile, Bill of material items, class, and characteristic. Dependency feature two views, the Basic view and dependency editor. Dependency feature four types:

- Precondition
- Action
- Selection Condition

- Procedure

Dependency editor personify where the coding written and relates to the dependency. Dependency feature the following status:

1. Released
2. In preparation
3. Locked

T-code for dependency is: CU01

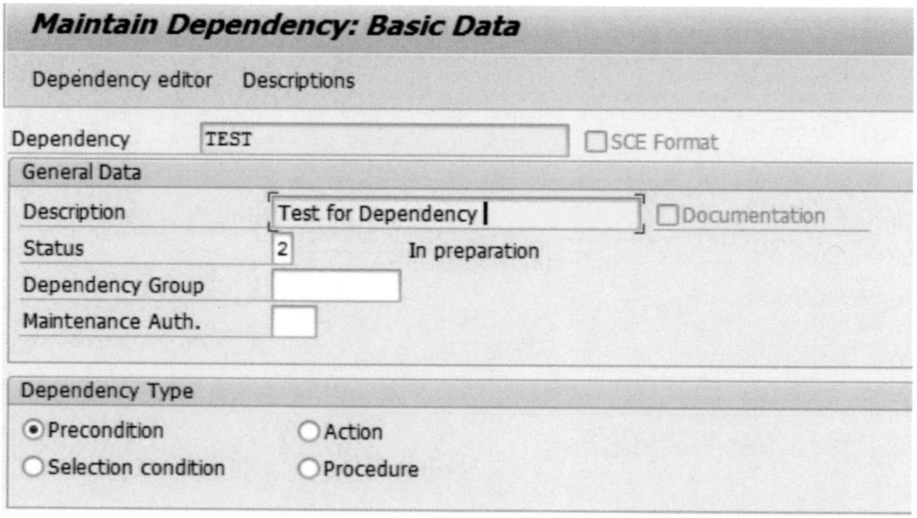

Maintain Dependency: Basic Data

Dependency editor   Descriptions

Dependency: TEST   ☐ SCE Format

General Data

Description	Test for Dependency	☐ Documentation
Status	2	In preparation
Dependency Group		
Maintenance Auth.		

Dependency Type

◉ Precondition   ○ Action
○ Selection condition   ○ Procedure

Dependency for pricing is written in precondition.

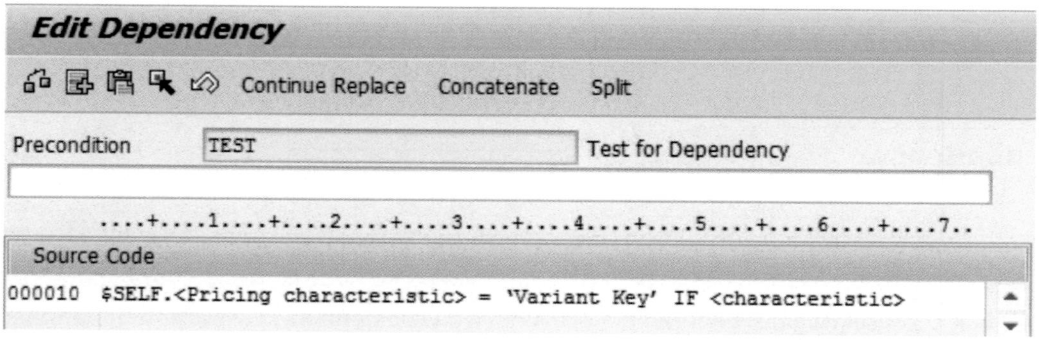

Edit Dependency

Continue Replace   Concatenate   Split

Precondition: TEST   Test for Dependency

```
....+....1....+....2....+....3....+....4....+....5....+....6....+....7..
Source Code
000010  $SELF.<Pricing characteristic> = 'Variant Key' IF <characteristic>
```


The syntax $SELF is utilized for characteristics and variant to be defined in dependency.

Syntax: $Self. <Pricing characteristic> = 'Variant Key' IF <characteristic>

= ‘characteristic value’

For each additional variant the $SELF statement able to be added as follows. Additional controls are available for the dependency like, $ROOT and $Parent.

$PARENT & $ROOT:

The statement “$PARENT” is utilized to bill of material related dependency. The parent could be one level above, but it does not mean it’s the highest level.
The statement “$ROOT” is utilized for the main item which it refers to the header material.

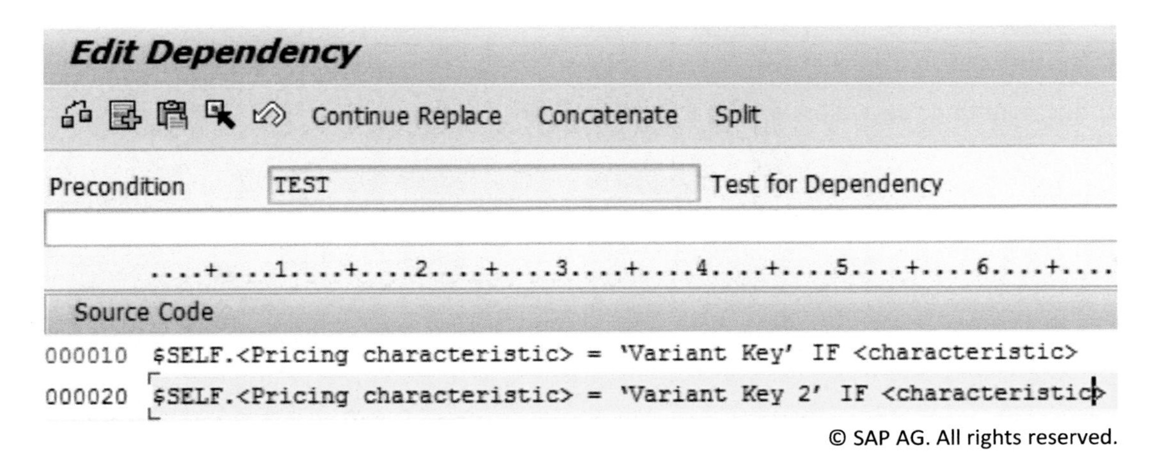

To validate the correct dependency syntax check button (figure Ch 1.1) or shortcut (CTL+F2) able to be utilized to indicate for any errors.

Check Button **Figure Ch 1.1**

With the help from check the syntax able to be fixed and the dependency will work accordingly. After the dependency is written and syntax checks the status of dependency, it needs to be updated to “released”.

Variant Configuration Tricks:

Variant Configuration required many steps like connecting dots between, class, dependency, tabs, characteristics and variant conditions. All the elements of Variant configuration able to be managed with one single t-code.

T-code: **PMEVC**

This variant configuration able to be done with a single t-code. This t-code should have many more function that might not be available from standard variant configuration.

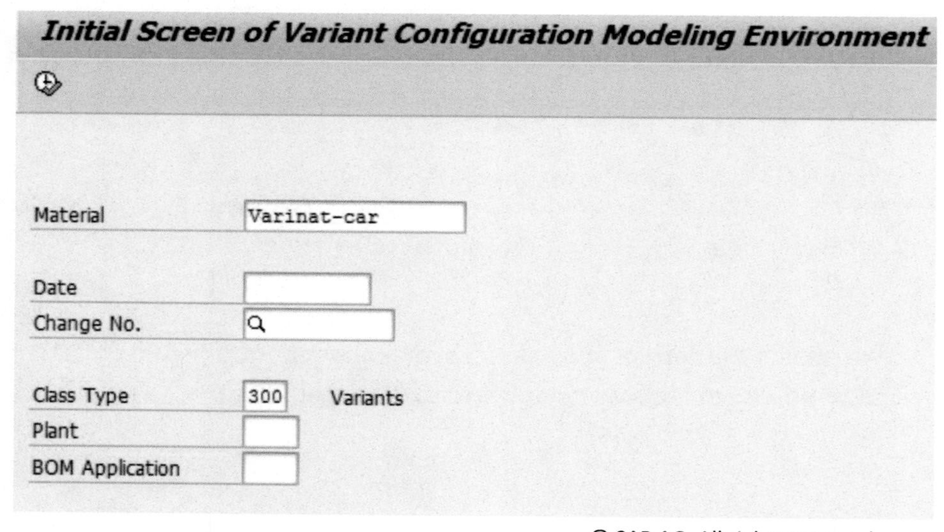

Configuration related Icons

Screenshot	Description	Notes
	Material Configuration	It will open a new screen with item sub item details
	Dependency Object	Dependency able to be written in class or characteristic etc.
	Class	Class
	Variant in characteristic	Variant in characteristic
	Bill of Material	BOM
	BOM item	Bill of material item
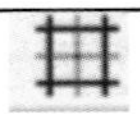	Constraint Net	Constraint Net
	Constraint	Constraint
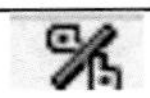	Procedure	Procedure
	Precondition	Precondition
	Selection Condition	Selection Condition
	Material	Material Master

Parameters (Save clicks):

Parameter ID is utilized as a user own data, meaning it will be specific to the user. If the user wants to auto populate the data in the processing of the transaction, it able to help in time and less clicks and keyboard entry for the user. If the same field value is different every time than maintaining the field value to auto populate does not make sense.

Parameter ID able to be searched in table TPARA

SAP standard parameter ID sample:

Description	Parameter ID
Parameters for shipping Point	VST
Sold to party in the sales order	VAU
Purchasing Group (MM)	EKO
Currency unit	FWS
Sales organization	VKO
Distribution Channel	VTW

Screenshot: for Parameter maintenance

T-code: **SU3**

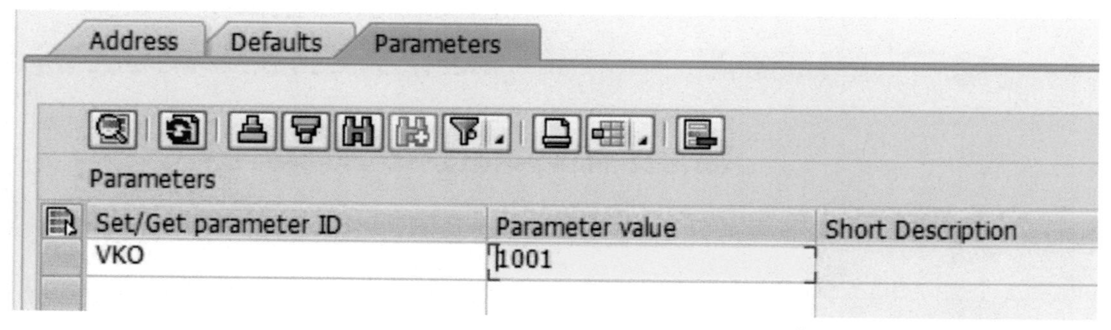

The above screenshot represent the parameter ID and parameter value able to be managed according to the values that are maintained in the system.

The default values of the date format, time format, decimal notation and numbers able to also be set from the Defaults Tab.

Address | Defaults | Parameters

Start menu
Logon Language
Decimal Notation X 1,234,567.89
Date Format 2 MM/DD/YYYY
Time Format (12/24h) 1 12 Hour Format (Example: 12:05:10 PM)

Spool Control
OutputDevice
Print immed.
Delete After Output

Personal Time Zone
Time Zone

Startup Transaction:

With this setup, the system will start with the transaction automatically every time the user logs, on. To setup the transaction, go to easy access Menu and click on "Extra" and select "Set start Transaction".

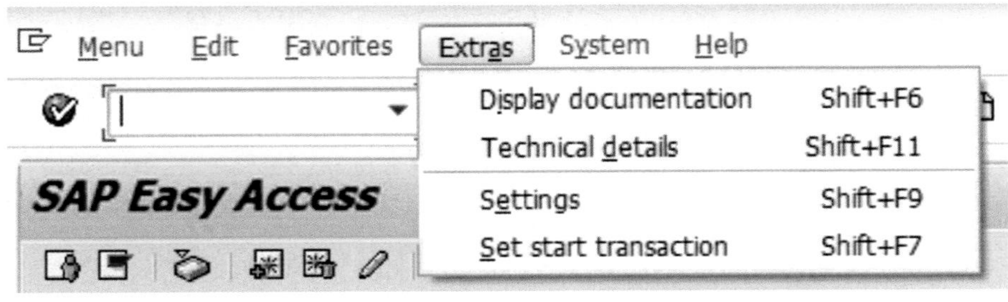

This transaction code represent utilized for this function.

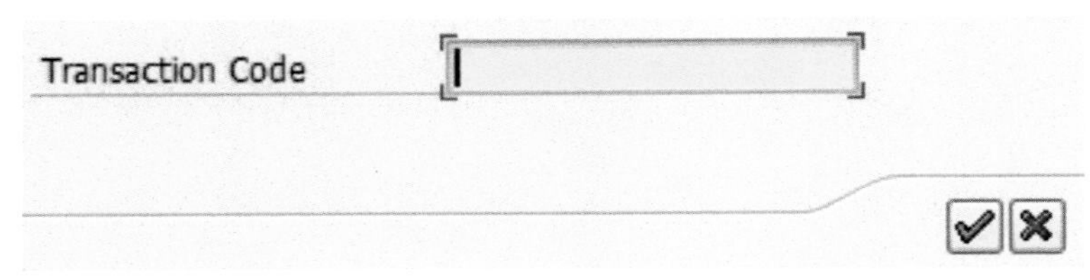

With that this transaction will be there from a log on the GUI.

SAP ICONS:

Throughout the SAP transactions and configuration, users interact with many icons.

Here are few examples of ICON description.

T-code: ICON
With this, the user able to see what this icon means.

Display View "Icon maintenance": Overview

Icon maintenance

+	+	+	+
	ICON_PRINT	Print	Print
	ICON_CREATE	Create	Create
	ICON_CHANGE	Change	Change
	ICON_DISPLAY	Display	Display
	ICON_DELETE	Delete	Delete
	ICON_TEST	Test	Test
	ICON_SEARCH	Find	Find
	ICON_COPY_OBJECT	Copy <object>	Copy <object>
	ICON_EXECUTE_OBJECT	Execute <object>	Execute <object>
	ICON_SELECT_DETAIL	Choose <detail>; Detail	Choose <detail>; Detail
	ICON_INSERT_ROW	Insert Row	Insert Row
	ICON_DELETE_ROW	Delete Row	Delete Row
	ICON_MESSAGE_INFORMATION	Information message	Information message
	ICON_MESSAGE_WARNING	Warning	Warning
	ICON_MESSAGE_ERROR	Error message	Error message
	ICON_MESSAGE_QUESTION	Question	Question
STOP	ICON_MESSAGE_CRITICAL	Critical message	Critical message
	ICON_DISPLAY_MORE	Multiple Selection (Active)	Multiple Selection (Active)
	ICON_ENTER_MORE	Multiple selection	Multiple selection
=	ICON_EQUAL	Equals	Equals
≠	ICON_NOT_EQUAL	Not equal to	Not equal to
>	ICON_GREATER	Greater than	Greater than
<	ICON_LESS	Less than	Less than
≥	ICON_GREATER_EQUAL	Greater than or equal to	Greater than or equal to
≤	ICON_LESS_EQUAL	Less than or equal to	Less than or equal to
[]	ICON_INTERVAL_INCLUDE	Include range	Include range
][	ICON_INTERVAL_EXCLUDE	Exclude range	Exclude range

Click on change pencil icon and the user able to upload their own icon.

Messages Table:

All the messages are stored in table T100

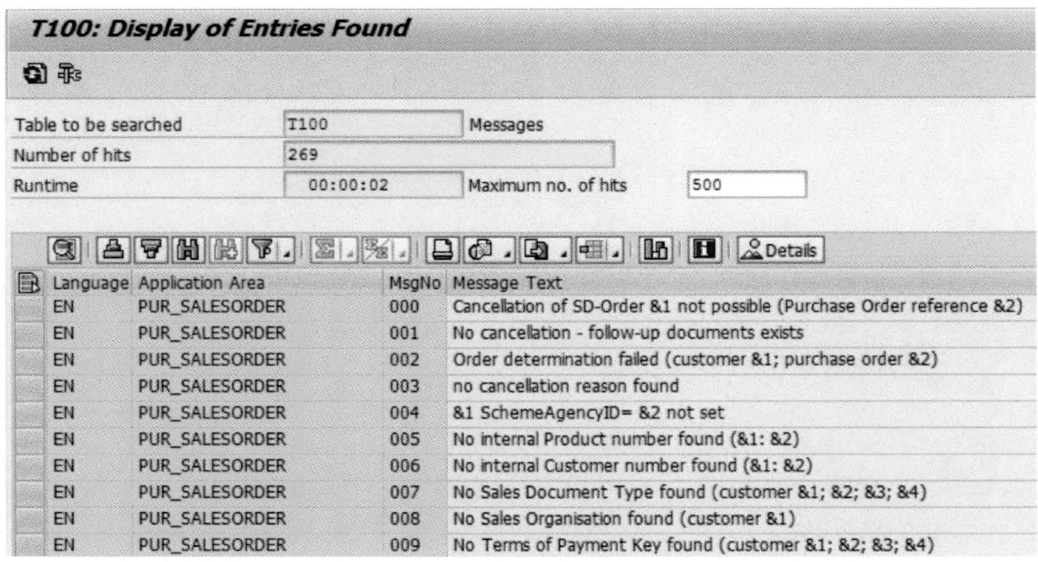

Reports:

Reports able to be searched with T-code SAP1. This will update the easy access menu to "SAP Easy Access Report Selection".

T-code: **SAP1** all the sections will have only reports.

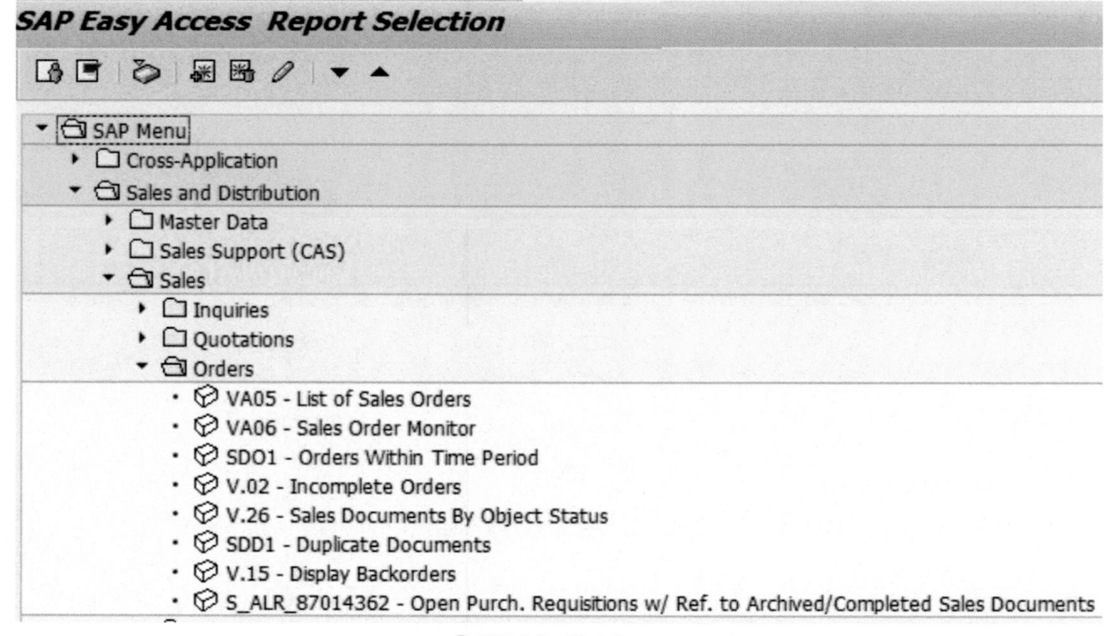

To display additional reports, use info catalog T-code: SAP2.
T-code: **SAP2**

This transaction displays all the Info catalog reports.

SAP Easy Access Info Catalog

Table View:

The table view function helps understand data stored in the table according to the master data and transactional date or enterprise structure tables.

To View the Table the following T-codes are following:

- SE16 (Old t-code)
- SE16N (Upgrade of SE16 and feature many options for data mining)
- SE11 (Data Dictionary view, belong to technical views)

Table View Old (SE16)

This represent a very basic yet powerful table with full potential use of every function of the table view.

If we use a table, it only displays limited fields in the initial screen.

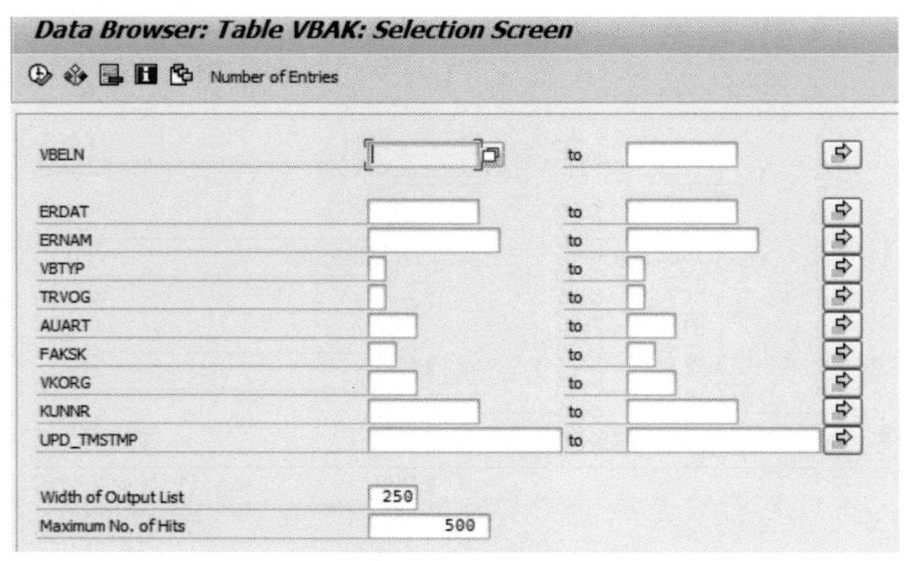

Additional field able to be added via Menu option and settings (Field selected)

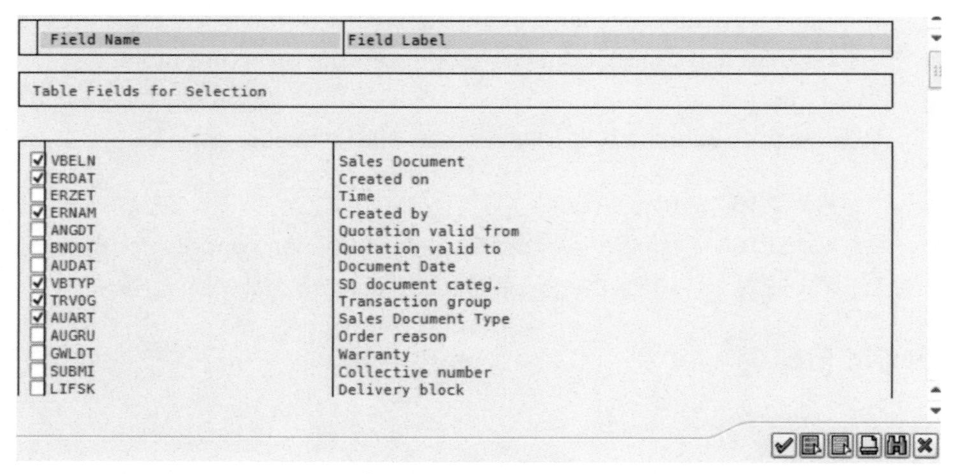

SE16 represent an old data viewer and able to be utilized, but it does show all the detail information on the first screen and it requires additional steps to use the data viewer.

New Table View (SE16N):

The New table view T-code SE16N allows for far more functionality and contains the first screen compare to old data view (SE16)

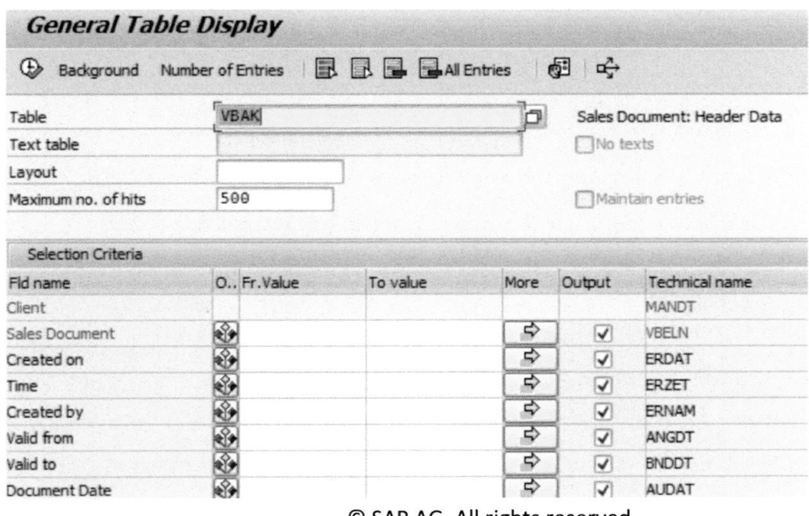

The table view starts with the field name, which represent more understandable compare to technical name of the field.

The table view feature an optional icon that make many controls that able to control the field value. It also feature the same control to other entries inputted in more icons. If the output represent selected, the table view will show the field results in the table display. The value range able to be entered into the view according to the range selected from and to.

The Option Icon feature many options that able to be selected, it will display a dropdown with options.

The more Icon feature multiple entries that able to be entered in manually or past into it. The more icon able to also be utilized with options for each entry for the controls.

Output

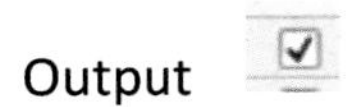

This icon able to change the colors and this icon representation based on the selection and entries that reflect the status.

Interface:

Third party Application interface:

SAP represent the leading ERP application software with the capability to integrate with any other application. SAP feature flexibility toward third-party application integration with industry standard and with standard interfaces. It allows third-party interface connectivity with application component with many technologies. The interface feature required to establish the connectivity between applications to transfer or transact. The interface feature many connectivity mediums available. The following are a few types available:

- **EDI**
- **BAPI**
- **RFC**

These are a few of the many interface technology available by SAP ERP. The interface able to be synchronous or as asynchronous which means that the interface able to be real time or based periodically (every hour, daily, weekly, etc.). The interface able to also be utilized for the master data or transactional data. Real time interface updates the application in real time or as soon as the data comes in, which at that point gets processed and sent back. In an asynchronous interface, data doesn't get processed in real time; instead it gets processed in batches or just updates the table as a requirement. SAP feature an EDI capability with IDOC processing with is the industry standard.

VOFM Routines:

VOFM transections represent utilized for formulas and routines utilized in SAP. Routines are utilized in pricing, pricing procedure, condition type and almost in all the configuration. The SAP system feature standard routines but new routines able to develop by ABAPER as per requirements.

T-code: VOFM

Chapter 10 Summary

In chapter 9 we covered the following topics:

- EDI
- User Exit
- BADI
- Rebate Process
- LSMW
- Cross Match
- BAPI
- Condition Technique
- Third-party Drop ship
- Variant
- SQVI
- Edit Table
- Debugging
- Variant Configuration
- SQVI
- Interface
- Routines and Formulas

Notes

Index

About the Author: Syed Awais Rizvi

Syed is a senior SAP Sales and Distribution consultant and experienced with worked in numerous implementation projects. He has years of experience in the automotive, healthcare, security and various industries. Syed Awais Rizvi serves as the Chief Executive Officer of ITSAS LLC.

SAP Certified Sales and Distribution Consultant.

SAP Certified Project Manager.

IBM Certified System Administrator

Authors Publications

1) Quick SAP Basic Introduction End User Guide: Learn SAP GUI Navigation, Reports, Tips and Tricks with Basic SAP Skills

Published on Feb 2017

2) SAP Sales and Distribution Quick Configuration Guide: Advanced SAP Tips and Tricks with Variant Configuration (Color)

Published on May 2015

3) 12 Powerful Leadership and Management Skills: Leadership for Productivity and Project Management

Published on Oct 2016

4) Urdu Beginners Guide: Start Speaking Urdu Phrases with English Pronunciations Learn Urdu Quickly

Published on Jan 2017

5) How to Become Effective Business Analyst Practical Beginners Guide: Real-life Software Requirements and Design Techniques

6) SAP S/4Hana Business Partner: Customer: Beginners and Business End User Learning for Practical Usage

7) SAP Customer Master Ultimate Guide: Essential End User Guide; Customer Mater, Credit Management and Customer Hierarchy

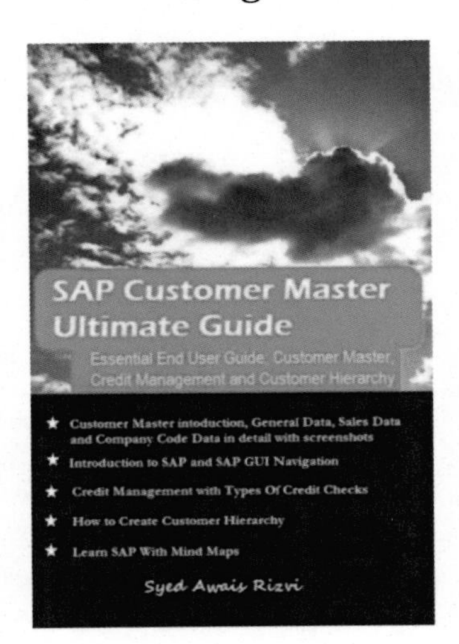

Please leave a review on amazon.com

YouTube Channel

http://www.youtube.com/c/SyedRizvi

Please leave feedback and comments at rizvir@gmail.com

Subscribe @ http://phtime.com/ for updates!

Thank you

Made in the USA
Las Vegas, NV
22 July 2022